THE KILLING OF WILLIAM BROWDER

THE KILLING OF WILLIAM BROWDER

Bill Browder, the false crusader for justice and human rights and the self-styled No. 1 enemy of Vladimir Putin has perpetrated a brazen and dangerous deception upon the Western world. This book traces the anatomy of this deception, unmasking the powerful forces that are pushing the Western world toward yet another great war with Russia.

ALEX KRAINER

EQUILIBRIUM
MONACO

First published in Monaco in 2017

Copyright © 2017 by Alex Krainer

ISBN 978-2-9556923-2-5

Material contained in this book may be reproduced with permission from its author and/or publisher, except for attributed brief quotations

Content editing by Alex Krainer and Boris Krainer. Cover page design, and copy editing by Alex Krainer.

Set in Times New Roman, book title in Imprint MT shadow

*To the people of Russia
and the United States, who
together
hold the keys to the
future of humanity*

*Enlighten the people generally,
and tyranny and oppressions
of body and mind will vanish
like the evil spirits
at the dawn of day.*

Thomas Jefferson

Table of Contents

1. Bill Browder and I 1
   Browder's 2005 presentation in Monaco 2
   Harvard club presentation in 2010 3
   Russophobia and Putin-bashing in the West 4
   Red notice 6
   Reading and rereading Browder's story 7
   It's all true! 7
   Bill Browder, the complex hero 8
   Russia is a terrible place and Russians terrible people 9
   Vladimir Putin is a greedy, brazen tyrant 12
2. Red Notice – play by play 13
   The opening chapters 14
   The plot thickens 19
   Chapter 18: "Fifty percent" 19
   Chapter 20: "Vogue Café" 23
   Chapter 21: "The G8" 24
   Chapter 22: "The Raids" 26
   Chapter 23: "Department K" 27
   Chapter 24: "But Russian Stories Never Have Happy Endings" ... 28
   Chapter 25: "High-pitched Jamming Equipment" 30
   Chapter 26: "The Riddle" 31
   Chapter 27: "DHL" 32
   Chapter 28: "Khabarovsk" 37
   Chapter 29: "Ninth Commandment" 39
   Chapter 30: "16 November 2009" 42
   Chapter 31: "The Katyn Principle" 43
   Chapter 32: "Kyle Parker's War" 45
   Chapter 33: "Russell 241" 46
   Chapter 34: "Russian untouchables" 47
   Chapters 35, 36: "The Swiss Accounts" and "The Tax Princess" . 48

Chapter 37: "Sausage-making" 50
Chapter 38: "The Malkin Delegation" 51
Chapter 39: "Justice for Sergey" 52
Chapter 40: "Humiliator, humiliatee" 53
Chapter 41: "Red Notice" 54
Chapter 42: "Feelings" 54

3. Russia in the 1990s: The missing context 56
   Russia decides to go from communism to capitalism 57
      The Harvard connection 59
      1992: the shock therapy gets underway 60
      Voucher privatization 62
      Loans for shares scheme 65
   Lawmakers' revolt and the constitutional crisis of 1993 67
      Yeltsin's violent crackdown 69
   The Americans came for the best of reasons 71
      IMF's strangulation of Russian economy 72
   The Enterprise 76
      Reagan administration cold warriors formulate the policy 77
      Preparing the ground in the Soviet Union 80
   Fallout: the economic genocide 84
   Did it have to be that way? 89

4. Enter Vladimir Putin 93
   Regime change 93
   Vladimir Putin's disastrous contribution to Russia's history 95
      Economic reforms 96
      Social and demographic improvements 98
      Impressions of modern Russia 103
   So, who is Vladimir Putin 109
      Working for the people 109
      A hard working leader 110
      Fight against terrorism 111
      Forgiving Cuba's debts 112

  Edward Snowden asylum *113*
  The corruption thing *114*
  Kursk submarine tragedy *117*
5. Bill Browder, the great pretender 119
  The superentrepreneur 120
   The Murmansk asylum *120*
   Thirty meetings in four days *121*
   Browder's excellent adventure in Davos *121*
  Protection in high places 123
  Bill's tall tale unravels 124
   U.K. High Court of Justice: Pavel Karpov v. William Browder ... *128*
   U.S. District Court – So. Distr. of New York: USA v. Prevezon ... *129*
   The tax fraud thing *130*
   Misrepresenting Sergei Magnitsky *132*
   Framing the Russians for the $230 million tax fraud *135*
  Edmond Safra's lieutenant 138
   Republic National Bank's money planes *138*
   For he's a jolly good felon... and so say all of us! *142*
   Browder and the West's criminal plunder of Russia *144*
  The $230 million tax fraud: whodunit? 145
   Working a lot with Renaissance Capital *146*
   Browder's defector lawyers *148*
   Laundering AVISMA's profits *149*
  Dirty dishonesty of Bill Browder 150
   Monopolizing "truth" *151*
   Desecrating Sergei Magnitsky *153*
   Escaping American gestapo *155*
6. War and peace 158
  The dangers of demonization 161
  Rise of the military industrial complex 163
  The endless cast of enemies and threats 165
  Our American friends and partners 169

The first U.S. – Russian alliance 171
   Russian intervention in U.S. Civil War (1861-1865) 173
   God bless the Russians 176
The bankers' revenge 178
   Scrubbing Russian-American friendship from history 180
Toward the new U.S. – Russian alliance 183
   Why I wrote this book 185
   Thank you. 189
Appendix I: Deflationary gap and the West's war addiction 190
   Methods of bridging the deflationary gap 191
   Averting depression through destruction of goods 191
   Producing goods that don't enter the market 192
   War: the irresistible solution 192
Appendix II: The top of the pyramid 195
   Rothschild is the new power behind Yukos 195
Bibliography 197

Introduction

This book has been a path of discovery. Without a doubt, its most significant aspect is the smouldering but needless conflict between Russia and the Western world. It is my fondest hope with this book to contribute to a peaceful resolution to that conflict. Although I grew up in the "communist bloc," in the former Yugoslavia, our cultural inclination was pro-Western and largely Russophobic. As a result, my views about Russia essentially matched the negative Western narrative. This all began to change in 2005 when I met Bill Browder, manager of the Moscow-based Hermitage Capital. He was the first person I ever heard speaking positively about President Putin. Because his account contrasted so sharply with the Western narrative, I started to pay attention. Since that time however, Browder has changed tack and became a hugely prolific anti-Russia activist. His relentless campaigning achieved a stunning success in 2012 when he lobbied the U.S. Congress into passing the Magnitsky Act, which was damaging to the relations between the U.S. and Russia. In 2015 Browder published the book titled *"Red Notice"*. Ostensibly a true account of his Russian experience, on closer scrutiny, *"Red Notice,"* turns out to be untrue in many important details.

This book is divided into six chapters. Chapter 1 recounts my three run-ins with Mr. Browder. Chapter 2 is a rather thorough review of Browder's book. I tried my best to make it readable even for those who haven't read *"Red Notice"*. Chapter 3 provides the context which Browder's book omits: the 1990s criminal plunder of Russia carried out behind the smokescreen of the "Shock Therapy." Chapter 4 summarizes the changes in Russia's economic, political and social life during the 17 years of Vladimir Putin's leadership. Chapter 5 re-examines William Browder's tall tale and his character, particularly in light of his more recent misadventures in UK, Isle of Man and US court cases. Chapter 6 re-examines U.S. – Russia relationship from its historical perspective. This again, turned out to be very different from what we were taught at school.

Acknowledgements

I remain deeply in debt to many historians, book authors, film makers, bloggers and researchers – those whose names appear in this book's bibliography, but also numerous others. Thank you.

1. Bill Browder and I

If a thousand old beliefs were ruined in our march to truth we must still march on

Stopford Brooke

I became interested in Russia, its leadership and its role in world affairs primarily through my work as a hedge fund manager. Although I never invested so much as a penny in Russia, I trade commodities for a living and Russia has always been a relevant player in commodity markets like oil, natural gas, grains and metals. Aside from conducting market research, my outlook on Russia was largely formed by western media portrayal of this country: I thought of it as a cold, dark, rusty place where corruption and crime ran rampant and ordinary people's lives were oppressive and miserable. I also had a very poor impression of Russia's leadership, especially of its president, Vladimir Putin. I suppose I was a typical unsuspecting consumer of Western Russophobic narrative.

Browder's 2005 presentation in Monaco

This all began to change in early November of 2005 when I was invited to a presentation by a hedge fund manager who ran Russia's largest foreign investment fund. The presentation was organized under the auspices of the International University of Monaco and the manager in question was William Browder of the Hermitage Capital Management. Up until then I had never heard of Mr. Browder and because I had little interest in investing in Russia I was about to skip the event altogether. As it happened, I went and I was surprised to find the presentation fascinating and impressively well delivered. Browder came across as a very intelligent man, a competent manager, and an earnest, no-nonsense character. I was taken aback to find that he spoke of Russia's president Putin in very positive terms.

I think that was the first time I heard anyone speak of Vladimir Putin in such relevant and positive terms. When I say "relevant," I mean that Browder wasn't saying that Mr. Putin was nice, spoke languages, or dressed well. Browder recounted examples where he and his team investigated and exposed corruption at large firms like Gazprom, Unified Energy Systems (UES) and Sberbank, and each time Putin's government took notice and acted swiftly to clean up and remove the corrupt management. This contrasted with my belief that Putin was the protector of Russia's corrupt oligarchs who brought him to power. Browder's account was entirely credible – he clearly had an authoritative vantage point into Russia's economic and political system.

This all left me wondering not only about the uniformly negative portrayal of Vladimir Putin in the west but also about some of Russia's oligarchs who tended to be lionized as maverick young reformers of Russia's ailing economy. Most notable among these was Mikhail Khodorkovsky, majority owner of the Russian oil giant Yukos, whom Vladimir Putin had arrested in October of 2003 on charges of tax-evasion. While western media usually treated Khodorkovsky as the victim of Putin's purge of political rivals, Bill Browder pretty much said that Khodorkovsky was a murderous thug and belonged in prison. That evening in Monaco Browder didn't change my mind about Russia or about Vladimir Putin, but he did plant a seed of doubt in my mind that perhaps there was an unfair negative bias toward Vladimir Putin in the West and an undue sympathy for the oligarchs, many of whom were essentially criminals. This is when I started to pay closer attention to Russian affairs.

The thing that none of us knew on that November day in 2005 was that Bill Browder himself was about to run into trouble in Putin's Russia. Only days after his presentation in Monaco he was detained at Moscow's

Sheremetyevo airport, had his visa revoked and was escorted onto the first flight back to London, barred indefinitely from entering Russia where he had lived and managed his firm. Although I was now vaguely aware of this affair which occasionally featured in financial press, I did not pay much attention to Bill Browder's story as it unfolded. But my path would cross with Mr. Browder's once more in June of 2010 during the GAIM[1] hedge fund conference, again in Monaco.

Harvard club presentation in 2010

This time I was invited to a dinner organized by the local chapter of the Harvard alumni organization where Browder was the keynote speaker. My understanding was that he would be presenting his new fund, the Hermitage Global, but Browder had another surprise in store: during his entire presentation he barely mentioned Hermitage Global and took the entire time to speak about the arrest of Sergei Magnitsky and his death in a Russian prison cell. His outlook on Russia changed markedly: in 2005, Browder was very bullish on Russia and said that every investor in the world should own shares of companies like Gazprom. Now, in 2010 he was very negative, explicitly warning investors to stay away from Russia. Not a word about his new fund, how or where it invested, or why investors should be interested; only Russia, Putin, Magnitsky... I was puzzled by the whole event, but I reasoned that Browder was so moved by Sergey Magnitsky's plight that he thought it much more important to tell *that* story than to talk about his new fund. I took that as a sign of conscience and integrity which made me like Browder even more than I did before.

Nevertheless, his presentation did not diminish my opinion of Russia or of its president. Since my first encounter with Bill Browder in 2005 my views of Russia gradually diverged from the negative image typically presented in the west. By now I thought that Russia's diplomatic conduct and geopolitical positioning were reasonable and constructive in spite of many challenges and provocations she endured since the collapse of the Soviet Union. Regarding Vladimir Putin, I simply thought he was a capable leader and a shrewd politician. I thought of him neither positively nor negatively as a person – the relevant bit was the way he discharged his duties as the Russian president, not whether he was a nice man or not.

---

[1] Global Alternative Investment Management

Russophobia and Putin-bashing in the West

Citizens of the democratic societies should undertake a course of intellectual self defense to protect themselves from manipulation and control, and to lay the basis for meaningful democracy

Noam Chomsky

In the meantime, western bashing of Vladimir Putin had gradually escalated, reaching fever pitch by 2014 when Ukraine's president Viktor Yanukovich was deposed in a U.S. orchestrated coup. Following the coup, Russia moved to annex the Crimean peninsula which triggered strong condemnation of Putin among western leaders, diplomats and media outlets, likening him to Adolf Hitler and insinuating that he had imperialist designs toward Eastern Europe. It became quite apparent that this was an orchestrated campaign using and reusing the same stories, talking points, same contexts and same omissions printed and broadcast almost uniformly across the western media.

Things got worse still when on 17th July of 2014 Malaysia Airlines flight 17 crashed over Ukraine, killing all 283 passengers on board and 15 members of the crew. Apparently, the airplane was shot down by an anti-aircraft missile or by a military fighter jet. Within hours and before even a preliminary investigation into the matter could begin, the western media and politicians in unison called out Vladimir Putin as the culprit for this tragedy. Leading newspapers and magazines rushed out a slew of front pages depicting Putin as a cold blooded assassin with shockingly accusatory titles as if his responsibility ware clear and undeniable.

- The Week: "Blood on his hands"
- The Sun: "Putin's missile"
- Daily Mail: "Putin's killed my son"
- Daily Mirror: "Putin's victims"
- Daily Express: "Putin's rebels blew up plane"
- Der Spiegel: "Stop Putin Now!"
- Newsweek: "The Pariah" [featuring a photo portrait of Vladimir Putin]
- Maclean's: "Getting away with murder"

BILL BROWDER AND I

This relentless demonization had a subtle effect on western public, even on well informed individuals among them. In my line of business I periodically attend conferences, discussion panels or informal gatherings with other hedge fund managers, traders and analysts to talk about world affairs. In such gatherings, people tend to be exceptionally well informed and most of them by far understood that they couldn't take the mainstream news at face value, particularly so with regards to Russia. In such gatherings I'd frequently encounter better understanding and more positive views of Russia and its leadership than in the mainstream. But even there, I noticed that most people tended to hedge their remarks with disclaimers of sort like,

- I don't like Vladimir Putin, but…
- I do not support Putin at all, but…
- Whatever you may think of Putin,…
- Vladimir Putin is a thug, but…

As if somehow it became wholly unacceptable in polite society to express positive views about Vladimir Putin without first explicitly denouncing the man. So on a number of occasions I asked people in such conversation to explain why, specifically they disliked Mr. Putin or thought that he was a thug. As I suspected, in each case I would get a vague answer reflecting the familiar mud slung daily at Mr. Putin by our media: somehow we all knew that he used to be a KGB agent, that his regime is adversarial to freedom and democracy, that he's a homophobe, that he has $17 or $40, or $70, or $400 billion stashed away somewhere outside Russia, that he had journalists and dissidents assassinated, that he shut down human rights organizations, etc. It was all just allegations peddled by the media seemingly always intent on inflicting damage on the image of Russia and especially of its president.

Throughout my life I've noticed how in a given place and time, certain 'things' become – for the lack of a better term – taboo: you can discuss them, but there is only one acceptable way to talk about them. When I lived in the United States in the late 1980s during the Ronald Reagan administration, you couldn't speak about communism in anything but negative and derogatory terms. Calling someone a 'communist' was an insult. But for a teenager who grew up in the 'communist' world, well indoctrinated about the wonderful wonders of communism, this was very strange. Back in Croatia a few years later I blundered onto the wrong side of another taboo. When Yugoslavia broke apart in the early 1990s and its constituent republics went to war against one another I stated in a discussion among my friends how I would always prefer a Serb who is a decent man over a Croat who's rotten – something I thought was a fool proof non-controversial statement. But my friends reacted with an awkward silence followed by an abrupt change of subject. Today, in the west that prides itself on free speech, there are many such taboos and most people dare not challenge them openly even if they disagree. Speaking well about Russia or Vladimir Putin has belonged in this category for many years.

It is important to understand that these taboos don't arise spontaneously. They are systematically infused into society by frequent and widespread repetition as well as loud and public rebukes and ridicule of anyone who dares to challenge them. Thus, numerous people who opposed NATO's policy of escalating tensions with Russia after 2014, like the (then) U.S. presidential candidate Donald Trump, UK's Labour Party leader Jeremy Corbyn, foreign minister Boris Johnson and a few others were labelled "Putin's useful idiots." Repetitive and widespread use of the same canned labels suggests that these campaigns were almost certainly coordinated at some level. Another example was when United Kingdom's Independence Party's home affairs spokeswoman Diane James said in a radio interview that she admired Vladimir Putin for standing up for his country. Her comments provoked such a storm of hysterical rebukes that she was pressured into correcting her stance: she had subsequently clarified that she *admired* Vladimir Putin but did not *like* him.

Observing these episodes made me realize that western antipathy toward Putin had less to do with the quality of his character and more with the unwritten commandment of Western public opinion that, "*thou shalt loathe Vladimir Putin.*" This all finally made me interested in Mr. Putin as a person. UKIP's spokeswoman Mrs. James was pressured into saying that she disliked him, but this didn't seem genuine or sincere. After all, anybody in the west can freely express admiration and liking for 'unsavoury' characters like Tony Blair, George Bush, Dick Cheney, Israeli Prime Minister Benjamin Netanyahu, Rwanda's president Paul Kagame or Russia's former president Boris Yeltsin. But for some reason, Vladimir Putin is off limits and we simply can't speak of him in positive terms.

Red notice

It was in this general Russophobic atmosphere in the west that my next 'encounter' with Bill Browder took place. It was the early months of 2015 and this time I didn't see Browder in person but received a copy of his book, "Red Notice." My wife read it before me and found it fascinating and compelling. She told me I absolutely had to read it and taunted me with something like, "let's see how you're going to feel about Putin and

BILL BROWDER AND I

Russia after you'd read this!" I tend to always guard against blindly trusting anyone or anything, so while I've come to support and admire Vladimir Putin as a statesman, I remained just as keen to learn the truth – *especially* if the truth should invalidate my present beliefs. I delved into Browder's book with great interest.

Reading and rereading Browder's story

It has to be said, "Red Notice" is a devilishly well written book. The story, which reads like a spy thriller takes the reader from Browder's troubled youth through his successful professional career that culminated with his building up the largest foreign owned hedge fund in Russia, an achievement that led ultimately to his becoming – in his own words – "*Putin's no. 1 enemy.*" "Red Notice" is also one of the few books I have ever read twice in its entirety, although this was not for its literary qualities. After I read it the first time, it had left me perplexed, with a feeling similar to that vague sense of wrong when you walk out of a shop, counting your money and thinking that you somehow got swindled, but you're not quite sure how. Part of my conflict was that I considered Bill Browder to be a sincere, decent man and I expected that he presented the true account of events. That account would have led me to believe that (a) Bill Browder was a very complex hero, a hybrid of spectacularly successful capitalist financier, a fearless fighter for justice, and a romantic family man, (b) that Russia was a terrible country and Russians terrible people, and (c) that Vladimir Putin is the greediest, most ruthless tyrant since Genghis Khan, and that he had turned his government into a lawless mafia state.

While I didn't (yet) doubt Browder's character and truthfulness, much of his story was so at odds with what I thought I understood about the issues and the people in it that just a few days after reading it I had to go back and read it over again. Like a cheated customer adding up his bill line by line, I sure enough started finding all kinds of odd things that slipped past my inner bullshit detectors on the first reading.

It's all true!

"Red Notice" disarms its readers' scepticism from the get-go by repetitively announcing how *everything* between its covers is true. Lee Child blurb on the front page says, "*Reads like a classic thriller ... but it's all true...*" On the inside cover, Geoffrey Robertson QC announces that Browder's story is "*absolutely true.*" Walter Isaacson tells again how it "*reads like a thriller, but it's a true, important and inspiring story.*" Tom Stoppard says the book is "*a true-life thriller...*" On the page following

Browder dedication of the book to Sergei Magnitsky, the publishers remind us that, *"the story in this book is true."* It did occur to me to wonder how all these people could possibly know that Browder's story is "absolutely true," but I was prepared to indulge the storyteller and believe his account.

Bill Browder, the complex hero

Browder paints a rather glowing image of himself. Already on page 1 he presents himself as a devoted father and a man of his word. From 1995 to 2005 he lived and worked in Moscow, but during that time he flew to London 260 times. The number 1 purpose for his trips was to visit his son, David. After divorcing David's mother, Browder made a commitment to visit him every other weekend *"no matter what"*. He had never broken the promise, he tells us. Only four lines later, Browder tells us that he is also a *very* successful hedge fund manager: *"I had made many people a lot of money."* And he didn't make money for those people just any old way – he did it by *"challenging the corruption of the oligarchs,"* who stole Russian companies and were robbing them blind. On page 160 he tells us how, *"... not only was I making lots of money, but I was also helping to make Russia a better place."*

On page 7, Browder reveals his tender, romantic side as he recounts a conversation with his second wife Elena, who recently gave birth to their first baby. *"Go to sleep, honey. You and the baby need the rest,"* says the tender father and adds, *"Goodnight. I love you."* Except Elena didn't hear this last bit – *"she'd already hung up,"* Browder tells us for some weird reason. Browder also tells us that he is a man of unwavering integrity and clear priorities.

In 1998 he confronts a rival investment group that attempted to defraud him and its investors in a fight to recover the money even at considerable risk to his own life. The situation was so serious that his largest investor, Israeli-Bazilian banker Edmond Safra sent Browder a squad of 15 heavily armed body guards with four armoured vehicles. His wife, who lived in London with their child beseeched him to leave Russia and return home, but Browder brushed her concerns aside: *"I have a responsibility to the people who trusted me with their money. I got them into this mess, I have to get them out."* In Browder's world, interests of his clients – whom he characterizes as people who *"had money and wanted more of it,"* – had a higher claim on his life than did his wife and infant son. He stayed in Moscow, fought his fight and won. Several times he reasserts his determination to recover his investors' losses. On page 132 he says, *"I had to make back all the money I had lost for my clients. I wasn't going to leave Russia with my tail between my legs."* On page 138 he says it again:

BILL BROWDER AND I

"*I'd stayed in Moscow for one simple reason: I was going to make my clients' money back no matter what it took.*" He proved successful in recovering his remaining clients' losses, but the "*no matter what it took*" part included divorce and the sacrifice of his family.

Browder is also quite a romantic conqueror. In chapter 16 he tells us about his conquest of his second wife, Elena Molokova. As he describes her, Elena was an attractive young woman with two PhDs who worked for an American public relations firm. Browder's friend, a Wall Street Journal reporter couldn't believe Browder was able to get not one, but two dates with Elena: "*Shit, Bill, that's an accomplishment in itself. Lots of people are after her.*" On the third date, Browder, "*grabbed her round the waist and pulled her towards me, and without any resistance we shared our first real kiss.*"

At the beginning of chapter 18, Browder shows himself as a true hero. One cold Saturday in February 2002 while running late to a tennis game, he (probably) saved a man's life. He sat in the back seat of his Blazer holding hands with his fiancée Elena when he spotted "*a large, dark object in the middle of the street.*" His driver, Alexei drove fast, but as they approached the object Browder saw that it was a man lying in the road, cars swerving left and right to avoid him. He shouted, "*Alexei, stop!*" But his Russian driver gave no indication of slowing down and Browder showted, "*Goddamnit, stop!*" As soon as he did, Browder jumped out of the car and knelt next to the man amidst cars "*zipping by and horns honking.*" The man was unconscious but Browder noticed that he was twitching and foam was bubbling from his mouth... he bent down and looped his arm under one of the man's shoulders and with his fiancée's and driver's help moved the man to the side of the road.

In chapter 38, towards the end of the book, Browder reveals what he's made of. Having devoted himself to his "*fight for justice,*" for nearly seven years, his business took a toll. He laments that his firm's investment business became only "*a shadow of its former self,*" but magnanimously accepts that it was all for a good cause: "*To build my fund back to what it had been would have required month after month of marketing trips and investment conferences. When I put the idea of doing this against that of getting justice for Sergei* [Magnitsky]*, justice won in a heartbeat.*"

Browder's star shines through the "Red Notice" all the brighter in contrast with the evil darkness of Russia – the book's main backdrop.

Russia is a terrible place and Russians terrible people

On my second reading of "Red Notice," I marked all the places in the book where Browder takes a jab at Russia or the Russian people. In 361 pages of text I counted at least 59 such jabs, some of them subtle, others borderline racist and overtly contemptuous of all things Russian to the point that Browder gives the reader a strong impression that he deeply despises the country where he lived ten years of his life and where he made his fortune. This impression is affirmed by Browder's disgraceful admission that after ten years in Russia he only learned "*taxi Russian.*"

Some of these jabs are rather metaphorical allusions like on page 2 when he tells us about his flights "*into the darkening country.*" As one day he walks to the office of one Boris Jordan, he tells us how, "*the sky is dark again.*" With great consistency, Browder contrasts this grey imagery of Russia with that of the West as if the places occupied two different planets: "*Where everyone was aggressive, angry and tense in Russia, everyone was tanned, relaxed and happy in Italy.*" In New York, "*the Twin Towers glistened in the bright morning sun.*" And California, "*was heaven. The air was clean, the sky was blue and every day felt as if I were living in some kind of paradise.*" And so on.

In Russia generally everything sucks according to Browder. Moscow's Sheremetyevo airport confronts the traveller "*with the crowds and the chaos,*" and even at the VIP lounge they serve weak coffee and overbrewed tea. No wonder returning to Russia made Browder feel "*cold and lonely.*"

As if all that weren't dismal enough, the reader may be shocked to learn that "*in Russia there is no respect for the individual and his or her rights. People can be sacrificed for the needs of the state, used as shields, trading chips, or even simple fodder.*" Russians are also terribly rude. Browder describes how in 1993 when he was taking a flight from St. Petersburg to Murmansk, "*a large stranger plopped down next to me. He didn't say a word, but he pushed my arm off the armrest between our seats and promptly lit a cigarette, taking pains to blow the smoke in my direction.*" They are rude and they're liars. You see, in Russia, "*People lie, politicians lie, everybody lies.*" In fact, everyone there is "*aggressive, angry and tense.*" and it should therefore be no surprise that "*Russian business culture is closer to that of a prison yard than anything else.*"

Browder is not sexist with his contempt for all things Russian. When writing about Russian women, he depicts them as *easy*: "*Russian girls wold throw themselves at you – and into your bed – almost upon meeting. There was no sport to it at all, no chase, no courting.*"

Russia is also a violent place and a "*rogue*" nation built upon an "*evil foundation.*" Its justice system is illegitimate and it has "*no rule of law,*" but rule of men who are "*crooks.*" In fact, Russian society is so rotten that acts of kindness are punished by law: "*a single act of Good Samaritanship could lead you to a seven-year prison sentence.*" Every Russian knows this and consequently "*most Russians didn't operate on high-minded *principles...*" Instead "*Everything in Russia was about money. Making it, keeping it and making sure no one took it.*" "*With all the evil going on in Russia,*" it's little wonder that, "*Russian stories never have happy endings.*" This is why, "*Russians are familiar with hardship, suffering and despair – not with success and certainly not with justice*"

When describing places he visits in Russia he usually describes them with derogatory language. When he visited Murmansk in 1993, he tells us how the bathroom in his hotel smelled like urine, and "*the mattress was lumpy and sunken in the middle, as if it hadn't been changed in twenty-five years.*" When he came for an appointment at the Moscow Oil Refinery (MNPZ), he describes the building as old and ugly with filthy walls and floors missing tiles.

Even business cards are laughable in Russia. Browder laments that if he'd been a London investment banker, his Rolodex, "*would have been bursting with embossed cards on thick stock.*" Instead, Browder's collection was humbler. Some business cards "*were printed on cardboard. Others were orange or green or light blue. Some looked as if they'd been printed on a home computer. Two cards were stuck together because of cheap ink.*" But Braveheart Browder adds with an air of rugged heroism, "*Still, I went through them.*"

Dealing with Russians is very difficult and you have to be incredibly focused to have even a chance of finding out what you need (especially if you didn't bother to learn the language). You see, the Russians tend to "*talk pointlessly for hours,*" because "*only bad things could come from passing real information to anyone*".

Russians are crooks, and they may steal even when it makes no financial sense, "*because it is the Russian thing to do.*" To illustrate, Browder tells us the famous Russian proverb about "*a poor villager who happens upon a magic talking fish that is ready to grant him a single wish.*" As the villager tries to make up his mind what he wants most, the fish warns him about an important caveat: whatever he chooses, his neighbour will receive double. "*Without skipping a beat, the villager says, 'In that case, please poke one of my eyes out.'* " You may not have caught the subtle moral of this "*proverb,*" since it conveys the uniquely Russian sentiments of envy and jealousy[2] which are entirely alien to the Western soul. Thankfully, Browder is patient enough to explain it for us: "*when it comes to money, Russians will gladly – gleefully even – sacrifice their own success to screw their neighbour.*"

---

[2] German word, "schadenfreude," meaning gladness at someone else's misfortune would be more appropriate here but English language does not have the equivalent word.

Vladimir Putin is a greedy, brazen tyrant

While "Red Notice" does a harsh hatchet job on the Russian president, the book mentions Vladimir Putin relatively rarely. We only get the first real glimpse into Putin's character in the pivotal chapter 18, aptly titled "Fifty Percent." Namely, here Browder explains for the reader the way Putin extorted money from Russian oligarchs: first he threw one of them, Mikhail Khodorkovsky, in prison as a warning to others, and then demanded 50% of the action from them lest they also ended up in prison. But Browder essentially pulls this entire idea out of his own bottom: *"It could have been 30 percent or 70 percent,"* he writes, *"or some other arrangement." "I wasn't there,"* admits Browder: *"I'm only speculating."* This particular kind of speculating can also be called spinning tales or making groundless insinuations.

Having painted a thoroughly ugly picture of Russia throughout his book, Browder then lays the responsibility for the dismal state of affairs in that nation squarely at Putin's feet. In chapter 31, ("The Katyn Principle") Browder tells us how in April of 1940, Soviet troops executed some twenty two thousand Polish prisoners but when the war was over, they blamed the atrocity on the Germans, manufacturing evidence and repeating the lie so often that their version of events became unchallenged. The relevance of that Soviet episode to Vladimir Putin's Russia is that, *"... when Vladimir Putin came to power in 2000, instead of dismantling this machine of lying and fabrication, he modified it and made it all the more powerful."*

My second reading of Browder's book raised several critical red flags and so I started researching more thoroughly into many of the issues and historical episodes within which Browder's story unfolded. This is ultimately how this book materialized.

2. Red Notice – play by play

When someone is crossing the yard coming for you, you cannot stand idly by. You have to kill him before he kills you.

Bill Browder

In Red Notice, Browder presents a multifaceted story that takes the reader along on the journey through his rather amazing Russian experience and its gripping aftermath. The story is very well told and packaged, so much so that the reader must be forgiven for forgetting that they are reading *Bill Browder's* story and not an objective rendition of reality. On my first reading of it, I realized I might easily have bought his tale if I didn't already know some aspects of it. The story's well-packaged complexity made it a bit laborious to deconstruct and highlight the suspicious parts, which is why my review below turned out somewhat lengthy.

While raising suspicions isn't the same as proving falsity, the two years that have lapsed since Browder's publishing of Red Notice, much has happened that actually *proves* that some key aspects of his account are false. We'll discuss these in part 5 of this book, "*Bill Browder, the great pretender.*" First, let's familiarize ourselves with Red Notice. It may be a thankless task, but don't worry, I've tried my best to make it as readable and entertaining as I could.

The opening chapters

Browder opens with the story about his deportation from Russia in November of 2005. Having arrived at Moscow's Sheremetyevo airport, as he did 260 times before, instead of passing through passport check counters, he was taken to a detention room where he spent the whole night waiting, only to have two immigration officers escort him onto the first flight back to London. His Russian visa was revoked indefinitely.

In the second chapter, he tells us about his family, starting with his grandfather Earl Browder who was a labor union organizer. In 1926, by invitation of the Bolshevik government, Earl Browder went to the Soviet Union where he stayed for six years. In 1932, upon returning to the United States he took charge of the American Communist Party and ran for President of the United States in 1936 and in 1940. Comrade Browder even appeared on the cover of the *Time* magazine in 1938 but in the 1950s he suffered political persecution under Senator Joseph McCarthy's anti-communist witch hunts. Browder's parents were both left-leaning PhD scientists as was his older brother. Bill himself grew up as the black sheep of the family. *"In my family,"* he writes at the end of chapter 2, *"if you weren't a prodigy, then you had no place on earth."* His parents sent him to *"a string of psychiatrists, counsellors and doctors."* Young Bill ultimately rebelled and thought that the best way to stick it to his parents would be to *"put on a suit and a tie and become a capitalist."*

In the chapters that follow Browder describes how he advanced along this path, from his boarding school days through college education at the University of Boulder in Colorado, his first job at a management consulting company [3] in Boston and graduate studies at Stanford University. In the late 1980s he started his professional career. At that time, the communist block [4] was facing a grave social and economic crisis. Sensing opportunity, Browder sought out consulting projects in Eastern Europe and by 1990 his employer, the Boston Consulting Group sent him on assignment to Poland, where he made his first personal financial investment in the post-communist world and acquired the taste for equity bargains. His investment in Polish privatization program appreciated tenfold in a short time, giving him the sensation he characterizes as *"the financial equivalent of smoking crack cocaine. Once you've done it, you want to repeat it over and over and over as many times as you can."* (38)

In 1991, Browder went to work for the billionaire media magnate Robert Maxwell who, at the time, was setting up an Eastern Europe

---

[3] Bain and Company
[4] Primarily the countries of Eastern Europe and the Soviet Union

investment fund. With this job, Browder was directly responsible for part of Maxwell's investments and he travelled extensively across the former communist bloc. However, in November of 1991 Maxwell mysteriously died while vacationing off the Canary Islands. It soon turned out that Maxwell's business empire sat on a mountain of debt he was unable to repay. To keep in business, Maxwell resorted to fraud, including raiding £460 million from Maxwell Communications Corporation's pension fund which left his 32,000 employees and pensioners destitute. The BBC called Maxwell the biggest fraud in British History. For Browder, having worked for Maxwell was toxic for his career. For a while he found that no other employer would touch him and he only managed to get a job in mid-1992 with Salomon Brothers, another scandal-prone investment bank. They hired Browder on a simple but daunting premise: *"You generate five times your salary in the next 12 months... Otherwise you're sacked."*

This was the job that finally brought Bill Browder to Russia. While the bank was covering activities and deals in all of Eastern Europe, Browder discovered that nobody was covering Russia, so he declared himself *"the investment banker in charge of Russia"*. With only three months on the job he took on an assignment for the Murmansk Trawler Fleet which was being privatized as part of the Russian "shock therapy" economic transition. The firm, owning one hundred trawlers worth about $20 million each, was offering half interest to investors for $2.5 million. This deal rekindled Browder's passion for investment bargains and rather than returning straight to London after his assignment he flew to Moscow to learn everything he could about the Russian privatization program.

To his astonishment, he found that the Russian government was selling about 30 percent of each of some 27,000 Russian companies for a sum total of $3 billion. This implied that the valuation of the entire Russian economy – the treasure trove containing some of the world's most abundant reserves of natural gas, oil, coal, iron ore, tin, lead, gold, silver, palladium, platinum, diamonds, timber, rare earth minerals and arable land – was being sold for only $10 billion, corresponding to one sixth of Wal-Mart's market capitalization at that time. After a few days in Moscow, Browder rushed back to Salomon Brothers to try to convince his bosses and colleagues that they were *"giving money away for free in Russia."* But his co-workers showed very little interest, and his persistent pitching of the investment opportunities in Russia seemed to make things worse for him: *"... I completely ruined my reputation inside Salomon Brothers. No one wanted anything to do with me because I was that 'crazy fuck who wouldn't shut up about Russia.'"*

As his first year at Salomon was drawing to a close, Browder was worried that he'd be sacked as he failed to generate much revenue for the firm. But then suddenly, he received a call from a senior colleague in New York who wanted to hear his Russia story. When he did, he said it was the most amazing thing he'd ever heard and the same day he got Browder $25 million to invest in Russia. This is where things start to get interesting for Bill Browder. He was soon on his way to Moscow, just in time to get in on Russia's massive privatization program. The scheme involved a voucher system whereby the government granted one privatization certificate with a face value of 10,000 roubles to each of about 150 million Russian citizens. The sum total of these vouchers could be exchanged for about 30 percent in each of Russia's 27,000 state companies. The government imposed no restrictions on who could participate in the program and any foreigner with money could buy as many vouchers as he could get his hands on.

To fund Browder's investment initiative, Salomon Brothers wired $25 million to a Russian bank owned by one of its employee's relatives.[5] Because voucher transactions were done in cash, Browder would withdraw the cash in *"crisp $100 bills"* stuffed in canvas bags, one million dollars at a time, and use an armoured car with security guards to take the money to Moscow's voucher exchange. Voucher exchange was at a large hall several blocks from the Red Square and it consisted of a series of concentric circles of tables with an electronic trading board hanging from the ceiling. Trading was fully open to the public and anyone could buy or sell vouchers.

Because Russian authorities made little effort to educate the public about the privatization, ordinary Russians were unsure about what to do with their vouchers. What the Russians *did* know was that inflation was eating up the value of their salaries if they were lucky enough to receive them, and most of them were ready to sell the vouchers for a few dollars or some food. Enterprising individuals with some cash went around towns and villages across Russia and bought the vouchers from people at steep discounts to resell them to consolidating agents in larger towns. These agents resold their hoard of vouchers to wholesale dealers in Moscow who consolidated them into bundles of twenty five thousand or more and sold them at the voucher exchange roughly for their face value. This is where Bill Browder spent $25 million of Salomon Brothers' cash.

But buying vouchers was only the first step in the privatization process. Investors then had to exchange the vouchers for the actual shares of Russian firms. This was done at Russia's unique voucher auctions. They were unique because buyers had no idea the price they would be paying for the stock shares until the auctions were finished. *"If only one person*

---

[5] A very fortuitous circumstance – what were the odds?

showed up with a single voucher," writes Browder, *"then the entire block of shares being auctioned would be exchanged for that one voucher. On the other hand, if the whole population of Moscow showed up with all their vouchers, then that block of shares would be evenly divided among every single voucher that was submitted at the auction."* The system was not only susceptible to abuse as Browder points out, it was *designed* for just such abuse. Resourceful managers only needed to find creative ways of keeping other investors away by making the auction sites difficult to find or scheduling the event at awkward times. Many auctions were arranged in such a way that only company management and privileged insiders would show up and walk away with the ownership of the firm, for next to nothing.

Only a few months after Browder invested Salomon Brothers' money in what he called, *"the most undervalued shares that had ever been offered anywhere in history,"* The Economist published an article titled, *"Time to bet on Russia?"* which triggered a wave of interest in Russian stocks among western investors. Browder's $25 million portfolio soon appreciated to $125 million turning him into hero at Salomon. Suddenly, he was sought after on all sides, invited to make presentations and share his ideas on investing in Russia to investors worldwide, including some of the biggest names in asset management like George Soros and Julian Robertson. One of Salomon's clients who saw Browder's presentation was an Israeli billionaire Benny Steinmetz. He was so impressed with Browder's presentation that he offered to help bankroll his own investment management shop, bringing along a small group of investors, the most important among whom was the Syrian-Israeli banker Edmond Safra. After much footwork on his part, which he recounts in its most interesting detail in chapters 7, 8 and 9, Browder did manage to set up a hedge fund operation and an office in Moscow, starting his career as an independent asset manager. In 1996 he moved to Moscow and launched Hermitage Capital with a $25 million seed investment from Safra and Steinmetz. Within weeks from investing these assets Boris Yeltsin's won his re-election as Russia's president and Browder's fund vaulted up 125%.

But with such spectacular bargains to be found in Russia, her capital markets attracted a veritable feeding frenzy of foreign investors and domestic oligarchs. In this environment it wasn't long before Browder had a dangerous run-in with a group headed by one of Russia's wealthiest oligarchs, Vladimir Potanin. Potanin was associated with George Soros, Russian-American investment banker Boris Jordan, the Harvard Institute for International Development and a number of other powerful individuals. He was close enough to Russia's center of power that he openly boasted about wielding control over the Yeltsin government. When Browder confronted Potanin's group over an illegal stock share issue that would have diluted and effectively robbed Browder and his investors, the situation became so dangerous that on barely half day's notice Edmond Safra sent 15 heavily armed bodyguards with four armoured cars for Browder's protection. Against the seemingly slim odds in his favour, Browder prevailed in this clash when the Russian Federal Securities and Exchange Commission annulled Potanin's firm's share issue.[6] Browder's victory over a larger, more powerful rival marked his rising star.

In 1997 Hermitage Fund gained 235% to become that year's best performing fund in the world. Even more impressively, the fund was up 718% from inception, and its assets under management grew from the initial $25 million to over $1 billion. Unfortunately for Bill Browder, this was when his fortunes reversed in an equally spectacular fashion. In 1997, a severe financial crisis hit east Asian markets and the fallout from that crisis affected Russia as well. In January of 1998 Hermitage Fund lost a whopping 25%. Before the year was out, the fund was down 90%, having sustained a $900 million loss. Humiliated and shunned, Browder took his blows in strides and remained in Moscow, determined to recover his clients' money. This all was too much for his first wife Sabrina, who finally wanted a divorce.

Things also went badly for his partner and mentor Edmond Safra who, along with losing money in Hermitage Fund played a bigger game in Russia. Less than a year after the Russian default in 1998, Safra had to sell his Republic National Bank of New York to the banking conglomerate HSBC and only a few months later – in December 1999 – he died at his Monaco apartment, possibly assassinated by one of his nurses. Browder dubbed 1999 as the worst year of his life, but to his credit he soldiered on and reinvented both his love life and his investment management career. Less than six months after his wife asked for divorce, Browder had his heart set on a Russian woman Elena Molokova, whom he met at one of his presentations in Moscow. He describes his long but successful courtship in chapter 16 titled "Tuesdays with Morrie."

With Elena conquered, Browder's life brightens and he opens the next chapter with the sentence, *"It's amazing how being in love changes things"* Reenergized, Browder put what was left of his fund to work by investing in shares of Russia's most valuable companies and seeking to unlock their value by investigating and exposing management corruption and theft of

---

[6] The firm in question was Sidanco but here the story has a small inconsistency. At first, the conflict is over a dilutive Sidanco share issue (p. 111). Upon resolution, Browder cites a *Financial Times* headline, "Watchdog Annuls Sidanco Bond Issue."

company assets. Browder illustrates the strategy with the fascinating example of Gazprom whose top management had effectively stolen oil reserves equivalent to those of Kuwait. Although in terms of oil reserves Gazprom was eight times the size of Exxon Mobil and twelve times the size of BP, in 1999 it traded at a 99.7% discount to western oil firms per barrel of reserves. Corruption was the key to the low valuation of Russian companies and Browder embarked on a bold but brilliant strategy of picking up the shares of such firms, and attacking corruption – a clever, Russian version of activist investing.

Investigating malfeasance was possible tanks to the fact that, as Browder puts it, *"Russia was strangely one of the most transparent places in the world."* Once his team figured out how to get the raw information about asset sales and purchases from the various government bureaucracies, they were able trace who stole what in considerable detail and they subsequently exposed their findings in the financial press. Browder reports that his and his team's research was so detailed and so compelling that all major financial publications picked up their reports. Their research exposing corruption at Gazprom was published in hundreds of articles in Russian and foreign press. This is where Vladimir Putin's government comes into the story.

The fallout from Browder's Gazprom reports was slow to materialize as both Russia's public Audit Chamber and the western auditing firm PricewaterhouseCoopers gave Gazprom a clean audit and provided arguments that justified management's conduct. While it appeared that the management might weather the storm unscathed, Vladimir Putin's government stepped in. On the occasion of company's annual general meeting on 30th June 2001, Vladimir Putin fired the company's CEO Rem Vyakhirev and replaced him by Alexey Miller who immediately announced he would secure Gazprom's remaining assets and recover what had been stolen. Over the next four years Browder's considerable investment in Gazprom appreciated 100 *times*. The new investment strategy was paying off and Browder's star was on the rise once more.

The plot thickens

Sadly, this is where the mood of the story turns dark and the plot of the book starts to feel dodgy and deceptive. The ensuing sections comb over some of the many suspicious details of Browder's tale.

Chapter 18: "Fifty percent"

In this chapter Browder gives us a shockingly crude account of the way Vladimir Putin abuses his power in Russia for his own personal enrichment. He does so right after telling us an unrelated story about himself, his own Jack Ryan[7] moment of sorts.

On a cold Saturday in February 2002, while running late to his tennis game, Browder saved a man's life. As he sat in the back seat of his car holding hands with his fiancée, he saw *"a large, dark object in the middle of the street."* His driver, Alexei drove fast, but as they approached the object Browder saw that it was a man lying in the road, cars swerving around him. He shouted, *"Alexei, stop!"* But as his Russian driver wasn't slowing down, Browder shouted, *"Goddamnit, stop!"* Browder then jumped out of the car and knelt next to the man amidst cars *"zipping by and horns honking."* It turned out that the man had an epileptic attack and to get him out of danger Browder put his arm under one of the man's shoulders and with his fiancée's and driver's help moved him to the side of the road.

This story – whether true or invented – served two important purposes. First, it creates contrast between Browder and his surroundings: he acts decisively to save a stranger's life while indifferent Russians speed by, *"horns honking."* When the police arrive, they virtually ignore the epileptic man and want only to blame and punish somebody for something. *"For the average Muscovite,"* explains Browder, *"a single act of Good Samaritanship could lead to a seven-year prison sentence. And every Russian knew this."* Russians, it seems, must be scrupulous never to commit acts of Good Samaritanship lest they end up in a gulag. Russia, you see, is just such a horrid place.

The second reason for this digression is for Browder to make himself likeable. If you ever studied psychology of persuasion, you may have learned that you are much more likely to persuade an audience if you can get them to like you. Thus, Browder tells us how he saved a man's life and goes on to further garnish his image of a moral hero by explaining his investigation of Russian corruption as more Good Samaritanship: you see, he was working selflessly, risking his life to fight corruption simply to make Russia a better place. The fact that this work turned out to be so very profitable for him was perhaps just a fortuitous coincidence. Browder strains to make himself so very likeable and trustworthy to the reader because he is about to make an incredible and utterly vicious accusation against Vladimir Putin. It is an accusation based – as he himself admits it – on nothing but his own speculation.

---

[7] Second lieutenant Dr. John Patrick "Jack" Ryan, a CIA agent, is the quintessential American hero created by author Tom Clancy in his novels. Ryan is an intelligent, courageous and moral hero committed to fighting against evil forces in the world. His heroics inspired a number of successful Hollywood films.

After priming his readers' credulousness with all this self-aggrandizement, Browder ambushes them with his fantastically ugly smear of Vladimir Putin. He recounts the story about the October of 2003 arrest of Mikhail Khodorkovsky, Russia's richest man. Browder's feelings about the arrest were mixed; in Russia, rich people didn't tend to spend much time in prison, and if Khodorkovsky *"miraculously stayed in jail and this was to be the beginning of a crackdown on the oligarchs, it meant that Russia had a chance at becoming a normal country."* As we now know, Khodorkovsky stayed in jail for nearly ten years, and that really *was* the beginning of a crackdown on the oligarchs. But Browder explains it otherwise: it was no crackdown after all. *"It all came down to the personal negotiation between Vladimir Putin and Mikhail Khodorkovsky, a negotiation in which neither law nor logic played any role."*

Browder then asks rhetorically: *"Why was Putin doing this?"* The likeable hero of his own story then explains: after Khodorkovsky's arrest, other Russian oligarchs essentially wet themselves with fear and *"one by one"* went to Putin to ask what they could do to make sure they also didn't end up in prison. *"I wasn't there, so I'm only speculating,"* says Browder, but he imagined that *"Putin's response was something like this: 'Fifty per cent.'"* He further clarifies that it wouldn't be 50% for the government or for the presidential administration but 50% for Vladimir Putin personally. *"I don't know this for sure. It could have been 30 per cent or 70 per cent or some other arrangement."* Or it might have been zero percent. Or it might be that all these oligarch meetings with Putin only took place in Browder's own vindictive imagination.

The allegation that Russia's president used his power to extort the country's oligarchs for his private gain is an extremely serious one. It is much too serious to be based on, *"I'm only speculating..."* And the reason why this shot up a red flag for me was that just in the preceding chapter Browder boasts about how he and his team were able to piece together asset transfers and ownership for any company or individual stockholder because Russia was *"one of the most transparent places in the world."*

Because he smeared Putin in this way, Browder also needed to explain why he was such a big Putin supporter before he got expelled from Russia. At that time, he believed that Putin was acting in good faith to clean up the country because his own experience confirmed as much: after exposing corruption at Gazprom, Vladimir Putin fired and replaced Gazprom's top management. When Browder exposed how the CEO of UES[8] was selling company assets to his friends at huge discounts, Putin's government halted

---

[8] United Energy System

the sales. When he outed the Sberbank management for similar misdeeds, Russia changed its laws to disable such management abuse.

So if Putin's government in actual deed cracked down on oligarchs and worked to clean up Russia, what made Browder change his mind about Vladimir Putin? For one thing, he may have felt that his expulsion from Russia was unfair.[9] But he contrives a different explanation – one that frankly insults the average reader's intelligence. You see, after Khodorkovsky's arrest, Bill Browder continued with his activist investing: buying shares in companies and then investigating and exposing corruption of their management. But now – since Putin was appropriating large chunks of Russian economy for himself, Browder wasn't merely going against a gaggle of corrupt managers – now he was going against Putin himself.

How does that make any sense at all? Browder's activism led to a clean-up of corruption at Gazprom, and that clean-up was done by Putin's government, resulting in a 100-fold increase in Gazprom's share price. Similar actions with other firms probably led to similar outcomes. If these firms were now Putin's personal fiefdom, Browder's activism would result in an exponential rise in Putin's wealth. In effect, Browder's and Putin's business interests would be so beautifully aligned that Putin should have made sure that Browder stayed in Russia forever to work his magic unmolested. He might even have offered to hire Browder himself. He should have, at the very least provided him full protection. But no – Putin has him expelled instead.

So in the same chapter, Browder shows Putin to be brazenly greedy and also not greedy. Well, if Putin wasn't acting out of personal greed, there could be two other explanations for Browder's expulsion from Russia. One would be that Vladimir Putin is spectacularly stupid. The other, that Browder was actually found in violation of Russia's laws and was expulsed to disable his activity. As even my Golden Retriever now understands, Vladimir Putin is far from being a stupid man and Bill Browder is far from being the moral, law-abiding hero he impersonates.

After I read this chapter the second time, I wrote the following in my notes: "Upon closer scrutiny, this chapter is an ugly, vulgar, deceitful write-up where a lot of stuff is distorted and contrived in a deceitful and malicious way... it must have been the work of a ghost-writer."

---

[9] In fact, in the next chapter he'll show that he's rather bitter about this: "*I'd spent the previous ten years painstakingly building my business brick by brick, foregoing a social life, ... treating weekends like work days, all to create a $4.5 billion investment-advisory business. I couldn't let the cancellation of my visa destroy it in one fell swoop.*" (164)

Chapter 20: *"Vogue Café"*

Chapter 19 briefly recounts Browder's initial attempts to reverse his Russian visa revocation by appealing to the UK Foreign Office and to the HSBC bank.[10] While neither HSBC nor the Foreign Office were able to help him, he learned through their intervention that he got expulsed from Russia because the Russian government designated him as a national security threat. Simon Smith, a Foreign Office diplomat also warned Browder that he would have to keep the affair strictly out of the press if there was any hope for him to regain entry into Russia.

In the following chapter, titled "Vogue Café" Browder's story starts to read like a spy novel as Russian *deep state* actors begin to enter the narrative. The first such instance was when Vadim, Browder's head of research who apparently has no surname, meets with one "Aslan" at the Vogue Café on Kuznetsky bridge in Moscow. Aslan was from the government, perhaps the FSB and apparently knew *"everything"*. He told Vadim that FSB was after Hermitage's assets and also that there was *"a war going on inside the government, and his group was in conflict with"* whoever was harassing Browder.

Meanwhile, several high ranking officials earnestly tried to help Browder's cause. First, there was German Gref, then Russian Minister for Economic Development. He intervened with the head of the FSB, Nikolai Petrushev, but Petrushev encouraged Gref to mind his own business. Then the head of Russia's security markets regulator, Oleg Vyugin wrote on Browder's behalf to Russia's deputy prime minister but someone high up apparently snubbed him too. Vyugin met with Browder personally in London, and a subtle gesture Vyugin made during that meeting convinced Browder that it was none other than Vladimir Putin who ordered him kicked out of Russia: *"He stared at me and raised his eyebrows ever so slightly. He then pointed a slender finger at the ceiling and said nothing more."* Well, duh! That gesture can only refer to one person: Vladimir Putin! Browder is careful not to suggest that Vyugin actually said any such thing, but only that, *"that was the only way I could interpret his mysterious gesture."* So here again we have an allegation against Putin based entirely on Browder's interpretation of another man's mute gesture. I can't help wondering why Browder did not simply ask Vyugin whether it was indeed Vladimir Putin who ordered his expulsion from Russia. Then he could report Vyugin's answer, sparing himself the embarrassment of pulling baseless allegations out of his back end.

---

[10] HSBC took Edmond Safra's role as Browder's business partner after buying out Safra's bank.

After Vyugin, it was Vladimir Putin's chief economic adviser, Arkady Dvorkovich who earnestly took up Browder's case and convinced several people in the presidential administration that cancelling Browder's visa was a mistake that could be damaging to Russia's interests. Dvorkovich even managed to put the issue on the agenda for the National Security Council meeting with Vladimir Putin in the winter of 2006. This initiative was, however, sabotaged in a rather extraordinary way. Namely, just four days before this meeting, reporters from Washington Post, Financial Times and Reuters started inquiring with Browder about the rumors of his expulsion from Russia. To provoke a response from Browder, Reuters' reporter Elif Kaban called repeatedly, claiming to have solid information about his expulsion. Although Browder followed Foreign Office advice not to go public with the news of his expulsion from Russia, just one day before the Security Council meeting with Vladimir Putin, Reuters published the story, *"Hermitage CEO Browder Barred from Russia."* [11]

This detail of Browder's story actually indicates that Putin probably *did not* order Browder's expulsion, and that he really had no idea who Bill Browder was. Arkady Dvorkovich was about to bring Browder's case to Vladimir Putin's attention at an important national security meeting, and just in time to damage Browder's cause, western press somehow got alerted to Browder's expulsion and published the story... *"This was exactly what Simon Smith* [of the UK Foreing Office] *had warned me about,"* writes Browder, *"and now it was happening. There would be no way for the Russians to save face, no way to back down."*

It appears that there really was a turf war within the Russian government: while the reformer Dvorkovich wanted to help Browder believing that this was in Russia's interest, another group wanted to make sure that this didn't happen, so they tipped off the press just ahead of the pivotal meeting with Putin. Had Vladimir Putin really been the moving force behind Browder's expulsion, there would have been no need for the sabotage of Arkady Dvorkovich's effort because Putin himself would have shot him down instantly even if the issue had been allowed onto the security meeting agenda. The fact that someone had to go out of their way and sabotage Dvorkovich by breaking Browder's case to the press indicates that Vladimir Putin wasn't privy to this turf war, and probably knew nothing about Browder's expulsion.

Chapter 21: "The G8"

Chapter 21 opens as follows: *"When the Russian government turns on you, it doesn't do so mildly – it does so with extreme prejudice."* Browder uses

---

[11] According to Browder, this story broke on 17 March 2006. (179)

Mikhail Khodorkovsky as a case in point, the same man whom in 2005 he called a crook and probably a murderer. Russian government went after Khodorkovsky and by early 2006, ten people connected to his company, Yukos, were arrested while dozens more fled Russia. *This*, Browder assures us, is why he took prompt action to get all of his clients' money and his key personnel *"out of Russia as quickly as possible."* The interesting bit is that even though the terrible Russian government turned on Browder "with extreme prejudice," he was able to get all of his key people and their families out of Russia within a month's time. It was a bit more complicated with the money because they had to sell billions of dollars of Russian securities without alerting the markets, as this would have depressed the prices of those securities. Nevertheless, over some two months' time they pulled it off and Browder writes proudly how, *"Hermitage had successfully removed all its money from Russia without our enemies ever knowing."*

Unfortunately, with Browder thrown out of Russia, many of his clients thought he could no longer effectively manage their funds and many of them requested redemptions of their investments in Hermitage Fund. The business he built over the previous ten years was starting to unravel and Browder's only hope of saving it was to regain entry into Russia. A slim chance of that was still open as the UK's Foreign Office continued working on his case, and their efforts culminated with the surprise announcement that Britain's Prime Minister Tony Blair himself was to raise Browder's case with Russia's President Vladimir Putin during the G8 Summit in Saint Petersburg scheduled for the 15th July of 2006. Six days before the summit, British daily *Observer* even published an article titled, *"Blair to Rise Fund Manager's Case with Putin."*

Unfortunately for Browder, just before the Summit, a major international crisis erupted when Israel launched an air raid and incursion into Lebanon. This was an event of major importance and it reshuffled all delegations' agendas for the G8 summit. As a result, Tony Blair never confronted Vladimir Putin about Bill Browder. Instead, it was a journalist from Moscow Times, Catherine Belton who confronted Putin at the post summit press conference, asking him why Browder's visa was denied. Vladimir Putin's response indicated that he didn't know why any particular person might be denied entry in to Russia and imagined that they might have broken the nation's laws. In his book however, Browder ventures to "translate" Vladimir Putin's words: *"We never mention enemies by name, and that includes Bill Browder. I am now instructing my law-enforcement agencies to open up as many criminal cases against him as possible."*

Browder's translation is a very imaginative stretch from Mr. Putin's original words, but as we shall explore later in this book, they reveal a lot more about the translator than they do about Mr. Putin.

Chapter 22: "The Raids"

In January 2007, Browder attended the Davos World Economic Forum where he met Russia's then first deputy Prime Minister, Dmitri Medvedev and pled personally for help with his Russian visa. Medvedev graciously consented and promised Browder that he would submit his visa application to the Federal Border Service with his own recommendation to approve it. About three weeks later, in February 2007, Browder was contacted from the Moscow branch of the Interior Ministry, by Liutenant Colonel Artem Kuznetsov who wanted to meet with Browder in person, suggesting that the sooner Browder could answer his questions, the sooner his problems would disappear.

By this time however, Browder was again flying high and raising significant capital[12] for his new firm, Hermitage Global. Browder thought that Kuznetsov's inquiry was not legitimate, that he was probably seeking to extract a bribe, and decided to ignore the presumptuous Russian cop. Perhaps this wasn't one of Browder's best decisions.

On the 4th June 2007, while Browder travelled to Paris for a meeting with Hermitage Global's directors, Artem Kuznetsov brought 25 plainclothes police to raid Browder's offices in Moscow. At the same time, another police squadron raided the offices of the law firm Firestone Duncan with whom Browder had done a lot of business over the years. Apparently, the police were after the files for "Kameya," a Russian company owned by one of their clients through which Browder advised them on investing in Russia. As he tells the story, Browder was horrified – not so much about the raids themselves – but because Maxim,[13] one of Firestone Ducnan's employees got beaten up and injured by the police.

---

[12] Browder tells us on p. 188 of Red Notice that by the end of April 2007 he had raised $625 million. Hedge funds used to charge their investors a 2% annual management fee. With $625 million under management, Browder could look forward to generating over $1 million per month in revenues. That's before so-called performance fees kick in, which are usually 20% of any gross capital gains.

[13] I'm not sure why Browder tells us that "Maxim" was beaten up. In a Hermitage Capital presentation dated March 2009, leaked by Wikileaks the person beaten by Kuznetsov's cops was identified as Victor Poryugin. In other words, in his book Browder changes this man's identity for some reason. Could it be so that some curious someone couldn't look up Poryugin and inquire about his version of events?

Entering again his Jack Ryan role, Browder pledged that *"We're not going to let these bastards get away with this."* But, *"More importantly,"* he was *very* concerned about Maxim's health and closes the chapter concluding that they were now all *"in deep shit,"* and that the 4th June 2007 raids were only the beginning of their troubles.

One of the oddities of this chapter is Browder's lawyer in Moscow, the American Jamison Firestone. He came to Moscow in 1991 aged only 25. Landing in the chaos of the Russian transition, he founded a law firm together with another young American, and until Kuznetsov's raids pretty much did well for himself.[14] Browder tells us that he liked Jamie Firestone and makes subtle contrast between this fit, handsome, *"straight-talking,"* honest American and the ghoulish Russians whom he describes as having *"great skill in talking without saying anything."*

Chapter 23: "Department K"

In the first paragraph of this chapter Browder tells us that Russia is a violent place, and makes contrast of himself in the very next paragraph as he shows us again what an up-standing fellow he is. In the aftermath of the police raids on his office, his *"first concern was Maxim"* You know, the junior lawyer at the law firm he hired in Moscow. To his great relief, he learned that Maxim's injuries were not life threatening. Less importantly, he also learned the official reason for the police raids: the tax crimes department of the Moscow Interior Ministry had opened a criminal case against Ivan Cherkasov, Hermitage's Chief Operating Officer. They accused him of underpaying $44 million in taxes related to a Russian company named Kameya, which Hermitage Capital controlled and through which it transacted its investments. As soon as Browder explains this to the reader, he goes on writing, *"No matter how illegitimate the Russian criminal justice system may seem from the outside..."* I found this sentence confounding as I couldn't quite conceive how or why the Russian criminal justice should look *illegitimate*. It could look harsh or lenient; it could be efficient or inefficient; it could be biased; it could be many things, but Browder's use of the word *illegitimate* only made sense as a narrative diversion: if Russian criminal justice system was coming after his firm, then it must be illegitimate and wrong.

Chapter 23 also introduces Sergey Magnistsky, the pivotal character of Browder's drama: Browder presents Magnitsky as – to his knowledge – the best tax lawyer in Moscow, and tells us that he was rumored never to

---

[14] Firestone's partner was Terry Duncan who got killed during the 1993 attempted coup. Browder claims Duncan paid with his life for attempting to evacuate the wounded.

have lost a case. Hmm… *rumored?* As an important client and business partner of his law firm, Browder could easily have ascertained whether these rumors were indeed true. Instead, he gives us gossip, but not the fact. Sergey Magnitsky's assignment was to review all of Kameya's tax returns. He quickly established that Browder's COO Cherkasov had done nothing wrong, and should be in the clear legally. All the same, Cherkasov now needed a lawyer to defend himself against the Interior Ministry's charges, and for this role they hired one Eduard Khayretdinov.

Browder describes Khayretdinov as the Russian version of the Marlboro man, someone you wanted on your side if things went wrong. His opponent was the 33-year old major Pavel Karpov, Interior Ministry's lead investigator in this case. As these events unfolded over the first half of 2007, financial press got wind of the rumors surrounding Browder's legal issues and on the 15th June 2007 the *Financial Times* broke the story, "Russia Probes Browder Firm over Taxes." From this article, Browder learned that he himself was targeted in the investigation as the mastermind of Kameya's tax avoidance scheme. Browder's research man Vadim subsequently learned from his FSB contact "Aslan," that he and his firm were in fact being targeted by FSB's *Department K*: agency's economic counter-espionage unit. Finally the gravity of his predicament dawns on Browder and he concludes the chapter ominously: *"I am being pursued by the Russian secret police, and there is nothing I can do about it. ... They are the <u>secret police</u>. Worse, they have access to every tool imaginable, both legitimate and illegitimate. The FSB doesn't just issue arrest warrants and extradition requests – it dispatches assassins."*

Chapter 24: "But Russian Stories Never Have Happy Endings"
In mid-August 2007 just weeks after all these events, Browder took his family on vacation in the South of France where he perhaps hoped to forget Maxim's injuries and his mounting troubles in Moscow. Meanwhile, the Department K proceeded methodically to raid Browder's bankers in Moscow: Credit Suisse, HSBC, Citibank and ING, apparently looking for Hermitage assets. Although Browder found this amusing, since he had already pulled Hermitage's assets out of Russia, he still gave these events priority over spending time with his family. He laments: *"As I learned about each of these raids I was drawn further and further from my family. Instead of de-stressing, singing lullabies to Veronica and Jessica, and playing with David in the pool, I spent most of my holiday on conference calls as we tried to figure out what our enemies were going to do next."*

Perhaps I'll be unfair to Mr. Browder, but it does seem that he has a penchant for ditching family time. Even though he *"almost had to laugh at the amateurishness"* of the Russians raiding after assets that were long gone, he continued to obsess about what his "enemies" were up to. And it was not like he had nothing else to think about: Browder had by this time raised *at least* $625 million for his new hedge fund, Hermitage Global, and his prospects in London were again looking very promising.[15] His family, his team, as well as his clients' money were all safely out of Russia, and his lawyers assured him that it would be impossible for the Russian state to seize his personal assets. It is hard to imagine why at this point Browder still obsesses about the busywork of a bunch of Russian officials rather than enjoying the time with his family? Indeed, his fixation with *"the grave things going on in Russia,"* seems extraordinarily odd. Unless of course, there are details that Browder isn't telling us about. To my mind, *either* he is making a convoluted excuse for not wanting to sing lullabies for his daughters or he forgot to share with us some key details of this story. Knowing that Browder was a devoted family man, I should have to suspect the latter.

My suspicions are greater still when Browder tells us that, upon his return to London he closeted himself away with his team to *plan their next steps*. In October 2007 he went to Korea to look at some potential investments, but his mind remained mostly fixated on the grave things in Russia. After a few meetings in Korea, he abruptly cut his trip short and returned to his war room in London. He found out that his firm had become the victim of a "Russian raider attack." Raider attacks entailed stealing entire firms by taking control of their official documents,[16] stripping them of assets, loading them with debt, or extracting cash from the Russian state by claiming tax returns. Browder alleges that Artem Kuznetsov, Pavel Karpov, and their collaborators perpetrated just such an attack on his firms. During the police raids on their lawyers' offices, they confiscated Browder's firms' seals, registration files and ownership certificates, used them to transfer ownership of the firms, fabricated false transactions, and ultimately stole no less than $270 million from the Russian state by claiming tax returns against these fictitious deals.

---

[15] Browder told us as much in chapter 22 (p. 188). The typical fee structure for global macro hedge funds at the time was "2+20," which meant that the manager earned an annual 2% management fee (i.e. $20,000 per million of assets under management) and a 20% cut of gross returns. This implied that Browder could be looking forward to earning at least $1 million per month.

[16] Specifically, the raiders would be able to take control of a firm by stealing its corporate seals, its original charters of incorporation, the certificate of registration with state registrar, and the certificate of registration with the tax authority.

At first, Browder finds this hysterical and has a hearty laugh: a bunch of corrupt cops couldn't touch him or his money and instead used his companies to steal money from the Russian state which he despises. It is Sergei Magnitsky who warns him that the story is not over: *"Russian stories never have happy endings."*

Chapter 25: "High-pitched Jamming Equipment"

Chapter 25 opens with some tortuous account of Browder's legal troubles in Russia. Since Kuznetsov, Karpov, and their associates had "obviously" stolen his companies,[17] Browder brought on board Vladimir Pashtukov, another lawyer to help them file a case with the Russian authorities against these rogue cops. Pashtukov now came to London to help prepare the criminal charges against Karpov and Kuznetsov. He drafted a 244-page criminal complaint against *"the bad guys,"* as Browder has now labelled Karpov, Kuznetsov, and their associates. For contrast it might be appropriate from this point on to label Browder and his team as *the goodfellas*. Thus, the *goodfellas* filed two copies with the general prosecutor of the Russian Federation, two with the head of the State Investigative Committee, and two with the head of the Internal Affairs Department of the Interior Ministry. The State Investigative Committee seemingly took these complaints seriously and in January of 2008 they indicated that that they would open a preliminary investigation and bring Kuznetsov and Karpov in for questioning.

Two months later, the bad guys opened their own case against Browder in the Republic of Kalmykia where his fund had registered two investment companies. Russian authorities were charging Bill Browder with two counts of tax evasion in 2001. Browder assures us that his companies paid taxes correctly, that the tax authorities audit confirmed this, and that the charges against him were *"clearly trumped up."* Nonetheless, the process against Browder was now in motion.

Now, this chapter's title, "High-pitched jamming equipment," refers to an odd detour from the book's storyline. It is related to the story about Browder's meeting with one Igor Sagyrian, president of Renaissance Capital, one of the largest investment funds in Russia. On 30th November 2007, Sagyrian called up Browder and asked to meet him in person on a rather short notice. His objective was to get Browder's consent to let Renaissance Capital liquidate his stolen companies, which would somehow make all of his problems in Russia go away. Sagyrian flew to

---

[17] For simplicity I will refer to these stolen companies as Browder's. For the sake of accuracy, they were probably owned by his clients or their representatives in Russia and Browder or his firm merely administered them on his clients' behalf.

London and met Browder at the Dorchster hotel where after much small talk he made his silly proposal. Browder did not take him up on the offer and Sagyrian hastily cut the meeting short and excused himself. According to Browder, that was it. Nothing more happened in consequence of that meeting.

I couldn't help wondering why Browder even included this episode in the Red Notice. Perhaps it was just for the added drama in case the book became a Hollywood film, or perhaps there is another reason. For now, please just make a mental note of this meeting which we'll revisit in part 5 of this book. Whatever Browder's motivation to tell us this story, he uses it to strike yet another naughty jab at Russia. Namely, the reason why Sagyrian requested to meet Browder in person was because he did not dare discuss things over the phone: "... *I'm on a mobile phone. You are a lucky guy, you live in the UK, but I'm in Russia and I would prefer to meet in person.*" Poor Sagyrian lived in Russia, in fear of aggressive government surveillance. But Browder is a *lucky guy* because he lives in the free world where governments scrupulously respect citizens' privacy and would never, ever snoop on their communications. This little jab may have had its desired effect with some readers, but since Red Notice's publication, we know it to be laughable. According to Craig Murray, former British Ambassador, residents of Great Britain live under closer surveillance than any other people in the world and *all* of their e-mail, internet and telephone conversations are now monitored, recorded and stored. British government in fact employs more secret police per capita than does Russia. On his blog, Murray wrote that, "*British people are watched on closed circuit television more often than any other people in the world. Under the 'Prevent' programme, 'radicals' like me can only speak in universities under monitoring so intense and conditions so onerous that organisers give up, as I can personally witness.*" [18]

Over the recent years, revelations by whistleblowers like Edward Snowden, William Binney, Russel Tice and others largely corroborate Murray's claims and prove Sagyrian wrong in thinking that Browder is a lucky guy.

Chapter 26: "The Riddle"

This appropriately titled chapter opens with more slander of Russia. Browder mentions how Winston Churchill characterized Russia as, "*a riddle wrapped in a mystery inside an enigma,*" but maintained that the key to understanding it was to understand its national interest. Browder simplifies this by explaining that nowadays Russia's actions are "*guided*

---

[18] (Murray 2016)

by money, specifically criminal acquisition of money by government officials." Presumably, this is in contrast to Browder and his *goodfellas* whose actions are ever guided by selfless altruism.

Browder proceeds to deconstruct the scheme that the bad guys used in their criminal acquisition of money using the firms they stole from him. Hermitage earned $973 million in profits for 2006, through its three Russian subsidiaries: Rilend, Parfenion, and Makhaon. Their combined tax bill for the year was $230 million, and Browder claims they paid them in full. But as the bad guys took control of Hermitage's three subsidiaries, they arranged, with the help of phony courts and impostor prosecutors, judges and defence attorneys, to obtain legal judgments against the firms in the exact amount of their profits for 2006: $973 million. The effect of these judgments was to retroactively zero out Hermitage's firms' profits. This way the bad guys could now apply for a full refund of taxes Browder's firms previously paid. The refunds were soon approved and settled, and the tax authorities paid out $230 million to the bad guys into two obscure Moscow banks from where they quickly disappeared offshore. As Browder will inform us later, this was *"the single largest tax refund in Russian history."*

Browder provides a rather detailed account of how this theft was carried out, claiming that his team even obtained copies of the wire transfers from the tax authorities to the bank accounts of Hermitage's stolen firms. All this makes Browder's account seem quite compelling. However, since this story *is* Browder's story, it is fair to ask: what if important parts of the story are untrue, or if he omitted some critical details? What could be the reason for Browder's dogged determination to mire himself in what he calls the *"dirty dishonesty of Russia,"* at the time when he had such great prospects for his new fund in London? The *bad guys* in Russia stole money from the government which Browder despises, and not from his firms or his clients. Furhtermore, at that time Sergey Magnitsky was very much alive and a free man. So why squander so much time and resources in fights that didn't need to be fought? It seems that Browder hasn't told us the whole truth in Red Notice.

Chapter 27: "DHL"

Browder starts this chapter by opining that it was Vladimir Putin himself who authorized his expulsion from Russia and probably also the theft of his assets. But he then proceeds to tell us a story that's rather revealing about Russia under Putin.

On 23rd July 2008, Browder and his team started filing detailed complaints about the tax-rebate fraud with *"every law enforcement and regulatory agency in Russia."* [19] They also sent the story about it to the New York Times and the Russian business newspaper Vedomosti. *"The story quickly got picked up widely, both in Russia and internationally."* A few days later, Browder was invited for a telephone interview with Russia's leading independent radio station Echo Moscow. Over the 45-minute interview, Browder was able to *"methodically"* go *"through the whole ordeal: the raids, the theft of companies, the false court judgments, involvement of ex-convicts, police complicity and most importantly, the theft of $230 million of taxpayers' money."*

Did you catch that? In Putin's Russia, after more than eight years of the tyrant's rule, the man who had been declared a national security threat can speak on public radio unhindered for 45 minutes. Matvei Ganapolsky, his interviewer who expressed shock and consternation about the corruption Browder exposed, was nevertheless unafraid to have the enemy of the state on his show and to broadcast his interview. Apparently, he was right to be unafraid: as I write these lines in September 2016, Ganapolsky is still very much alive, a free man, and continues to contribute to Echo Moscow.[20] This is indeed remarkable because it suggests that Russia perhaps does have a respectable degree of media freedoms and that dissenting voices *do* get heard. This is quite contrary to the way Russia is presented in the West.[21]

The chapter's main feature is an intrigue with a mysterious DHL parcel sent from London to Moscow. On 21st August 2008, Hermitage's three Moscow-based lawyers – Sergey Magnitsky,[22] Vladimir Pashtukov, and Eduard Khayretdinov – called Browder and reported that their offices had been raided (apparently at the same time). Browder singled out Khayretdinov's news as the most disturbing. While he was away from his Moscow office, a DHL package arrived and within an hour of its arrival, the police raided the place. When they found the DHL parcel, they took it and left, suggesting that the parcel was what they were after.

---

[19] Here, Browder contents himself to tell us that they sent the complaints to every law enforcement and regulatory agency in Russia. He was much more specific about the legal complaints his team filed on 3rd December 2007, telling us exactly where they sent how many copies (see p. 210).
[20] His most recent article on Echo Moscow website was dated 24th August 2016.
[21] In fact, western media are arguably less free than those of Russia. As I write these lines (September 2016), the U.S. presidential campaign is underway and in the recent weeks at least two journalists in the U.S. have lost their jobs for daring to question the U.S. establishment candidate Hillary Clinton's health.
[22] Browder insists on presenting Magnitsky as a lawyer although he was an accountant and worked for Firestone Duncan as an auditor, not lawyer.

Now, the whole intricate plot seemed rather strange to me: Khayretdinov wasn't at his office during the raid and he called Browder from his dacha. For some reason, he was aware that the DHL parcel was seized. Khayretdinov evidently reported this to Browder, who for some reason found this news very disturbing even though he'll spend the next page of the book convincing us that the DHL wasn't sent from his office. So why was Browder so vexed about some parcel he didn't send? As he explains, the reason they even knew about the DHL package was because Khayretdinov's secretary *"had the foresight to make a copy of the waybill and fax it"* to the *goodfellas* in London. I found that thoroughly amazing: a secretary working at a legal office where much paperwork and post comes and goes, gets her day interrupted by a police raid (not likely a pleasant experience) and her reflex is to make a copy of the DHL waybill she had received an hour earlier and fax it to a client in London?? This easily qualifies the woman as the most diligent and foresightful secretary in the history of mankind, especially as that client in London claims they never sent the parcel.[23]

As it happened, it was only thanks to that fax that the *goodfellas* were able to look up the parcel on DHL website where, to their shock and dismay they learned that the parcel's return address was their own office in London. *"Of course,"* writes Browder, *"it hadn't actually been sent from our office."* Instead, it was sent from a DHL depot in South London so the *goodfellas* immediately contacted the London Metropolitan Police explaining what had happened. The same day, Detective Sergeant Richard Norten came to Browder's offices bringing a DVD with the DHL depot's security camera footage. The recording showed two *"Eastern European-looking men,"* sending a bunch of documents they brought in a plastic bag, *"emblazoned with the logo of a department store in Kazan, Tatarstan."* A few observations are in order at this point: first, as an Eastern European man myself, I am not sure what exactly makes Eastern European men so conclusively discernible in security camera recordings. Second, what's the deal with the Kazan, Tatarstan plastic bag? Well, this extremely fortuitous detail was helpful to Browder's diligent detective work because Kazan was exactly where the Russian authorities would summon Browder's lawyers Khayretdinov and Pashtukov for hearings at the local Interior Ministry headquarters only three days later.

So, here's what Browder leads us to believe: some Eastern European-looking bad guys flew over from Tatarstan to London, carried a bunch of documents in a plastic bag from a Tatarstan department store, went to the

---

[23] I'd like to meet another secretary who of her own initiative makes a copy of the waybill when they receive a box from DHL?

DHL depot, and sent them to Khayretdinov's office in Moscow. Then the DHL parcel was seized by the police, all in order to frame Browder for some misdeed of which he is clearly innocent. But there may be a simpler explanation for what took place: Hermitage employees sent the DHL parcel to Khayretdinov, and some of the documents in that parcel incriminated Browder or someone working for him. After all, Browder did have several Eastern European men in his employment.

Finally, reading Browder's account of this event, I couldn't help admiring the surprising diligence of the London Metropolitan Police. Their detective came to Hermitage offices only a few hours after receiving their call, by which time he had already obtained the security camera footage from the DHL depot. It is odd that a report about two Eastern European-looking men sending a DHL package to Russia could become such a top priority investigation for the London police. Just how busy they are was made clear on Monday, 22nd August 2016 when an unidentified man broke into the Ecuadorian Embassy in London. Many believed that the break-in was an assassination attempt at Julian Assange, an Australian journalist living at the embassy under Ecuador's asylum. In spite of the seriousness of this incident, London Metropolitan Police, whose nearest police station was located only two minutes' walk from the embassy, took more than two hours to arrive at the premises.

Either way, the important detail of Browder's story was that shortly after the infamous DHL parcel had been seized by the police, his two lawyers, Eduard Khayretdinov and Vladimir Pashtukov both received summons to report to the interior ministry in Kazan for questioning. Browder informs us that Kazan police *"had the reputation of being one of the most medieval and corrupt in Russia."* They were in fact so awful, they *"made Midnight Express*[24] *look like a Holiday Inn."* The men who worked there, Browder assures us, *"were notorious for torturing detainees, including sodomizing them with champagne bottles, to extract confessions."* By western standards, such practices would be regarded as *enhanced interrogations* and as such deemed morally acceptable and legally defensible. Still, Browder felt *"absolutely terrified."* Of course, he was primarily concerned with his lawyers' safety, so much so that he tried hard to persuade them both to leave Russia as soon as possible. He was especially worried about Pashtukov because of his frail health, so he called him and said anxiously, *"I'm worried about you, Vladimir."* Browder's

---

[24] "Midnight Express" was a 1978 film about a young American student who got caught in Turkey for attempting to smuggle drugs out of Turkey. The film portrays Turkish justice system, police and prison in a disturbingly unflattering light.

right-hand man Vadim meanwhile worked on Khayretdinov, but according to Browder, neither man shared his worries and showed no intentions of fleeing Russia.

If we are to believe Browder, both of these men – top notch, experienced lawyers – felt assured that they were protected, that the summons they received weren't legal, and that they were in no danger. In fact, Vladimir Pashtukov told Browder that leaving Russia would be the worst thing he could do. However, as the pressure from the bad guys continued to mount, his lawyers' confidence wasn't reassuring enough for Browder. Khayretdinov had meanwhile been under surveillance for several weeks. Says Browder: "*The people following him hadn't even bothered to hide it.*" When both lawyers received the second summons to appear in Kazan, Browder felt "*pretty sure*" that if they failed to show up for questioning, "*the corrupt cops would issue arrest warrants for both of them.*" That was an impressively confident interpretation of how the Russian judicial system worked for a man who never bothered to learn to speak Russian during the ten years he lived in the country. Nonetheless, he ultimately managed to persuade both Pashtukov and Khayretdinov to flee Russia. It goes without saying that he did so purely out of selfless concern for their health and safety, and never, never in a million years did he get them out in order to sabotage the Russian investigation into his business.

Following all this drama, I couldn't help wondering about the people who were following Khayretdinov. Who were they? Why did they not bother hiding? After all, if they hoped to find out something by following Khayretdinov, they would certainly have tried to conceal their surveillance. If they didn't bother hiding it, their purpose must have been to intimidate Khayretdinov and make him feel like he is in danger. And what was the point of going to such lengths to intimidate a lawyer who was simply acting as Browder's defense attorney? What if these men were not the police? When Browder went to war against the oligarch Vladimir Potanin over his investment in Sidanco and things heated up a bit, on less than a 12-hours' notice he got a 15-men armed security squad with four armoured vehicles to protect him 24/7. With that in mind, was it beyond Browder's means to arrange for a handful of thugs to spook his lawyers and help them decide to leave Russia? This certainly seemed like a possibility I couldn't dismiss out of hand.

Browder's tale continues with the story about Vladimir Pashtukov's escape from Russia. In essence, this is what happened: Pashtukov went to Moscow's Sheremetyevo airport with his family, boarded a flight to Milan and left. However, Browder's account of Pashtukov's trip is full of tension and suspense which he deviously uses to deliver yet another vicious jab at Russia. The suspense climaxes late in the evening on Sunday, 31st August

2008 when Pashtukov approaches passport control at the airport. The agent behind the counter was "*a young man with red cheeks, bright eyes and a sheen of sweat on his forehead,*" writes Browder as if he were there himself. "*Papers!*" the agent said without looking up.

I found it hard to believe that this really happened. I am no stranger to international travel, including to Russia, but I don't recall even once hearing a passport control agent anywhere exclaim, "papers!" When travelers approach passport control they understand what's expected of them and normally have their passports ready in their hands when they approach. It would be entirely silly and unnecessary for an agent sitting there to say, "papers" several hundred times a day. So why does Bill Browder build up this scene for us? He does it because the image of a state official demanding *papers* is reminiscent of the proverbial Gestapo officer in Nazi Germany barking, "*ihre papiere bitte!*" at rounded-up civilians. Browder reinforces this image in Red Notice with contrast: Vladimir Pashtukov makes a friendly casual remark to the agent, "*Crazy night here at the airport...*" who, in response, "*grunted something incomprehensible,*" and after checking and stamping the passport with red (!) ink, shouted, "*Next!*" as if that were necessary either.

For the author to embellish in this way a scene he never witnessed, with the obvious intent to insinuate that Putin's Russia is akin to Hitler's Germany is indeed a devious and malicious ruse and an affront, not only to Russia, but also to his readers. Reading this chapter made me additionally suspicious that Red Notice had been heavily ghost[25]-written by a person or a team of people highly skilled at psychological manipulation in order to weave a toxic mix of suggestive distortions and half-truths through Browder's story, aimed at demonizing Russia and its political leadership. The more I read into Browder's book, the more convinced I was that this purpose was premeditatedly woven into the story.

Chapter 28: "Khabarovsk"

Browder's fantastical tale continues with a detailed account of Eduard Khayretdinov's escape, first from Moscow and then from the country altogether. Again, the tale involves much suspense: "*The people after him were closing in and Moscow was getting too hot.*" But in fact, just like Pashtukov, the man simply went to the Domodedovo airport, paid for his ticket in cash, passed through security check without a hitch and took

---

[25] In fact, I suspect that Lee Child played a role in ghostwriting the Red Notice. He lent his name to Browder's credibility with the front cover blurb stating that Red Notice, "reads like a classic thriller... but it's all true and it's a story that needs to be told."

off.[26] He first stayed at Khabarovsk for several weeks under some former client's protection before taking a flight out of Russia to London on 18th October 2008. Even though their lawyers were now safe, the *goodfellas* couldn't well leave things alone and they kept trying to figure out what the bad guys were up to. In early September they procured copies of materials from the court in Kazan where apparently Browder and Khayretdinov were being charged with tax fraud. Browder uses only a single paragraph to elaborate this and his explanation barely makes sense. Apparently, one of the court documents was a witness statement from one Viktor Markelov, a convicted murderer who became the new owner of one of Browder's firms. He swore to the court that he did everything at the direction of another man who died two months *before* the theft. That man worked under instructions from Eduard Khayretdinov who got his orders from Browder himself.

This is our first indication that there *is* a legitimate investigation into the matter going on in Russia and that Khayretdinov's involvement with the *goodfellas* was deeper than simply being their defense attorney. Whatever the case, the *goodfellas* were *very* anxious for Khayretdinov to leave Russia. While he was hiding in Khabarovsk they were unable to communicate with him directly, but Vadim managed to reach out to some of Eduard's contacts in Moscow passing a simple but chilling message: *"New information has come to light. Your life is in danger. Please leave as soon as possible."* Finally, some bloke, one of Khayretdinov's *"most trusted confidants,"* makes a trip to Khabarovsk to meet him and deliver in person the following message: *"We've tried everything... I wanted to tell you face to face – you must leave Russia. You're in danger of being killed."* The super-aggressive Russian secret police apparently didn't think to keep an eye on Khayretdinov's most trusted confidant, but for the time being let's pretend still that Browder's story makes sense.

It may well be that the *goodfellas* were just *that* anxious to save Khayretdinov's life and protect him from danger. But it's also plausible that they were just anxious to cover their tracks and make sure Khayretdinov wouldn't be questioned in Kazan. When Khayretdinov's confidant tells him how *"they"* tried everything, it remains unclear just

---

[26] I thought it quaint that Khayretdinov could buy his ticket in cash, handing over nearly 57,000 roubles (about 1,500 British pounds) to the lady at the counter, who took the money *"without any reaction,"* handed him his ticket with a smile and wished him a good trip. In the "free world," she would probably have had to file a *suspicious activity report* of one kind or another, file it with the transportation security authority and Khayretdinov would likely get to spend a few hours detained, forced to explain himself to a bunch of government goons.

who exactly tried *what*. What *is* clear is that they are extremely eager to spook him into leaving the country.

If we unsuspectingly follow the trail of breadcrumbs Browder lays out for us, we'd have to think that Khayretdinov, this outstanding criminal lawyer with an unsurpassed track record in defending some of the most difficult criminal cases, was now being framed on totally bogus charges and was as helpless as deer in the headlights? We'd also have to conclude that Russian investigators were laughably incompetent. While Browder and his band of *goodfellas* manage to communicate with Khayretdinov in hiding through his Moscow contacts, the bad guys who kept him under tight surveillance failed to pick up on any of this communication and let him slip away onto an international flight out of Russia. Well, paint me excessively suspicious, but the farther I read, the harder I found it to buy Browder's tall tale.

The final point of significance in this chapter was that it properly introduces Sergey Magnitsky. The supposed tax lawyer, who was only briefly mentioned in chapter 24, appears like an honest and courageous man, indignant about the bad guys' theft of $230 from the Russian taxpayer. Like Browder's other two lawyers in Moscow, Magnitsky also "*steadfastly refused*" to leave Russia in spite of Vadim's attempts to convince him to go.

Lastly, this wouldn't be a complete chapter if it didn't end with another pointed jab at Russia. Browder delivers: "*Russia had no rule of law, it had rule of men. And those men were crooks.*" If you say so, Mr. B!

Chapter 29: "Ninth Commandment"

"Ninth Commandment" relates the beginning of Sergei Magnitsky's ordeal with the Russian state security apparatus. The story of his arrest includes a rather bizarre, but significant detail about the attempted arrests of his assistants Irina Perikhina and Boris Samolov. On the morning of the 24th November 2008 the police came knocking at Perikhina's door. Instead of answering, "*she continued to brush on mascara and apply lipstick.*" It is unclear just *how* Browder knew why Perikhina failed to answer the door, but she did this long enough that the police gave up waiting and left. In the manner of an adolescent explaining why dog ate his homework, Browder offers a comical explanation of Perikhina's conduct: "*Like any self-respecting thirtysomething Russian woman, she wouldn't be caught dead talking to anyone without her make-up on.*" Myself, I thought Perikhina's conduct too bizarre: most people in that situation would attempt to communicate with whoever was at their door to let them know that they needed a moment to get ready. They might be especially scrupulous if they knew that the people knocking were the police – unless of course, they had a reason to hide from the police.

Magnitsky's other assistant, Boris Samolov was lucky because he didn't live at his registered address when the police came for him. This too seemed suspicious: it reminded me of the war days in Croatia in the 1990s when many young men lived away from home in order to avoid being drafted into the military. In dealing with state bureaucracies, making sure you weren't present at your registered address was a good way of avoiding to receive a draft notice, a court subpoena, or getting arrested. Browder tells us nothing more about either Samolov or Perikhina, which begs the question of why he even included them in his book since they have no bearing on any other part of the plot.

He tells us that Perikhina and Samolov were Magnitsky's assistants, implying that they worked under his direction and supervision. But what if they weren't just Magnitsky's assistants? What if they received their assignments straight from their employer, Mr. straight-talking American, Jamison Firestone or even from Browder himself? And what if Sergei Magnitsky knew nothing about some of these assignments? If so, we would have to consider the possibility that something illegal was indeed cooked up at the Firestone Duncan offices, that Perikhina and Samolov had a role in it, and therefore knew to avoid getting arrested. That would imply that Magnitsky may have been set up to take the fall for whatever shady business was being cooked up between Bill Browder and the office of Firestone Duncan.

Indeed, Browder will later tell us that the Russian Interior Ministry assigned no less than nine investigators to this case indicating that this was a very major affair. Either way, Sergei Magnitsky seemed confident that he had done nothing wrong and neither hid nor attempted to flee. When the police came for him, he opened the door and waited as they searched his apartment. When they finished, they confiscated his files and arrested him. Thus began Magnitsky's ordeal with the Russian state security apparatus – a story that will have a tragic ending.

What's otherwise different about this chapter is that Browder's story regains some credibility as he relates Magnitsky's ordeal and his courageous defiance toward his oppressors. To the extent that Browder's account is true,[27] Magnitsky believed that law and justice were on his side and refused to implicate any of his colleagues or clients in any malfeasance. Browder tells us that in prison Magnitsky endured cold and sleep deprivation, was denied contact with his family, and when his health took a toll was denied adequate medical treatment.

---

[27] As we'll later find out, Browder's account is far from truthful.

RED NOTICE – PLAY BY PLAY

That Magnitsky would suffer such indignities in Russian prisons is not hard to believe, not because these were Russian prisons, but because they were prisons, period. With a few honorable exceptions, prisoners tend to be treated harshly all over the world and this is not unique to Russia. It may indeed be something of a human universal: if you divide a group of people and give one group power over another, the empowered group will often subject the other group to harsh treatment. This much was shown in the famous Stanford University prison experiment, run by psychologist Philip Zimbardo in 1971. Zimbardo converted the basement of the university's psychology department into a makeshift prison and recruited 24 normal, healthy university students. The students were then divided by coin flips into two groups: prisoners and guards, the roles they were meant to play during their two-week confinement. Harassment and humiliation of the "prisoners" started so soon that the prisoners rebelled within the first 24 hours of the experiment. The "guards" crushed the rebellion with physical force, breaking into the cells and stripping the prisoners naked. Within the first 36 hours, the first "prisoner" had a nervous breakdown and each remaining day of the experiment another prisoner suffered the same. Things deteriorated so quickly that the experiment had to be discontinued after only six days.

The participants in Zimbardo's experiment were students who understood that they were role-playing and that none of their "prisoners" were criminals or deserved harsh treatment for any reason. Yet somehow their harassment and humiliation started almost immediately and continued to escalate until the experiment was aborted. Far worse abuses take place in real prisons around the world, as we saw from the infamous Iraqi prison Abu Ghraib where the American prison guards subjected their Iraqi detainees to shocking cruelty.

None of this is to excuse or justify what happened to Sergey Magnitsky, only to consider his plight in a broader context. In most, if not all criminal justice systems in the world, when a person is accused of a crime and imprisoned, his accusers strive to prove his guilt and secure a conviction. That is how they build their careers. When your accusers are men and women who swore to protect the fatherland from all enemies, foreign and domestic, and especially where those people are ambitious zealots, you may be stuck in a Kafkaesque nightmare from which it is difficult to emerge unscathed. In fact, in this chapter Browder does introduce just such a character: Major Oleg Silichenko whom he describes as the embodiment of the aggressive zealot of the state security apparatus.[28]

---

[28] Whether Browder's characterization of Major Silichenko is fair or unfair, unfortunately we cannot tell.

Sergey Magnitsky probably worsened his predicament by standing up to his accusers. His defiance benefited chiefly our storyteller Bill Browder, whose greed and ambition produced the chain of events that ultimately led to Magnitsky's death. That seems to have inflicted a moral injury on Browder. As he confesses, Magnitsky's ordeal was something he never stopped thinking about. Over the months, as the situation gradually worsened, Browder's inability to help Magnitsky in any meaningful way caused him much anxiety. For the reader of Red Notice, this actually improves the prose as it finally brings out Browder's humanity. As he learns of Magnitsky's worsening conditions, he tells us that a part of him[29] wished that Magnitsky would just give the Inteior Ministry what they wanted. This glimpse into Browder's better nature contrasts favorably with the numerous glowing portrayals of himself as a shrewd businessman, a romantic hero, or a devoted family man – portrayals that feel embellished so that we would like and trust Bill Browder as he sells us his tall tale.

Finally, this wouldn't be Browder's tale if this chapter didn't also pack some quality anti-Russia slander. Browder tells us about his efforts to pressure Russian officials by helping a Council of Europe investigation into the matter, by intervening with the UK Foreign Office, and by attempting to get the U.S. Helsinki Commission to slip Magnitsky's case as an item for U.S. President Barack Obama to raise with his Russian counterpart Dmitry Medvedev. All these efforts had little effect because, as Browder laments, *"With all the evil going on in Russia,"* nobody cared about some tax lawyer getting shredded in the wheels of Russia's criminal justice system.

Indeed, for Browder everything in Russia is extra-evil. When Magnitsky was moved to Butyrka, the infamous maximum-security prison, Browder tells us that Butyrka *"was like Alcatraz, only worse."* It is unclear just how Butyrka was worse than Alcatraz, or how the author knew this to be so, but his judgment was probably based more on his consuming contempt for all things Russian than on his expertise on the quality of prisons around the world.

Chapter 30: "16 November 2009"

This chapter opens with another clear expression of Browder's moral injury: he can't not think of Sergei Magnitsky and writes, *"guilt coated me like tar... Even today I can't step into my bathroom without thinking of*

---

[29] I do hope that this part of Browder was very nearly all of him because if too much of Browder actually preferred for Magnitsky to go on protecting him at the cost of his own life, I would be much less impressed with his humanity.

Sergei." Browder proceeds to tell us how in Russia the police abuse their official status to steal money and terrorize their victims, and smears an impressive mix of defamation through the chapter about events leading up to Sergei Magnitsky's death on 16th November 2009.

Barely a month prior, on 14th October, Magnitsky submitted a formal, 12-page testimony to the Interior Ministry where he detailed [30] the role of officials in financial fraud and subsequent cover-up. In this testimony Magnitsky wrote, *"I believe all members of the investigation team are acting as contractors under someone's criminal order."* Browder clearly wants us to assume that this someone is none other than Vladimir Putin. This was very courageous on Magnitsky's part because, writes Browder, *"People in Russia are regularly killed for saying much less."* Sadly, Sergei Magnitsky did in fact die several weeks later. All the same, Browder's account about how this happened leaves me with some doubts.

On the day of his death, Magnitsky was so ill that he was taken to a medical facility to receive emergency care. *"However, when he arrived, instead of being taken to the medical wing he was taken to an isolation cell and handcuffed to bedrail. There he was visited by eight guards in full riot gear."* They beat him viciously with their rubber batons. About an hour later a doctor arrived and found Sergei dead on the floor.

In the end of the chapter, Browder cites Magnitsky's words from his prison diary where he decries his punishment which was imposed, *"merely for the fact that I defended the interests of my client and the interests of the Russian state."* He finally tells us that Magnitsky was killed *"because he loved Russia."* In all, chapter 30 was difficult to read. Magnitsky's suffering at the hands of the state security apparatus does appear Kafkaesque and rather credible in the way it is related. The reasons I found some key aspects of it hard to swallow will become clearer as Browder's story continues to unfold.

Chapter 31: "The Katyn Principle"

By this point, Browder is pushing the farther limits of what he expects his readers to swallow. Chapter 31 opens with a graphic version of the story of the Katyn massacre in 1940 when the NKVD, the fearsome Soviet secret police[31] killed about 22,000 Polish prisoners of war, then blamed it on the Germans. The Soviet version of this atrocity was at first accepted and upheld as the official history until 1990. From that historical event,

---

[30] Browder uses the word "documented," probably to make it sound more compelling, but I question how much of a major financial fraud you could document in only 12 pages.

[31] Which at one time allegedly employed Browder's own grandfather.

Browder telescopes straight to 2009 to claim that the *"machine of lying and fabrication"* functioning on the "Katyin principle" still formed *"Russia's evil foundation."*

When Vladimir Putin came to power, instead of dismantling this machine, he modified it and made it more powerful – and Sergei Magnitsky's case exemplified this. What Browder forgets to mention regarding the Katyn massacre is that it was Vladimir Putin himself, who in 2010 made an unequivocal public statement about the Soviet responsibility for this atrocity and urged reconciliation. Following his initiative, the Russian Duma officially declared that the massacre of Polish prisoners of war was carried out by the NKVD at Joseph Stalin's orders.

From that grim digression, Browder returns to his storyline. He tells how Magnitsky's mother Natalia learned of her son's death when she came to visit him in prison the next morning. Then he tells us how he took the news: *"Sergei's death was so far beyond my worst nightmares that I had no idea how to cope. The pain I felt was physical, as if someone were plunging a knife right through my gut."* Then he tells us about the state cover-up of Magnitsky's death which appears credible to the extent that we are talking about the national security state in action.

A doubt crept into my mind again when Browder tells about Magnitsky's mother, widow and aunt coming to see Sergei's body. They found it covered with a white sheet and when his mother uncovered his body, *"she was shocked to see dark bruises on his knuckles and deep lacerations on his wrists."* Recall, on the day of his death, Magnitsky was supposedly visited by eight guards in full riot gear who viciously beat him with rubber batons. Did they all just beat his wrists and knuckles? I may be naïve, but I would think that lacerations on the wrist could be from handcuffs. Bruised knuckles could result from punching a hard object like a wall or a door – something an imprisoned man might do out of frustration. Vicious beating with rubber batons by eight guards should have left more damage than bruised knuckles and lacerated wrists. And if Magnitsky really was viciously beaten by eight guards with rubber batons, I doubt whether his family would be allowed to see his body.

Given the impression of Russia that Browder strains to create in his book, you might think that Magnitsky's death must have been an unremarkable event since, *"People in Russia are regularly killed,"* for minor offenses. But Magnitsky's death was not a routine business in Russia: on 25th November 2009, Russian President Dmitry Medvedev ordered an investigation into Magnitsky's prison death and two weeks later his spokeswoman announced that 21 prison officials would be dismissed from their jobs. Browder deemed this investigation a sham, but this wasn't the only investigation into Magnitsky's death. A non-governmental organization called Moscow Public Oversight Commission (MPOC) conducted an independent investigation. MPOC lead investigator, Valery Borschev interviewed all the guards, doctors and inmates who had anything to do with Magnitsky and filed this report with five different government agencies. Borschev's report completely contradicted the official version of events, but Browder fails to tell us anything about it.

As he did in chapter 27, Browder again unwittingly gave us a glimpse of Russia that clashes with the idea of a totalitarian dictatorship he is so anxious to convey. First, the death of a Moscow prison inmate was a significant enough event for the President of the Russian Federation to order an official investigation. Then, a non-governmental investigator was allowed free access to interview Magnitsky's guards, doctors and fellow inmates, and when this investigator produced a report that contradicted the government findings, he was not afraid to file it with five different government agencies. Finally, Russian newspapers Novaya Gazeta published Sergei Magnitsky's unedited prison diaries on their front page where every Russian could see and read them! All this in Vladimir Putin's totalitarian dictatorship? To me this seems more like an advanced society with a respectable degree of media freedoms and a viable system of government checks and balances.

In the end, Browder recaps Magnitsky's plight saying that he was, "*a middle class tax lawyer... His only misfortune was to stumble across a major government corruption scheme...*" Perhaps Magnitsky's main misfortune was stumbling across Bill Browder.

Chapter 32: "Kyle Parker's War"

The rest of Browder's book is about his "fight for justice" for Sergei Magnitsky. In chapter 32, Browder goes to Washington D.C. since the UK government doesn't seem too keen on fighting for his cause. Neither is the U.S. State Department, but he manages to find an ally in a certain Kyle Parker at the U.S. Helsinki Commission, the "*human rights battering ram*" of the U.S. establishment. In fact, the U.S. Helsinki Commission is more like the progressive front of the U.S. deep state structures. It works to further American foreign policy objectives behind the façade of fighting for human rights. It is in fact slightly suspicious that Kyle Parker, the young idealistic human rights crusader just happens to speak perfect Russian and has a firm grasp on everything that's going on inside Russia. "*He could just as easily have worked for the CIA,*" says Browder.

Browder and Kyle Parker resolved to get the U.S. State Department to invoke the *proclamation 7750* which imposes visa sanctions on corrupt foreign officials. This proclamation was enacted by President George W. Bush in 2004. However, State Department officials were not enthusiastic at first. Browder takes advantage of explaining their disinterest to deliver yet another smear against Russia. He laments that the policy of the Obama administration toward Russia had been one of *appeasement*. Here again he deviously draws the parallel with the British policy toward Hitler's Germany in the run-up to World War II. But in making this claim Browder grossly misrepresents reality. Obama administration's policy toward Russia could more accurately be characterized as hostile and provocative. Some of these provocations resulted in serious geopolitical crises and wars like those in Georgia in 2008, Syria in 2011 and Ukraine in 2014. Under Obama administration's leadership, the NATO alliance undertook very aggressive NATO force buildup along Russia's borders.

Eventually, to overcome State Department's reluctance to invoke the Proclamation 7750, Kyle Parker suggests that he could ask senator Ben Cardin to demand this in an official letter to the then Secretary of State Hillary Clinton.

Chapter 33: "Russell 241"

Browder and his team got quite excited about this possibility because, *"If this happens, it means that we'll have the US government on our side!"* That was going to be a morale boost, especially for the Russians on Browder's team, because you see, *"Russians are familiar with hardship, suffering and despair – not with success and certainly not with justice."* And now the young American human rights crusader Kyle Parker was challenging this Russian gloom and fatalism. Senator Cardin's letter to Clinton stated that 7750 would be *"an important message to corrupt officials in Russia and elsewhere that the US is serious about combating foreign corruption and the harm it does."*[32]

For Browder, this was a small victory in his fight for justice, but also an important step in fighting corruption in Russia where all of Putin's *"key lieutenants had used their jobs to become enormously wealthy, and many had done some very nasty things to get rich."* Ordinary Russians, Browder assures us, *"were celebrating."*

Cardin's letter was only the beginning of the campaign. Kyle Parker carried on and in May of 2010 arranged for Browder to testify about the Magnitsky case in front of the Tom Lantos Human Rights Commission in the House of Representatives. More footwork by Kyle Parker got Browder an appointment with Senator John McCain at his office on Capitol Hill on 21st September 2010. When Browder came to see McCain and shared his story, the old Senator said: *"You've been a real friend to Sergei. Not many*

---

[32] LOL

people would do what you're doing, and I deeply respect that. I will do everything in my power to help you get justice for Sergei. God bless you."

I thought this was truly extraordinary: here is a Senator elected by the people of Arizona to represent them in U.S. Congress, taking time out of his busy schedule to meet with a British subject and pledge full support in his fight for justice for a Russian tax accountant. You would think the people of Arizona had so few grievances, Mr. McCain could extend his benevolence even to British subjects seeking redress for troubles they encountered in Russia. You might also wonder why Kyle Parker became so involved in Browder's crusade. As Browder explains, it was because he was just *that moved* by Sergei Magnitsky's plight. A few months earlier Browder sent him some tribute to Sergei that he wrote after his death and Parker read it on the metro. He read it over and over… He was heartbroken and cried right there on the train. And then he read it to his wife and she also cried. *"This murder,"* said Parker, *"it's one of the worst things that's happened since I started my career."*

Imagine that – with U.S. wars in Iraq and Afghanistan raging, with photographs and eyewitness accounts of torture and abuse coming out from the many U.S. black operations sites around the world, with weddings and funerals getting massacred wholesale from American predator drones, and with numerous terrorist attacks occurring regularly around the world during those years, the worst thing Kyle Parker came across in his career was Sergei Magnitsky's murder! Browder was indeed extremely fortunate to make an ally of just such a man. But by this point, his story has turned into something that even Maya, my golden retriever could not swallow if I wrapped it in premium organic bacon. My urge to toss the book in trash became more and more difficult to resist with every new page.

Chapter 34: "Russian untouchables"

Some of the same men who raided Hermitage Capital also raided the business of one Ekaterina Mikheeva and her husband Fyodor. Fyodor was also kidnapped, apparently by the same man who took possession of one of Browder's firms in 2007. The kidnappers demanded a $20 million ransom, but rather than paying up, Mikheeva called the police who rescued Fyodor and arrested the kidnappers. This story is yet another in the series of Browder's oddities. We are led to believe that these raiders worked for the Russian secret police and their actions are coordinated from some very high place, if not *the man* himself. But here their victim simply calls the police, and the police storms their hold-out and arrests them – a strange fate for the fearsome secret police thugs working for some mysterious somebody high up in Russian power hierarchy. But then the story gets still more complicated: for some reason, Mikheeva's husband Fyodor was later himself arrested and thrown in prison where he shared the cell with one of his former kidnappers. Browder doesn't know what happened to him or who was involved, but did know that Fyodor was eventually found guilty of fraud and sentenced to eleven years in prison.

Although Browder does not explicitly link what happened to Mikheeva and her husband with Karpov and Kuznetsov,[33] it was ostensibly their story that induced the *goodfellas* to focus *all* their *"energy on finding anything they could about Kuznetsov and Karpov,"* intensifying their *"battle with these two men."* Capable and sophisticated as they were, Browder and his team were able to dig up a truly impressive trove of details about the two cops. As Browder lays them out, the reader is led to the conclusion that they were indeed corrupt and appeared too wealthy for their modest state salaries. The *goodfellas* then packaged their findings about Karpov and Kuznetsov in several internet videos which were released in June of 2010. Within three months, more than 400,000 people saw the videos and the Russian weekly *New Times* magazine even published a big story on Kuznetsov titled, "Private Jets for the Lieutennant Colonel." These findings soon led to official investigations of Kuznetsov and Karpov by the Internal Affairs Department of the Interior Ministry, but these were concluded without any sanctions, which is why Browder labeled them as *"untouchables."*

In all, this chapter was in part a satisfying read, but a let-down at the same time. While the reader gets some gratification in Browder & Co's clever and creative unmasking of the allegedly corrupt cops, Browder's credibility sinks lower still in the process. During this time, Browder was running a high-profile London hedge fund with hundreds of millions of dollars under management. As he reminded us more than once in his book, he had such an exemplary sense of loyalty toward his clients that when his professional obligations conflicted with his family life, Browder sacrificed his marriage in order to attend to his clients' interests. But now he and his team were focusing *"all"* of their energy on the battle with two relatively low-ranking Russian police officers. For the man who casts himself as such a model professional, this amounts at the very least to a flagrant dereliction of duty toward his clients.

Chapters 35 and 36: "The Swiss Accounts" and "The Tax Princess"

Chapters 35 and 36 relate the story connected to a former private banker from Russia who contacted Browder through Jamie Firestone. His name

---

[33] The two policemen who who were investigating Browder's firms and whom Browder held responsible for Sergei Magnitsky's death.

was Alexander Perepilichnyy and he had been a Moscow private banker for a number of wealthy Russian clients but somehow lost much of their money. One of his clients was a certain Olga Stepanova.

Browder informs us that Mrs. Stepanova was *"the lady at the tax office who signed the refund cheque"* paid by the Russian tax authority to the stolen Hermitage subsidiaries. The reason why Mr. Perepilichnyy brought Mrs. Stepanova to the *goodfellas'* attention was because she opened a criminal case against him, accusing him of stealing her money. Once the *goodfellas* took aim at her, they discovered that she was inexplicably wealthy for a salaried state official and they dug up enough dirt on her to make an internet video that got even more traction than their previous videos about Karpov and Kuznetsov.

But the really odd part about the Perepilichnyy story was that as soon as Stepanova brought criminal charges against him, he packed up and moved his family to Surrey to *"lie low."* Lying low and maintaining a family in the wealthy Surrey County would be very expensive for an immigrant without a livelihood. While Browder makes it seem like he was an innocent victim of a witch hunt by corrupt Russian state officials, it is likely that Perepilichnyy did embezzle much money from his clients and escaped to London to avoid arrest. Another oddity is that again we see the *goodfellas* completely immersed in digging up dirt and making videos about a middle rank Russian official. Shouldn't they be busy running their hedge fund?[34] Apparently not.

In telling these stories, Browder didn't neglect to throw in more ugly smears on Russia and the Russian people. He assures us that, *"most Russians don't operate on high-minded principles... Everything in Russia was about money. Making it, keeping it and making sure no one took it."* That stands in stark contrast with Bill Browder and his *goodfellas* who did everything they did out of selfless desire to make the world a better place. He also made sure to mention the 2006 assassination of Alexander Litvinenko who, as a *"well-known Putin critic was poisoned by FSB agents at the Millennium Hotel..."* That statement was false on at least two accounts. First, Litvinenko was not a well-known Putin critic. He only became known *after* he was poisoned and western media almost instantly jumped on the story to demonize Russia and Vladimir Putin. Second, as to who might have poisoned him, several theories have been advanced since

---

[34] Ordinarily in the hedge fund business, as soon as your clients suspect that you are losing focus, they are likely to redeem their investments. Browder and his team clearly weren't too worried about this and one wonders if their clients – whoever they were – weren't just sponsoring them to focus on the work of demonizing Russia as their full time occupation.

that time and it is extremely unlikely that the poisoning was the work of Russia's FSB. [35]

Chapter 37: "Sausage-making"

While the *goodfellas* were entertained with the Perepilichnyy revelations in London, the relentless Kyle Parker was busy drafting the Magnitsky Act in Washington. His labors were rewarded when on 29 September 2010 United States Senators Ben Cardin, John McCain, Roger Wicker and Joe Lieberman introduced the Act in the Senate. Browder claimed that this encouraged scores of other victims of Russian human rights abuse to come out and write to the Act's sponsors, asking that the names of their abusers be added to the list of sanctioned people. *"The senators quickly realized that they'd ... inadvertently discovered a new method for fighting human rights abuses in authoritarian regimes in the twenty-first century: target visa sanctions and asset freezes."* Claiming that the bill sponsors hit on the Russian regime's Achilles heel, Browder rejoiced that, *"What had started out as a Bill about Sergei had morphed into a historic piece of global human rights legislation."*

Most of the rest of the chapter covers the relatively un-interesting intricacies of the process of pushing the Magnitsky Act through Congress, but Browder also throws in new details about Sergei Magnitsky's death after his mother Natalia saw Sergei's autopsy report. She was able to copy six color photos of Sergei's body after he died, *"showing the same injuries that Natalia had seen when she went to view her son's body in the morgue."* Interestingly, she also copied an official document authorizing the use of rubber batons on Sergei. Browder presents this as conclusive proof that Magnitsky was killed in prison: *"What we knew – that Sergei had died violently at the hands of the state – was now undeniable."* Nonetheless, I still felt unconvinced. Is there such a thing as a signed official authorization to beat someone with rubber batons? Would state officials trying to cover up the murder include this document with the autopsy report and let the victim's mother make a copy of it? Would they even

---

[35] One interesting lead was offered by the former French intelligence operative Paul Barril who stated in an interview that the British intelligence agency MI6 and the CIA ran a program codenamed "Operation Beluga" whose objective was to discredit Russia and Vladimir Putin and that Litvinenko was assassinated in order to frame Russian leadership. Litvinenko's associate Boris Berezovsky, Russian oligarch in exile in London was a party to the operation and was subsequently also killed when he became a risk to expose the operation (Source: "Bombshell: French Counter-Terror Boss: 'I have proof who killed Litvinenko'" OpEd News, 27 March 2016).

allow her to see the body after his death? None of it seemed very credible to me. Even supposing that Browder told us the whole truth, there's still that important detail that Sergei's injuries – bruised knuckles and lacerated wrists – didn't seem consistent with a brutal beating with rubber batons. Unless, of course eight gentle guards (in full riot gear) beat Sergei Magnitsky on his wrists and knuckles with their extra-soft rubber batons.

It would be wrong and distasteful to make light of Mr. Magnitsky's tragedy and this is not my intention, though I do have difficulty with Browder's version of events. By this point in the book his credibility has sunk so low that I find it hard to believe him anything at all. All of his stories seem embellished to have the greatest possible effect in demonizing Russia. I was prepared to believe that Sergei Magnitsky died of preventable medical conditions he acquired under harsh prison conditions. By not providing him with the necessary medical care, the state apparatus gravely wronged a man who was at this point still not found guilty of a crime. However, Browder's version goes much further than that and by exaggerating and distorting he sins against truth. That too is wrong and two wrongs don't make a right. Rather than seeking justice for Sergei, Browder gives the impression that he is cynically exploiting Sergei's death and his family's tragedy to vindicate himself and to inflict as much damage as he can on Russia and its legitimate leadership.

Browder tells us that Sergei Magnitsky loved Russia. I imagine that if he were still alive, he might ask Bill Browder to desist with his relentless campaign of defamation and to focus his passions instead on loving his family and managing his lucrative hedge fund business.

Chapter 38: "The Malkin Delegation"

As the Magnitsky Act was in the works, the Russians sent a delegation led by Vitaly Malkin to Washington to try to dissuade American lawmakers from passing it. The delegation turned out to be ineffective, and it was ultimately inconsequential to the whole story. I suspect that Browder chose to tell us this story simply because he took pleasure in seeing the Russian initiative embarrassed and defeated.

For that same reason, he adds one more uninteresting story in this chapter: in London, Major Pavel Karpov hired a very expensive law firm to file a suit against Browder. He remained unconcerned, seemingly out of a sense of superiority: *"I could imagine some silver-tongued lawyer lecturing a bunch of unsophisticated Russians on what spending £1 million on this lawsuit would do for all their problems with Bill Browder and the Magnitsky Act."* As we'll find out later, Browder's posturing here is false and disingenuous. He *was* in fact very worried about Karpov's suit and his lawyers strained mightily to have it dismissed by the court. They succeeded, but the process nevertheless inflicted major damage on Browder's credibility

A bit more interestingly however, Browder finally gives us an update about his hedge fund career: by 2012, his investment business *"was a shadow of its former self. ... To build my fund back to what it had been would have required month after month of marketing trips and investment conferences. When I put the idea of doing this against that of getting justice for Sergei, justice won in a heartbeat."* That is truly amazing: in a heartbeat, Browder sacrificed the future of his business, which was making hundreds of millions of dollars in profits[36] in order to fight for justice for Sergei Magnitsky. That must count as one of the most remarkable acts of selfless altruism I've ever come across.

Chapter 39: "Justice for Sergey"

The generally uninteresting chapter 38 ends with a dramatic line: *"Alexander Perepilichnyy is dead."* In this chapter Browder does his part to insinuate that Mr. Perepilichnyy was killed by the Russians, based again purely on his own speculation. This is apparently good enough for him to imagine that it was *"reasonably likely that a Russian assassin was on the loose in the U.K."* and to declare ominously: *"our enemies had brought their terror to us."* I suppose this was a well-chosen place in the book to introduce the word "terror" and subtly associate it with Russian state...

As it was, while the Russians were busy spreading their terror in London, Browder took a trip to the United States to spread enlightenment. At Harvard Business School he delivered one of his presentations about the events in Moscow leading up to Sergei Magnitsky's death. *"The mood in the room changed as I spoke. By the end, I noticed that some of the students were crying."* After his presentation, professor Aldo Musacchio told Browder how that was the first time in his career that he ever saw students cry after a case study." I will ask the reader to keep in mind the image of Browder's lecture imparting fear and loathing toward Russia to future leadership elites who in their soft-hearted sentimentality shed tears over Sergei Magnitsky's tragedy, oblivious to the broader context in which that whole story was brewed up. As it will soon become apparent, their very University played the pivotal role in creating that context.

After the Harvard presentation, Browder went to New York where on 6th of December 2012 he watched the C-SPAN transmission from the U.S. Senate in his hotel room. On that day, the Magnitsky Act was enacted by the 112th Congress of the United States. For Browder, the passing of the Act was almost anti-climactic, but he underscores just the kind of

---

[36] Recall, just in 2007, Hermitage Capital earned $937 million in profits!

achievement this was on his (and Kyle Parker's) part: "*Since 2009, 13,195 Bills had been proposed, and only 386 had made it out of committee and voted into law. We had completely defied the odds.*" Browder credits "*Sergei's bravery, Natalia's heart, Kyle's commitment, Cardin's leadership, McCain's integrity, McGovern's foresight, Vadim's brilliance, Vladimir's wisdom, Juleanna's savvy and Elena's love.*" Myself, I would only be more judicious about using the word *integrity* in the same sentence with [Senator John] McCain; they somehow seem to clash.

Chapter 40: "Humiliator, humiliatee"

Thus, as a result of Browder's and Parker's relentless lobbying, the humiliator (Vladimir Putin, of course) becomes the humiliatee. Browder writes how, "*In Putin's totalitarian mind, ... Putin overlooked... that the United States was not Russsia.*" This was the time for Bill Browder to gloat and celebrate, but he celebrated by taking his crusade for justice northward to advocate for a Canadian version of the Magnitsky Act.

Browder sees his crusade with black-and-white moral clarity and proposes that, "*you are either on the side of truth and justice or you were on the side of Russian torturers and murderers.*" This style of advocacy was right out of George W. Bush's playbook when he announced the Global War on Terror in 2001 and gave the world a choice: "*Either you are with us, or you're with the terrorists.*" [37]

In chapter 40 Browder shares yet another glimpse into the totalitarian nature of Putin's regime and his control of the press in Russia. He describes one of Vladimir Putin's famous 4-hour press conferences. At the 20th December 2012 conference, a Los Angeles Times reporter confronted Mr. Putin on the Magnitsky Act and the stolen $230 million asking, "*What happened? ... That money could have been used to rebuild orphanages,*" at which the hall "*erupted in applause.*" Significantly for Browder, Vladimir Putin mentions Bill Browder by name during that very conference stating that he was suspected by the Russian law-enforcement agencies of economic crimes in Russia. At this, Browder's "*heart skipped a beat.*" He knew that when his name "*passed Putin's thin lips,*" his life had changed forever.[38]

---

[37] George W. Bush spoke these words before the U.S. Congress on 21 September 2001. The nations around the world were given the choice: support us in whatever we chose to do or we'll consider you our adversaries...

[38] I've looked at many photographs of Vladimir Putin and Bill Browder. I think that an accurate measurement of their lips would show that Vladimir Putin's lips are in fact much more full and lush than Browder's. Psychologists say that we always resent in others that which we most dislike about ourselves.

Chapter 41: "Red Notice"

On 22nd April 2013, Russian authorities issued an arrest warrant for Bill Browder and issued a formal petition for Browder's arrest with the Interpol. On 24th May, his lawyer informed Browder that the Interpol rejected Russia's application; it announced that, *"The Interpol General Secretariat has deleted all information in relation to William Browder following a recommendation by the independent Commission for the Control of Interpol's Files."* As Browder informs the reader, this rejection was almost completely unprecedented: the Interpol rarely rejected notices, and if they did, they never publicly announced this.

Apparently, *"Putin's fantasies"* about what Browder and Magnitsky had done, *"was all a show, a Potemkin court. This is Russia today. ... A place where lies reign supreme. A place where two and two is still five, white is still black, and up is still down. A place where convictions are certain and guilt is a given. Where a foreigner can be convicted in absentia of crimes he did not commit. ... This is Russia today."* Or so says Mr. Browder, and we can believe him because everything he wrote in his book is true.

Chapter 42: "Feelings"

Browder tells us about the time he broke down and cried for Sergei Magnitsky at the home of a documentary film maker Hans Hermans in Holland after watching the final version of his film titled "Justice for Sergei." This, he tells us, was where he finally let his emotions out and the point at which his emotional healing could begin. The main thing that had brought him comfort, *"has been the relentless pursuit of justice."* He garnishes his sense of achievement further, stating that his fight has improved the way Russian prison guards treat prisoners as they *"worry about being too brutal in case they end up being held responsible for another Magnitsky."* Sergei's story has also *"given everyone in Russia, as well as millions of people around the world, a detailed picture of the true brutality of Vladimir Putin's regime."* And in fumbling the Magnitsky fallout, Russia lost face and damaged its relationship with *"many international institutions."* In what Browder proclaims to be a highly unusual step, the Russian authorities made the second application to Interpol to obtain a Red Notice issued for Browder, which was rejected like the first one.

While Browder despises Russia for being so very backward and uncool, it is more relevant to note that Russian authorities appear to be addressing their grievances through legitimate institutions of international law, rather than dispatching assassins, as Browder would have us believe when he writes, "*I have to assume that there is a very real chance that Putin or members of his regime will have me killed some day. ... If I'm killed, you will know who did it.*" Browder goes further still, pleading with the readers to help share and spread his story with as many people as they can, reproducing this appeal on the inside cover of the book.

In the story's epilogue, Browder relocates the Magnitsky family "*to a quiet suburb of London where Nikita was able to attend a prestigious private school and where Natasha could stop looking over her shoulder every day.*" In the finishing paragraphs, he pays special tribute to them: "*I am grateful for your friendship. Your bravery and determination in the face of unspeakable grief is awe-inspiring, and I know that Sergei would be proud of each one of you.*"

In April 2014 Browder scores another victory in his crusade for justice when the European Parliament passed a resolution to impose sanctions on 32 Russians complicit in the Magnitsky case. Following Estonian member of European parliament Kristiina Ojuland's speech and an applause to Browder and the Magnitsky family who were Parliament's guests that day, the resolution passed without a single objection raised. For our reformed hero, the satisfaction he felt there, getting some measure of justice in this unjust world was, "*orders of magnitude better than any financial success,*" he has ever had.

3. Russia in the 1990s: The missing context

Lenin was certainly right. There is no subtler, no surer means of overturning the existing basis of society than to debauch the currency. The process engages all hidden forces of economic law on the side of destruction and does it in a manner which not one man in a million is able to diagnose.

John Maynard Keynes

Browder's story omits the broader context of his Russian experience. Instead, he offers the same terse explanation he had regurgitated countless times in his various presentations and speeches, and it goes like this: after the collapse of the USSR, the government of Russia decided to go from communism to capitalism.[39] They thought that the best way to do this would be by giving everything away practically for free through various privatization schemes. Very rapidly, they transferred the nation's economic resources into private hands.

---

[39] This phrase, "going from communism to capitalism," became something of a mainstay talking point in the western media to explain what was going on in Russia as though this going was of such great value that it justified the unbelievably irrational and destructive conduct of the Russian government and disastrous advice of its western consultants.

But the unusual aspect of this transfer was that the private hands that received Russia's wealth were not the same ones that had built it up since there were no restrictions on who could participate in the privatization program. As a result, the crown jewels of the nation's productive resources ended up in the hands of a small group of oligarchs, most of whom covertly represented the interests of various western financiers.

It was this great wealth giveaway that drew Browder to Russia when he discovered that *"they were giving money away for free in Russia."* He arrived in Moscow in the early 1994 and spent $25 million of Salomon Brothers' money to buy bundles of Russian privatization vouchers. In only a few weeks' time, Browder's $25 million portfolio was worth $125 million – a hefty 400% return on investment. Things like that don't happen every day. In fact, they virtually never happen. How then, and why did they happen in Russia? Who decides to give away their country's wealth nearly for free? And how is it that an American investor can parachute into Moscow, pick up $25 million worth of uncirculated U.S. Federal Reserve banknotes and buy up large stakes in choice Russian companies? Browder's tale about Russia going from communism to capitalism is far too simplistic, and to more fully understand the extraordinary events he describes we need a more detailed analysis of their historical context.

Russia decides to go from communism to capitalism

> *I told Chubais, 'You are creating the conditions for a revolution.' Chubais said, 'You're too sensitive. No need to think about the people. Even if 30 million die, new ones will be born. Thirty million didn't find their place in the market.'*
>
> *Vladimir Polevanov, Chairman of the State Property Commission*[40]

Beginning in the late 1970s and through 1980s, Soviet Union experienced an escalating economic and political crisis. By 1985 when Mikhail Gorbachev came to power, there was growing pressure to reform the

---

[40] Polevanov interviewed in the film, "The Rise of Putin and the Fall of the Russian Jewish Oligarchs" by Alexander Genteleev.

system and free the economy from the shackles of state control. However, Gorbachev's gradual and piecemeal approach failed to produce the hoped for results.

A more radical approach was necessary and toward the late 1980s, a firebrand nationalist leader Boris Yeltsin rose through the communist party ranks to become Gorbachev's chief rival for executive power. Yeltsin had questionable loyalty to the Communist party and didn't hesitate to upset its many vested interests in the Soviet system. In the summer of 1990 he urged Gorbachev to draw up a "500 days" plan to rapidly transition USSR's system of public ownership and central planning to a capitalist market economy based on private property and entrepreneurship. To formulate such a plan, Yeltsin had put forth the 39-year old economist Grigori Yavlinsky who took on the assignment.

The plan proposed a set of neoliberal economic policies that included reducing government spending, abolishing price controls and legalizing private property. To undertake such a radical transition, the USSR needed very substantial financial aid from the leading Western powers. However, Gorbachev's numerous requests for such aid were consistently turned down and he ultimately withdrew his support for Yavlinsky's plan. The plan however had full backing from Boris Yeltsin. His push for radical reforms gained momentum in June of 1991 when he became president of the Russian parliament, and again after the August coup and counter-coup when Gorbachev was forced to resign as the Secretary General of the Communist Party and to cede his political authority to Yeltsin.

With Gorbachev and the old guard out of the way, Yeltsin wasted no time to push ahead with the reforms at breakneck speed. In November 1991, he assumed the role of Prime Minister and won the privilege[41] to implement the reforms through presidential decrees – even if such decrees would be illegal under Russian laws.[42] He appointed Yegor Gaidar as deputy Prime Minister and Minister of Economics and Finance, and Gaidar brought in Anatoly Chubais, a 36-year old economist from St. Petersburg. The new cabinet launched the transition program in January of 1992. The changes immediately plunged Russia into a dramatic crisis that would persist through the remainder of the decade to become the longest economic depression of the 20th century and the worst humanitarian

---

[41] This extraordinary privilege was granted to the president by the People's Deputies Congress decision No. 1831-1 on the Legal Support for the Economic Reform.
[42] For example, on 29 January 1992, Yeltsin issued the Presidential Decree No. 65 which simply stated that, "Everyone has the right to trade anywhere in whatever they wish." (Engdahl, How 'shock therapy' has ruined Russia 1993)

disaster since World War II. In this environment, a group of well-connected oligarchs and foreign financiers looted the better part of Russia's considerable wealth.

This tragedy was not simply a rash social experiment concocted by a group of corrupt politicians and their inept advisors. Russia's transition to capitalism was planned and directed by certain power structures attached to the U.S. government, and executed through various western political and financial institutions led by the International Monetary Fund (IMF), World Bank, Federal Reserve Bank of New York, International Finance Corporation and a number of other non-governmental organizations and academic institutions,. Among the latter, Harvard University played a very prominent role, lending the project the prestige of its name as well as an important degree of intellectual legitimacy.

The Harvard connection

When Gorbachev commissioned Grigori Yavlinsky to produce the "500 days plan," Yavlinsky had already been working on just such a plan with a group of Harvard University professors among whom were Jeffrey Sachs, David Lipton and Graham Allison. Allison was the founding dean of the JFK School of Government which from 1987 had been receiving CIA funding for research on intelligence and policy. [43] It is through this collaboration that Yavlinsky came to adopt the "shock therapy" for Russia in accordance with the economic reforms model developed by Jeffrey Sachs and David Lipton.

Harvard's involvement with the Russian transition program was not limited to intellectual support: an entire brain trust of consultants and operatives associated with the university set out to direct and supervise the implementation of Russian reforms. Harvard's operation in Moscow was run through the Harvard Institute for International Development (HIID) and directed by Andrei Schleifer, a 35 year-old Russian-born professor of economics. Schleifer was appointed to this post by his friend and mentor Lawrence Summers, then chief economist at World Bank and former Harvard professor. Summers, in turn was the protégé of Robert Rubin, another Harvard alumnus and Secretary of the Treasury under President Bill Clinton. In 1993, Clinton would appoint Summers as Under Secretary of the Treasury for International Affairs. Working under Rubin, Summers was the administration's point man on Russia policy.

Among other prominent members of Harvard's Russia task force were Marshall Goldman, the director of Harvard's Russian Research Center who was a frequent visitor to the Soviet Union over several decades;

---

[43] This is according to CIA's own unclassified documents (Lundberg 1995)

Robert Hormats, former Assistant Secretary of State and associate at Goldman Sachs and Kissinger Associates; US Vice President Al Gore, and Jonathan Hay, a recent Harvard Law School graduate who would be appointed to manage HIID's day to day operations in Moscow. The agency conveniently set up its Moscow offices right at the heart of Russia's government bureaucracy, at the Council of Ministers building, enabling HIID's executives to forge close ties with the key ministers, particularly Gaidar and Chubais. For its work during the four years from 1992 to 1996, HIID obtained $57.7 million from the U.S. Agency for International Development (USAID), [44] most of it by far without competitive bidding. It also helped disburse another $300 million of USAID grants to other contractors.[45]

1992: the shock therapy gets underway

Soviet leadership under Secretary General Mikhail Gorbachev was well aware of the necessity of reforming USSR's economy and began to cautiously implement market reforms starting in the mid-1980s.[46] However, as gradual reforms failed to return the economy to growth, by 1991 Yeltsin had resolved to go with the western-prescribed shock therapy.

His government launched the program on the 2nd January of 1992 with a two-pronged attack on price controls and government spending. For decades, Soviet State Ministry of Central Planning (Gosplan) had determined prices for consumer and industrial goods. The abrupt termination of price controls for 90% of consumer goods and 80% of industrial goods produced an almost immediate 500% price jump. Within the year, inflation reached 2,500%. By early 1993, domestic oil prices increased 85-fold, making the cost of fuel for transport and agricultural machinery prohibitive.[47] Food production collapsed and Russian produce almost vanished from consumer markets. At the same time, Russian markets were open wide to unrestricted competition from foreign imports, further eroding domestic production. The government also cut social spending by 40% in the first quarter of 1992, including drastic reductions

---

[44] USAID obtained these funds from the $350 million aid package authorized by President George Bush under the 1992 "Freedom for Russia and the Emerging Eurasian Democracies and Open-Market Support Act."

[45] (Wedel 1998)

[46] An important and fairly radical part of those efforts was the 1988 banking reform which triggered a wave of creation of cooperative and commercial banks, starting in August of that year. (Fedorov 1989, vol. 1, no. 4)

[47] (Engdahl, How 'shock therapy' has ruined Russia 1993)

in defense spending, social services, and pensions[48] which were halved to about $30 per month, leaving pensioners to cope on $1 per day. Even at that, pensions were not paid regularly. Almost overnight, ordinary Russians found many of life's necessities out of reach and millions of them faced hunger. Health services collapsed and an acute shortage of drugs and medical equipment appeared.

Ostensibly to counter inflation, the central bank stopped printing money and curtailed credit to firms, causing a severe contraction in money supply, forcing the Russian economy to grind along with only about 15% of currency it needed to operate. This liquidity crunch took place at the same time as prices of goods skyrocketed. Suddenly, nation's enterprises were unable to pay their workers and suppliers. The debt that companies owed to one another and to the banks ballooned by 8,000% in the first half of 1992,[49] causing a 20% contraction in industrial production and an 18% decline in the GDP. Millions of people received no wages for months and even years, [50] while much of the working population received compensation in goods like lightbulbs, macaroni, jackets, or other products that they had to exchange in the streets for things they needed.

The central bank further kicked the dying economy by increasing the interest rates it charged to member banks from 2% in late 1991 to more than 80% in April 1992. It also removed all restrictions on interest rates banks could charge to their clients.[51] This made it almost impossible for Russian firms to finance their operations or to invest in modernizing of the industry. As a result, business investment collapsed by nearly 50 percent in 1992 alone. [52]

With the economy in a dramatic contraction, hyperinflation in full swing and country's enterprises facing a severe cash shortage, the government's tax receipts collapsed. As the chief of Russia's Chamber of Accounts Venyamin Sokolov articulated it, *"You can tie our businessmen up, you can imprison them and beat them to near unconsciousness and still they will pay no tax, because they have no – and I repeat – no money."* [53] The consequence was that Russia's tax revenues collapsed and the government had to borrow money to finance its operations. Following the counsel of its Western advisors, Yeltsin's government borrowed by selling

---

[48] (Lindgren 1999)
[49] (Engdahl, How 'shock therapy' has ruined Russia 1993)
[50] (Williamson, Russia's Fiscal Whistleblower 1998)
[51] (Engdahl, How 'shock therapy' has ruined Russia 1993)
[52] After the 50% decline in 1992, business investment continued contracting: 12% in 1993, 23% in 1994, and 13% in 1995 (Gerber and Hout 1998)
[53] (Williamson, Russia's Fiscal Whistleblower 1998)

three-month ruble treasury notes to private investors at interest rates that started at 30% but rapidly rose well beyond 100%. This was unnecessary and spectacularly irrational; Russia's natural resources and government's monopolies were capable of generating enough economic rent to comfortably fund government operations. Short-term debt financing only made sense as an expedient to extract massive interest income from Russia's government: most of the bonds by far were bought domestically by private investors with money lent to them by the IMF. As Leonid Grigoriev, Russia's first envoy to the World Bank explained, "*Of course, the government was to return this money and that is why the yields on 3-month paper reached as much as 290%. ... It had nothing to do with the market and therefore such yields can only be understood as a payback, just a different method.*" [54] Russian government bonds or the "GKIs," became so remunerative that they attracted a veritable investor feeding frenzy, not only among the local banking oligarchs but also the Harvard Management Corporation and even many of the staffers of the HIID, IMF and other western agencies.

Voucher privatization

With the economy in disarray, agricultural production devastated, hyperinflation in full swing and ordinary Russians struggling to get by, the stage was set for the second phase of shock therapy: the speedy privatization of state owned enterprises. Funded with $325 million of US taxpayer dollars,[55] the voucher privatization scheme was approved in the summer of 1992 and the distribution of vouchers began on 7th October of the same year.

---

[54] Cited by journalist Anne Williamson before the Committee on Banking and Financial Services of the U.S. House of Representative on 21 Sep. 1999. (Sailer 2014)

[55] This is according to Anne Williamson September 21, 1999 testimony before the Banking and Financial Services Committee of the U.S. House of Representatives. (Sailer 2014)

RUSSIA IN THE 1990s: THE MISSING CONTEXT

Ten thousand rubles privatization voucher.

To give the privatization program a semblance of fairness and transparency, some 150 million vouchers were distributed to all Russians. But the actual transfer of ownership was apparently rather less generous than what was publicly disclosed and advertised. Anne Williamson who lived in Russia since 1987 as a freelance reporter gave a detailed account of how exactly the voucher privatization was implemented:[56]

> *"What GKI did was to value all state property at 150 billion rubles at 1991 prices and to divide that figure by a population of 150 million, leaving a share worth 10,000 rubles to each individual, the voucher's face value. Two thirds of the 150 billion whole was immediately excluded from privatization entirely. The remaining third was then divided again. Again, one half of that third was excluded. The remaining half of the third was the property privatized in 1992-94, but it too was divided.*
>
> *Small property - mostly municipal holdings - was auctioned for cash. Only what remained of the last division was subject to voucher privatization as it had been defined. However, of any single property privatized by voucher, 46% went to workers, 5% to management, 29% was sold at cash auctions and the remaining 20% - at a minimum - was left in the state's hands, meaning that at the*

---

[56] The paragraph cited is from Willamson's book "How America Built the New Russian Oligarchy" which was widely circulated and read in manuscript in the late 1990s, but which has meanwhile become unavailable either online or from any booksellers. The paragraph was quoted by journalist Bob Djurdjevic on his website Truth In Media. (Djurdjevic 1998)

end of the privatization process the state's largest shareholding dwarfed others' claims and therefore was the controlling shareholder of any "privatized" Russian asset.

The program had indeed put in place an expensive, time-consuming, distracting and destructive paper chase at the conclusion of which the government stood still mighty as the largest shareholder in any single allegedly privatized enterprise."

With regard to the vouchers distributed to ordinary Russians, the government made no effort to educate them about the vouchers or what they represented and most people were unsure what they should do with them.[57] As inflation steadily eroded the ruble's purchasing power, the vouchers' 10,000 ruble face value made it seem like they were rapidly losing value and most Russians were prepared to exchange them for a few dollars, a bit of food or a bottle of vodka. Moreover, the way these vouchers could be converted to actual dividend-paying shares of Russian firms was designed for abuse and fraud. Hundreds of voucher investment funds sprang up and deployed a small army of agents across Russia hustling the people to sell their vouchers. In this way they collected tens of millions of vouchers, bringing them back to Moscow where wealthy investors and their agents with hundreds of millions of newly printed American banknotes stood ready to buy them wholesale for token sums of money. By the end of 1994, large stakes in 65% of all officially registered companies were transferred into private hands. A handful of oligarchs appropriated the bulk of it, while top managers of many enterprises and foreign investors like Bill Browder took most of the rest.

Voucher privatization was followed by a long and often violent struggle over enterprise assets and financial flows. Where new owners could gain control over management, rather than developing their firms and investing in operations, they resorted to asset stripping and transferring their loot into foreign bank accounts. Around $25 billion per year was taken out of Russia in this way.[58]

---

[57] It is chiefly for this reason that Bill Browder even learned about the opportunities in Russia; namely managers of one of the large state companies (the Murmansk Trawler Fleet) hired Browder who at the time was working for Salomon Brothers and paid a $50,000 consulting fee so that he could tell them whether they should buy their company, which owned $1 billion worth of ships, for $2.5 million.

[58] (Hudson 1999)

Loans for shares scheme

While voucher privatization transferred company shares to private investors, the government became the controlling shareholder in all of them, creating a legal and political risk for the oligarchs' long-term interests. To remedy this situation, they cooked up the so-called *loans-for-shares* scheme. Supposedly a brainchild of Anatoly Chubais, this scheme was organized in 1995 and sold to the public as government's solution to short-term financing pressures. In reality, it was a massive transfer of ownership in Russia's most valuable resources to a small group of oligarchs known in Russia as "semibankirschina," or the group of seven bankers. These resources included giant deposits of oil and natural gas, gold, silver, platinum and diamond mines, world's largest paper, steel, automobile and aerospace factories and electric and telecom monopolies.

Under the scheme, banks like Vladimir Potanin's Oneximbank, Vladimir Gusinsky's Most Bank and Mikhail Khodorkovsky's Bank Menatep loaned money to the government and received shares in government-owned companies as collateral. The government was supposed to repay the loans after about three years, but if it failed to do so, the banks could auction off the company shares in their custody and split any profits with the government. However, because the very banks that held company shares in their custody also organized the auctions and controlled the bidding process, they were able to win the auctions in almost every case, buying up companies at prices that were barely higher than the minimum initial bids. In this way, Khodorkovsky took 78% ownership in the oil giant Yukos. With oil reserves the size of Kuwait, Yukos was worth at least $5 billion, but Khodorkovsky bought it for only $310 million. Boris Berezovsky walked away with Sibneft, another oil giant worth about $3 billion, for only $100 million. For $171 million, Vladimir Potanin became majority owner of Norilsk Nickel which controlled about a third of the world's Nickel reserves.[59] Not long after these auctions, Norilsk Nickel's annual profits reached $1.5 billion.[60] Potanin also took ownership of the oil giant Sidanco for $130 million. Only two years later, the firm was valued at $2.8 billion in international capital markets. Besides the seven bankers, Harvard Management Company (HMC)[61] and George Soros were the only other investors allowed to participate in the loans-for-shares auctions.[62]

---

[59] (Taibbi 1997)
[60] (Klein 2007)
[61] Harvard Management Company invested on behalf of the Harvard Endowment.
[62] (Wedel 1998)

To add insult to injury, it turned out that the bankers did not even use their own money to buy the companies – they bought them with public funds. Namely, before the auctions, several ministers in Boris Yeltsin's cabinet diverted large sums of government money from the state banks into the private banks owned by the oligarchs who used it as collateral to issue themselves credit to buy firms through auctions they rigged for their own benefit. As an example, Khodorkovsky's Bank Menatep obtained the money earmarked to fund the Russian Academy of Science. When Menatep was buying Yukos, Academy of Science employees stopped receiving their salaries.[63]

While Khodorkovsky's Menatep bank handled the public money meant for funding of the Russian academy of sciences, scientists went unpaid. Protest signs read: "A hungry physicist is a SHAME for Russia" and "Give scientists the salaries that they are OWED." (Kouprianova 2015)

Representatives of Western powers and financial institutions were well aware of the larceny perpetrated by the oligarchs and Yeltsin government, but they raised no objection. During his final trip to Moscow in the early

---

[63] (Taibbi 1997)

1995, Jeffrey Sachs himself warned Western officials about this blatantly corrupt scheme, but it appeared that none were moved by his warnings. He later wrote: *"I was stunned by the obtuseness of the response, from the IMF, and OECD visiting mission, and later from very senior U.S. officials, including Larry Summers."* [64] Nobody was inclined to interfere with this brazen theft of Russia's wealth, raising the suspicion that the process was intended to play out as it did. Through the whole privatization process from 1992 through 1996, the seven oligarchs gained control of 60% of the Russian economy.[65] At the same time, Russian government's proceeds from privatization amounted to about 0.15% of state revenues[66] while the vast majority of ordinary Russians found themselves left out with their hopes for a better life after communism forever shattered.

Lawmakers' revolt and the constitutional crisis of 1993

We created a virtual open shop for thievery at a national level and for capital flight in terms of hundreds of billions of dollars, and the reaping of natural resources and industries on a scale which I doubt has ever taken place in human history.

E. Wayne Merry, chief political analyst at the U.S. Embassy in Moscow (1990-1994)

Economic reforms and privatization were highly destructive for Russia. They were also achieved outside of the legitimate legal framework. To sidestep the government agencies and circumvent the parliament, Yeltsin's government worked through a network of private agencies and non-governmental organizations set up by Anatoly Chubais, his associates, and their western advisers. One of the most important of these organizations was the Russia Privatization Center (RPC), set up by the HIID and Anatoly Chubais under a presidential decree. RPC's directors were Andrei Schleifer and Chubais himself. Exemplifying corruption and conflicts of private and public interests in Yeltsin's cabinet, Chubais simultaneously

---

[64] (Sachs 2012)
[65] (Williamson, Don't Cry for Boris Yeltsin 2007)
[66] (Lindgren 1999)

headed the private RPC and the government's GKI (Federal Agency for State Property Management). This didn't seem to bother RPC's western sponsors; in addition to a $45 million grant from USAID, RPC obtained $59 million credit from the World Bank, $43 million from European Bank for Reconstruction and Development and further funding from the European Union, Japan and several individual European Governments.[67] HIID also helped establish the Federal Commission on Securities, also with USAID's money.

Another important agency was the Institute for Law-Based Economy which was funded by the World Bank and a $20 million grant from USAID. Its mission was to help develop Russia's legal and regulatory framework. While it failed dismally at that mission, it became notorious for writing Boris Yeltsin's presidential decrees. In total USAID bankrolled Russian reforms with $325 million of US taxpayers' money. The simple objective of all this, as Richard Morningstar, another Harvard alumnus involved in the project said it, was to "*win in privatizations...*"[68]

This framework of conflicting interests and corruption allowed Yeltsin's government to carry out the business of economic reforms and privatization unopposed by legitimate government institutions. USAID's Walter Coles put it simply enough: "*If we needed a decree, Chubais didn't have to go through the bureaucracy.*"[69] A further convenience of this network was that all actors could deflect accountability. Russian officials could defend their actions by claiming that they were following IMF or World Bank demands while Americans and other foreigners, when caught in any malfeasance, could blame the Russians for corruption.

Yeltsin cabal's blatant disregard for law ultimately provoked a violent confrontation with the Congress of People's Deputies, the legislative branch of Russia's government. In December of 1992, the deputies ousted Yegor Gaidar as prime minister and instructed the central bank to carry on issuing credit to the nation's businesses to keep them from shutting down altogether. Although Yeltsin's privilege to rule by decree expired at the end of 1992, on 20th March 1993 he granted himself extraordinary executive powers and announced a special government regime that would remain in place until the resolution of the political crisis. Three days later, Russia's Constitutional Court declared Yeltsin's measures illegal and on

---

[67] (Wedel 1998)
[68] Richard Morningstar was the Senior Vice President of Policy and Investment Development at the Overseas Private Investment Corporation. In April 1995 he was named as the Special Advisor to the President and Secretary of State on Assistance to the New Independent States of the former USSR.
[69] (Wedel 1998)

26th March an extraordinary session of the ninth Congress of People's Deputies initiated impeachment proceedings against the president.

Yeltsin managed to survive the impeachment vote but continued to rule by decree and the political crisis reignited after the summer recess. On 18th September he reinstated Yegor Gaidar as deputy prime minister but the parliament strongly rejected this nomination. On 21st September Yeltsin responded by dissolving the parliament, effectively staging a coup d'état. However, the lawmakers were not about to capitulate and the political crisis continued to escalate. After the Constitutional Court ruled that the president's actions were in breach of the constitution, the parliament held an emergency session during which it declared Yeltsin's decree null and void. The deputies stripped him of the presidency and swore in the vice-president Aleksandr Rutskoy as the new president. Rutskoy's first act was to dismiss Yeltsin and his key ministers from their cabinet posts. At a session held on 24th September, the deputies announced that new elections for Russia's presidency and parliament would be held by March of 1994.

Yeltsin's violent crackdown

Lawmakers' actions were likely to lead to a halt or even revision of the privatization process. Russia's new masters had too much at stake to allow Russian democracy to obstruct the project.[70] Boris Yeltsin responded with crude force, isolating the parliament building, cutting off its electricity, telephone lines and hot water. This provoked an open revolt among many Muscovites and tens of thousands of them descended into the streets in support of the parliament. Peaceful demonstrations went on for days and the numbers of protesters grew in spite of the news blackout of the protests. On the 28th of September, the interior ministry finally moved to suppress the demonstrations by force. This led to violent clashes between the people and the police. Still, neither the parliamentarians nor the protesters would back down. On 3rd October the protesters marched on Ostankino television station, seeking to break the media blockade and get the truth out to the rest of the Russian public. That might have catalyzed a nationwide revolt against Yeltsin's regime and the government moved ruthlessly to disperse the demonstrators. They opened live ammunition fire into the crowd that included the elderly, women and children, killing 46 and wounding 124 people.

The next day Yeltsin ordered a five thousand strong army division, flanked with tanks, armored personnel carriers and helicopters, to storm

---

[70] In a 2002 testimony during a lawsuit in Cambridge, Massachusetts Lawrence Summers characterized Russian transition in these words: "*The project was of enormous value...*" (McClintick 2006)

the parliament. When the army tanks opened fire into the parliament building, scores of deputies and staffers were killed and wounded. When the siege was over, the President's security had orders to kill the president Aleksandr Rutskoy and the speaker, Ruslan Khasbulatov. Yeltsin's personal bodyguard Alexander Korzhakov testified that he went into the parliament building with a loaded, unlocked pistol in his right pocket looking for Rutskoy and Khasbulatov, but was unable to use it as there were too many witnesses.[71]

The official death toll of Yeltsin's violent suppression of the uprising against his government was 187 killed and 437 wounded.[72] Unofficial figures might have been as many as ten times higher. In the days and weeks following the bloody storming of the parliament, Yeltsin issued a series of decrees to shore up his power, purging his political opposition, the Constitutional Court and the media outlets that supported the parliament. He took advantage of the crisis also to free the central bank from lawmakers' control and render it independent. On 12th December 1993, Yeltsin forced through a new constitution, granting himself broad powers to govern by decree and establishing a strong presidency at the heart of the Russian political system. Through this whole crisis, Yeltsin enjoyed full support and understanding from the Western powers in spite of his unconstitutional power grab, the murderous crackdown on the protesters and parliamentarians and a heavy-handed suppression of the political and media opposition. Former US President Richard Nixon, who was a close observer of events in Russia, testified that Russian officials had informed him that the United States government supported Yeltsin's violent crackdown against the parliament on condition that his government accelerate the economic reforms.[73] Indeed, shortly after the crackdown, the US Congress voted to donate $2.5 billion of American taxpayers' money to shore up Yeltsin's government. Through this bloody episode, western public was given the impression that Yeltsin was fighting an armed insurgency of hard core communist reactionaries while he himself was consistently portrayed as a committed democrat, modernizer of Russia and a friend of the west. That version of events was created through a concerted public relations effort, largely coordinated by the infamous PR behemoth Burson-Marstellar, courtesy of USAID and the unwitting American taxpayer.[74]

---

[71] (Bodykov 2013)
[72] "1993 Russian constitutional crisis." (Wikipedia, 1993 Russian constitutional crisis n.d.)
[73] (Simes 2007)
[74] (Wedel 1998)

RUSSIA IN THE 1990s: THE MISSING CONTEXT

The Americans came for the best of reasons

> *... if the notion of billions of barrels of proven oil reserves and billions of tons of gold fills your dreams with visions of red-hot cash flow and ice-cold vodka, then Boris Yeltsin just might find some work for you.*
>
> *Paul Hofheinz, Fortune Magazine, 23 September 1991*[75]

Shock therapy gave Russia one of the worst and longest economic depressions of the 20th century, an unprecedented humanitarian catastrophe for a peace time crisis, and a criminally inequitable privatization of public assets. The reasons why things happened this way in Russia generally aren't well understood in the west. Even among better informed intellectuals, the failure of shock therapy is often thought to be vaguely related to some sinister flaw in the Russian society. It is what Bill Browder characterized as *"the dirty dishonesty of Russia,"* or *"Russia's evil foundation,"* which spawned corruption and criminality of staggering proportions. In this toxic environment, the sweet fruits of western democracy and capitalism simply could not grow in spite of the generous benevolence of Russia's western friends.

Such a credulous version of events was never based on any coherent analysis of what transpired in Russia during the 1990s. Rather, it was based on purposeful perception management in the Western media. As late as April 2015, *Washington Post* provided a good example of this perception management. In an editorial board article, Washington Post informed its readers that in the 1990s, *"thousands of Americans went to Russia hoping to help its people attain a better life. The American and Western effort over the last 25 years – to which the United States and Europe devoted billions of dollars – was aimed at helping Russia overcome the horrid legacy of Soviet communism, which left the country on its knees in 1991. ... The Americans,"* write Washington Post editors,

---

[75] The quote from *Fortune* magazine is exact, but a correction is in order: neither Russia nor the rest of the planet Earth for that matter have *billions of tons* of gold. Perhaps Hofheinz didn't think *millions of ounces* sounded enticing enough.

"came for the best of reasons. ... a generous hand was extended to post-Soviet Russia, offering the best of Western values and know-how." [76]

Indeed, western role in Russian transition is almost invariably represented as generous benevolence. While many among Russia's western helpers did come with sincere and honorable intentions, the whole project, insofar as it was determined by its command and control structure, was simply a massive, bald-faced criminal enterprise.

IMF's strangulation of Russian economy

When Jeffrey Sachs drafted his shock therapy recommendations, he estimated that for the reforms to succeed, Soviet Union would need financial support of about $15 billion per year for many years. This money was needed for the state to continue administering essential social services like pensions, health care and food aid for the country's population. But while the IMF and U.S. government insisted that Moscow abidingly implement the draconian shock therapy measures, they stubbornly refused to provide the needed financial aid. Sachs also advocated debt relief for the USSR which, before its collapse in 1991 was already $60 billion behind in payments to foreign creditors. When he advised the Bolivian (1985-1986) and Polish (1989-1991) governments in implementing their own shock therapies, Sachs was able to negotiate a 50% debt write-off for Poland and a 90% write-off for Bolivia. By contrast, Russia would get no debt relief of any kind. To the contrary, at the G7 summit held in Moscow in November 1991, representatives of the seven leading western powers insisted that Soviet Union had to continue servicing its external debts at all cost, even menacing Yegor Gaidar that *"any suspension of debt payments would result in the immediate suspension of urgent food aid and that the ships nearly arrived at the Black Sea ports would turn around."* [77] Moscow's endeavor to comply with these payment obligations completely depleted the government's treasury within only three months' time (by February of 1992).

Sachs later reported that in December of 1991 he held discussions with the IMF urging its representatives to advance the financial support needed for Russia's transition, but they insisted that Russia didn't need any such assistance and told him that they had instructed the G7 accordingly. Sachs found the methodology on which the IMF had based their decision, *"primitive beyond belief,"* which led him to assume that the IMF was simply *"parroting the political decisions already decided by the United*

---

[76] (Hiatt 2015)
[77] (Sachs 2012)

States." He was right, of course: as we now know, US aid policy for Russia was indeed determined by two key US government agencies: the Treasury Department run by Robert Rubin with Lawrence Summers in charge of Russian affairs, and the National Security Council.[78]

To be sure, IMF did advance some loans to Russia during its transition period, but the amounts in question were too small and came too late to provide any meaningful economic or social relief. In all, between 1993 and 1999 the IMF lent Russia between $30 and $40 billion, a far cry from the $15 billion *per year* that were thought necessary to support her economic reforms. Furthermore, the bulk of IMF loans were given to the oligarch owned private banks which used them to fund capital flight, bond market speculation and betting against the ruble.[79]

There were further problematic aspects to the IMF loans: in 1995, with hardly any conditions attached, IMF advanced Russia a $6.7 billion loan through its Systematic Transformation Facility. Practically the entire $6.7 billion sum was used to finance Yeltsin's military assault on Chechnya.[80] That operation was a disaster but domestically it served the purpose of distracting the public attention from economic problems and political corruption. IMF's very next loan to Russia was a thinly veiled mission to rescue Yeltsin and his government from Russia's democracy. Namely the Chechen misadventure cost Yeltsin dearly in the December 1995 parliamentary elections and his party suffered a devastating defeat to the Communists. The president himself had become deeply unpopular. With his approval ratings languishing between 4% and 6%,[81] Yeltsin was in real danger of losing the June 1996 presidential elections, which again risked reversing Russia's transition and nullifying the privatization of its economy. To avert this, Yeltsin's cabinet hired a team of American political strategists with ties to the Clinton administration to advise his election campaign. As the Americans got to work in March of 1996, one of the first things they realized was that the Russian people were furious about the government's failure to pay state salaries and pensions for

---

[78] (Wedel 1998)

[79] As Dr. Michael Hudson explained in his 1999 testimony before the Russian Duma, the banks traded currency forward contracts, exchanging rubles for dollars at some future date, usually three months. As the ruble's exchange rate reliably declined, the banks made huge profits on these trades. The IMF justified financing this practice as supporting the ruble, but it was in effect a simple giveaway to the banks at the expense of the Russian people (Hudson 1999).

[80] (Sailer 2014)

[81] By the time Yeltsin handed the presidency over to Vladimir Putin, his popularity had sunk to barely 2% - making him possibly the most unpopular leader in history of mankind!

months on end. Washington got the signal and the IMF took action: it promptly released a $1 billion tranche of its next, $10.2 billion loan so that Yeltsin could pay all the salaries and pensions his government owed. The loan served the purpose of improving Yeltsin's unpopularity and making the rigged election appear a bit less suspect.

IMF approved its largest, $22.6 billion loan to Russia as late as 20th July 1998 as its bankrupt government slid inexorably toward default. The loan served two key purposes: large part of it was a gift to the oligarchs who helped themselves to the funds to convert their hoard of rubles into USD. Within four weeks they bought $6.5 billion and transferred most of it to foreign banks.[82] Most of the rest of IMF loan was a stealth bailout for western financial institutions which had some $200 billion worth of loans and investments in Russia. The banks feared the prospect of Russian default which would leave them with crippling losses. These risks became even more acute in the aftermath of the 1997 East Asian financial crisis that would engulf Russia in 1998.

In a testimony before the U.S. Congress, veteran investor Jim Rogers characterized IMF's assistance to Russia as follows: "*The activities of the organization are gussied up in sanctimonious prose about aiding the poor and raising the living standards of the third world. Don't be fooled. These bailouts are really about protecting interests of Chase Manhattan, J.P. Morgan, and Fidelity Investments.*"[83]

In addition to loading Russia up with unproductive debt, IMF also engineered Russia's hyperinflation and liquidity crisis. After eliminating price controls, IMF obliged Russia to maintain the ruble as the common currency for all Soviet Union successor states, giving each of the 15 new countries the incentive to issue ruble credits for their own benefit while fueling inflation for all others. Sachs reported that he strenuously argued with the IMF against this measure but "*for inexplicable reasons,*" he was consistently rebuked. The result was a one-year delay in the introduction of national currencies for the former Soviet republics, pushing Russia into hyperinflation and needlessly prolonging its economic depression. At this same time, the IMF engineered Russia's staggering liquidity crisis that made it almost impossible for enterprises to pay their suppliers and workers. Under IMF's dictate, Russian economy struggled along on less than one sixth of the currency required to operate an economy of its size.

The extent of IMF's iron-fisted control over Russian economy was exemplified in a letter from the IMF's representative Yusuke Horaguchi to

---

[82] (Browder, Red Notice 2015)
[83] From Jim Rogers' 10th September 1998 testimony before U.S. Congress (Lindgren 1999)

RUSSIA IN THE 1990s: THE MISSING CONTEXT

Russia's central bank chairman Sergei Dubinin. The letter specified the precise schedule of Russia's ruble supply along with "*harshly worded*" instructions regarding bank credits, the state budget, energy policy, price levels, trade tariffs and agricultural policies. Horaguchi's letter even included a warning that any acts of the parliament contravening the IMF mandates would be vetoed by president Yeltsin.[84]

It is clear that shock "therapy" was little more than a relentless, cruel strangulation of Russia's economy to facilitate looting of her vast industrial and resource wealth. Nonetheless, most Western-published analyses of this episode tended to treat it as failure of good intentions. While lamenting the outcomes and certain questionable practices, most analysts essentially attribute the failure of Russian transition to honest errors, Russia's endemic corruption, and perhaps inexperience in many of the drama's protagonists. In New York Review of Books, Robert Cotrell provides a typical example: "*One cannot really fault the youthful democratic movements for this failure. They were amateurs and innocents with a hazy grasp at best of what they wanted to achieve and no grasp at all of how concretely to achieve it.*"[85] Goldman Marshall of Harvard and the Council of Foreign Relations wrote: "*To be sure, there were unsettling reports of shady dealings during the takeovers, but most observers explained them away as inevitable side effects of such a far-reaching transformation.*" Naturally, Marshall fails to detail how or where he polled these "most observers," but his message to the readers is unmistakable: move along folks, there's nothing to see here – especially pay no attention to the fact that many of those thousands of Westerners who came to Russia "*for the best of reasons*," including Bill Browder, Andrei Schleifer and Jonathan Hay,[86] returned from Russia as multi-millionaires. Financial reporter Anne Willamson, who covered Russia for the New York Times and Wall Street Journal rightly remarked in her Congressional testimony that, "*Americans, who thought their money was helping a stricken land, have been dishonored; and the Russian people who trusted us are now in debt twice what they were in 1991 and rightly feel themselves betrayed.*"

---

[84] (Williamson, Russia's Fiscal Whistleblower 1998)
[85] (Cottrell 2001)
[86] During his time managing the HIID's Moscow operation, Andrei Schleifer and Jonathan Hay took advantage of their position and relationships to make personal investments in Russia. An investigation by the FBI and U.S. Justice Department found evidence of fraud and money laundering by Harvard's consultants. In 2004, Schleifer was found guilty of fraud and he agreed to pay a $31 million fine to settle the case. Not only did Harvard University persist in defending Schleifer over the 8 years of investigations and trials, it paid the bulk of Schileifer's fine and kept him on university's faculty.

The Enterprise

Now, why does the west applaud Gorbachev and Yeltsin? Do you think that the West wants Soviet people to live in luxury, be well fed? Not remotely! The West wants the Soviet Union to break up. Gorbachev and Yeltsin get a pat on the back because the West thinks they are destroying the country.

Alexander Zinoviev, March 1990 on French TV channel Antenne 2 during a debate with Boris Yeltsin

Western commentators usually focus on the period from 1991 to 2000 and blame the administration of Bill Clinton for mismanaging their aid to Russia. However, blaming the Clinton administration is a bit like reading a book from the middle rather than from the beginning. To understand U.S. government's role in the Russian tragedy, we have to go at least ten years back, to the beginnings of the administration of President Ronald Reagan. We must also distinguish between the legitimate U.S. government, and an illegal, parallel structure of power operating within it. For a long time, this "secret government" could not be discussed in polite society because its existence was deemed a wild conspiracy theory. But that all changed in the fall of 1986 when an American supply plane got shot down over Nicaragua and Reagan's illegal arm sales to Iran became exposed. These events brought to light the "Iran-Contra" affair. A full congressional investigation was launched and its proceedings revealed the existence of a parallel power structure operating unlawfully within legitimate government structure. For the first time, the actions of this network, also referred to as *shadow government, deep state* or *the Enterprise*, came out on record and could no longer be dismissed as mere conspiracy theory.

In his special report titled "Secret Government," journalist Bill Moyers described the organization as, "*an interlocking network of official functionaries, spies, mercenaries, ex-generals, profiteers and super-patriots who for a variety of motives operate outside of the legitimate institutions of government. Presidents have turned to them when they can't win the support of the Congress or the people, creating that unsupervised power so feared by the framers of our constitution.*" Late Senator Daniel Inouye characterized it as "*a shadowy government with its own air force, its own navy, its own fundraising mechanisms and the ability to pursue its own ideas of national interest, free from all checks and balances, and free from the law itself."* [87]

For the purpose of our analysis it is important to keep in mind the existence of this network as well as William Casey, the highest Reagan administration official directly associated with it.

Reagan administration cold warriors formulate the policy…

When Reagan took office in 1981, he appointed William Casey as Director of Central Intelligence (DCI).[88] Casey was Reagan's election campaign manager, but he was no ordinary party apparatchik. He had close ties in the political, financial and intelligence circles and counted among the most powerful people in the U.S. establishment.[89] It was Casey in fact who put forward the former CIA director and key Iran-Contras co-conspirator George H. W. Bush as the Vice President on the Republican election ticket. Reagan made Casey a member of his government, which caused some consternation in Washington since this was the first time in history that DCI would also be a cabinet member. Casey was charged with the mandate *"to build up C.I.A.'s ability to make military and political action outside the United States."*[90] This mission was important enough to justify a 17% rise in CIA's budget every year through the 1980s.[91]

Casey was a staunch anti-communist with very hostile views of the Soviet Union. This antagonism affected his work and at times caused serious tensions within the government and intelligence community, particularly at CIA's Office of Soviet Analysis (SOVA). Casey systematically demanded the most hardline interpretations of Soviet affairs in CIA's intelligence reports, even when evidence didn't support his case.

---

[87] (Moyers 1987)

[88] The Office of the Director of Central Intelligence (DCI) was active from 1946 to 2005. The Director managed and coordinated the activities of all intelligence agencies, acted as the principal intelligence advisor to the President of the U.S. and the National Security Council and also acted as the head of the C.I.A.

[89] During World War II, William Casey served with the Army Intelligence and the Office of Strategic Services (predecessor of the CIA). Under President Ford, he served on the Foreign Intelligence Advisory Board, an executive committee of the U.S. intelligence community. During Nixon administration, he headed the Securities and Exchange Commission. After that post he took charge of the Export-Import Bank, an independent Government agency created to facilitate exports of American goods and services. From 1976 to 1981 he was associated with the Rogers & Wells law firm which operated in New York and Washington.

[90] (Pace 1987)

[91] (Jeffreys-Jones 2013)

Analysts who resisted this pressure were intimidated and sidelined as communist sympathizers. Casey's anti-Soviet bias went so far that State Secretary George Schultz later reported that he came to distrust all intelligence documents related to the USSR. Senator Daniel Moynihan went further, outright accusing the intelligence agency of lying, *"repeatedly and egregiously."* [92]

Soviet economy was one of CIA's focal points of interest. The agency closely tracked Soviet economic developments and produced an annual report about it for the US Congress' Joint Economic Committee. Already in the late 1970s, CIA recognized serious economic problems in the USSR. Its 1977 report noted that, *"the combination of slowing economic growth and rising military outlays poses difficult choices for the leadership over the next several years."* [93] Conditions continued to worsen over the years and by the time Mikhail Gorbachev came to power in 1985, economic growth had faltered to nearly zero. Gorbachev was keenly aware of the need for a drastic reform of the system, but he was facing a minefield of economic, political, and social problems that had compounded for decades and defied any straightforward solutions. A report by the Directorate of Intelligence pointed out that Gorbachev's reforms could not, *"simultaneously maintain rapid growth in defense spending, satisfy demand for greater quantity and variety of consumer goods and services, invest in the amounts required for economic modernization and expansion and continue to support client-state economies."*[94]

Some six months into Gorbachev's term, CIA's newly created Societal Issues branch of the SOVA published a comprehensive report titled "Domestic Stress on the Soviet System," detailing the many issues affecting the Soviet society. The report noted that USSR was handicapped with an apathetic labor force plagued with rising criminality and alcoholism, and that its political system, parasitic bureaucracy and moribund leadership all obstructed economic growth and reforms. It emphasized mounting pressures from Soviet people's aspirations and the system's inability to provide them any real venues of fulfillment. The CIA understood that these tensions were potentially a threat to the stability of the regime itself: *"these tensions could eventually confront the regime with challenges that it cannot effectively contain without system change and the risks to control that would accompany such change."*[95] This report was so

---

[92] (Jeffreys-Jones 2013)
[93] (Lundberg 1995)
[94] The report in question was published in September 1985, titled "Gorbachev's Economic Agenda: Promises, Potentials and Pitfalls." (Lundberg 1995)
[95] (Lundberg 1995)

important to Reagan administration's Soviet policy that its lead author, Kay Oliver personally briefed the President about its findings and implications: that the Soviet system was unsustainable, that it needed drastic social and economic reforms, and that such reforms might destabilize the regime and cause the Communist party to lose political control over the country.

Western observers were aware that if Gorbachev pursued the necessary reforms in earnest, he would jeopardize communist party's control of the country and risk his own political suicide. Consequently, part of the foreign policy establishment thought that Gorbachev was merely posturing to buy time and get concessions and aid from the west. In 1987, NSA's Lieutenant General William Odom noted: "*It seems more and more clear that Gorbachev himself does not intend systemic change. ... If what one means by reform is a significant improvement in the standard of living for Soviet citizens and increased protection of their individual rights under law, that kind of reform cannot go very far without bringing about systemic change – the kind of change that Gorbachev cannot want.*"

But the doubters would soon have to reconsider their mistrust of the Secretary General: in the fall of 1988 Gorbachev, who was now under growing pressure from the old guard communists, called for multiparty elections and moved to outflank the hardliners by seeking his own appointment as president. It became clear that his reforms were for real and he meant business. However, Gorbachev was by now clashing with so many vested interests that a major conflict within the communist party leadership was building up. The circumstances compelled him to speed up the reforms, and his measures became visibly more hasty and erratic, generating an uncomfortable level of uncertainty that would have an adverse effect on the economy. As a result, in 1988 the economy again took a turn for the worse.

USSR's growing vulnerability presented a golden opportunity for the American cold warriors to vanquish their great geopolitical rival. For the hardcore anti-communist zealots and their financier overlords, this was too great an opportunity to ignore and they resolved to take an active role in managing the looming fallout. As Reagan's National Security Council Special Assistant Jack Matlock said, "*What you had to do was find a policy that would protect you if [true reform] didn't happen, but would take advantage of it if it did. And that's what we devised. It was a policy with no downsides.*"[96]

Since that time, some elements of that policy had leaked out into the public. Russian sources revealed an alleged 1986 CIA document titled

---

[96] (Lundberg 1995)

"*Change the Constitutional and Political System in Eastern Europe and the USSR.*" The document spelled out the key measures of the US policy. These included recruitment of collaborators from among influential representatives of the state apparatus, integration of public and financial institutions into political and economic system of the state, and "*setting control over financial flows and removing assets from the economies of developed countries.*" [97] As the events unfolded, they largely corroborated the authenticity of these leaked documents. So did various other American official sources.

Preparing the ground in the Soviet Union

Collapse of the USSR unleashed a wave of jubilation within the ranks of the American leadership, public servants and opinion makers. In their triumphalist rush to take credit for defeating the scourge of communism, many of them spoke openly, even boastfully about their actions, revealing rather a lot about what had actually taken place. One such zealot was Washington Post's David Ignatius. For a journalist, he was as close to the belly of the beast as a journalist could be. A graduate of Harvard and Cambridge, his Washington reporting covered the U.S. Department of Justice, the Senate and the CIA. His writing on CIA's activities particularly became subject of derision for its credulous tone and PR-ish bias. Veteran CIA operative Melvin Goodman called Ignatius "*Washington Post's long-time apologist-in-chief for the CIA...*" [98] This detail about Ignatius is relevant to our analysis because it indicates his allegiances and close connections within the intelligence community.

Shortly after the August 1991 anti-communist coup in Russia, [99] Ignatius penned an article in the Washington Post exalting the role of western "*pro-democracy*" operatives in bringing down the Soviet regime. Gushing over "*the great democratic revolution that has swept the globe,*" Ignatius makes a surprising revelation about the makings of this revolution: "*Preparing the ground for last month's triumph*[100] *of overt action was a network of overt operatives who during the last 10 years have quietly been changing the rules of international politics. They have been doing in public what the CIA used to do in private – providing money and moral*

---

[97] (Popov 2016)
[98] (Goodman 2017)
[99] This was actually a counter-coup as it was the communists who staged the initial coup.
[100] Ignatius is referring to the 19th August 1991 counter-coup where Yeltsin's reformist faction prevailed over the Communist old guard that attempted to reassert Communist hold on power.

support for pro-democracy groups, training resistance fighters, working to subvert communist rule." [101]

Ignatius singles out the work of the pro-democracy activist Allen Weinstein who began to organize Soviet dissidents already in 1980. Weinsten *"quickly became connected with the network of pro-democracy activists...Soon he was sponsoring conferences for dissidents, arranging visits for them to the United States and otherwise making trouble."* [102] Early on, Boris Yeltsin and his aides became drawn into Weinstein's *"transatlantic hospitality suite."* Weinstein remained in close communications with Yeltsin's circle, particularly during the critical August 1991 events. *"When Boris Yeltsin's aides were trying to rally support for their resistance in Moscow on Aug. 19,"* writes Ignatius, *"they needed to broadcast their defiant message to Russia and the world."* One of them faxed Weinstein in Washington, requesting that the American President issue a public statement of support for Yeltsin. Promptly, George Bush called Yeltsin to express his support and then went on television to describe their telephone conversation. Weinstein's ability to engage the President of the United States on such a short notice was indeed an incredible feat of power networking for a humble pro-democracy activist.

Of course, Weinstein was not the only operative "making trouble" against the USSR. Ignatius also credits William Miller of the American Committee on U.S.-Soviet Relations, George Soros of the Open Society Foundation, John Mroz of the Center for East-West Security Studies, John Baker of the Atlantic Council and Harriett Crosby of the Institute for Soviet-American Relations. National Endowment for Democracy (NED) headed by Zbigniew Brzezinski was the *"sugar daddy of overt operations."* [103] It had been active inside the Soviet Union for years – *overtly*, of course – financing various Soviet trade unions and the liberal "Interregional Group" in the Congress of People's Deputies. The Interregional Group was the first legally organized opposition group in the Soviet Union and was subsequently identified as the prime catalyst of "democratic reforms" in Russia.

---

[101] (Ignatius 1991) Ignatius may be a tad disingenuous in insisting that these activities were *overt* as opposed to *covert*. Things like training resistance fighters and working to subvert Communist rule could not have been done overtly. Perhaps just for effect, Ignatius merely misspelled the word *covert* by omitting the "c" – kind of like if I characterized his assertions as *rap*.
[102] (Ignatius 1991)
[103] (Ignatius 1991)

We can now vaguely discern how Boris Yeltsin, a communist party apparatchik from Sverdlovsk in Siberia, stumbled upon the whole plot of taking down the Soviet communist regime and privatizing Russia's wealth. The populist leader was well known as an ambitious careerist willing to, *"trample anyone to get to his goal,"* [104] and had racked up an impressive track record of making trouble for the communist party. Among other things, Yeltsin preached about multi-party democracy to the Komsomol, the Youth Communist League, where Russia's future oligarchs were recruited and groomed to take part in the privatization of Russia on behalf of their Western sponsors. In 1987 Yeltsin's troublemaking led to a collision with the Moscow communist authorities after he publicly criticized the party leadership for dragging their feet on reforms. Public criticism of the party dignitaries was a grave affront in the USSR. He was strongly reprimanded, barred from politics, and forced to return to Sverdlovsk to a simple business management function. During his exodus, but possibly even before that, Boris Yeltsin became closely associated with a circle of liberal dissidents and academicians led by Gennady Burbulis. Burbulis was the leader and one of the founders of the above mentioned "Interregional Group," which was funded by the U.S. National Endowment for Democracy. Burbulis became one of Yeltsin's closest associates and helped him resurrect his political career. In 1991, he managed Yeltsin's successful election for the Russian presidency (June 1991) and became the first Secretary of State in Yeltsin's cabinet.

Almost as soon as Yeltsin became president in 1991, the advance guard of Harvardites and other Westerners started to arrive in Moscow. They spent time at a dacha outside the city to recruit their Russian collaborators and chart the course of events that would determine Russia's tragic fate for the remainder of the decade.

We need not assume that everyone involved worked for the CIA or knowingly sought to harm Russia. In all likelihood, most of Russia's reformers were earnest people yearning for change from an unsustainable, unsatisfactory system that was collapsing on itself. Without a doubt, many of them were seduced by the promise of western style democracy and capitalism which appeared so much better at satisfying people's needs and aspirations. When Boris Yeltsin himself toured the United States in September of 1989, he was mesmerized with the glitz and abundance he saw in Houston and Miami. When his hosts took him and his entourage to

---

[104] This is how Yakou Riabov, first secretary of the Sverdlovsk communist party and Yeltsin's early political mentor described him in an interview featured in the documentary film, "Boris Yeltsin – the Formation of a Leader." (Alfandari and Leconte 2001)

a supermarket in Clear Lake in Texas, Yeltsin remarked with amazement that in Russia, even members of the politburo couldn't dream of such abundance and variety of goods as were available to any middle class American. This all must have made a profound impression on Boris Yeltsin and perhaps ignited in him the resolve to do whatever it took to make Russia also a land of wealth, abundance and technological advancement. If the Americans got it right, following their advice must have seemed as the right thing to do.

16 September 1989 - Boris Yeltsin and a group of Soviet visitors made a 20-minute visit at a Clearlake supermarket. Yeltsin browsed the aisles, tried free samples of produce, 'nodding his head in amazement.' Photo © Houston Chronicle

But where Russian reformers saw the lure, they did not see the hook. The generous outward friendliness of the American leaders disarmed the Russians who thought that as they left communism behind, they would now be friends and allies with the Americans. This illusion was probably reinforced by the real, sincere friendship of the majority of those Americans and other Westerners who went to Russia to share their know-how and help guide the reforms. But the people who were higher up in command of this project were neither altruistic nor friendly. Their mindset was entrenched in cold war animosities and their objective was to defeat, dismember, and loot Russia of its wealth, and leave it so weakened and impoverished that it could never again challenge American hegemony. Willam Casey's deputy Robert Gates[105] gave us a glimpse of this mindset in 1986, declaring: "*We are engaged in an historic struggle with the Soviet*

---

[105] Gates was the Deputy Director of Central Intelligence and specialist of Soviet studies William Casey's second-in-command. His remarks are from a speech he delivered on 25th November 1986.

Union ... *[The Soviets] use conflict in the third world to exploit divisions in the Alliance and to try to recreate the internal divisions caused by Vietnam in order to weaken the Western response and provoke disagreement over larger national security and defence policy."* [106] Gates accused the Soviets of targeting four areas of expansion: the middle-east oil fields, the isthmus of Panama Canal, the mineral wealth of South America, and the Western political and military alliance. In other words, Reagan administration saw the Soviet Union primarily as a rival in a global struggle for resources. The same Robert Gates would later acknowledge that the CIA had conducted a campaign of economic sabotage against the USSR and took credit for bringing about the fall of communism, which he considered, *"the greatest of American triumphs."*

Fallout: the economic genocide

> *Does America want Russia to raise its living standards and consume most of its fuels and raw materials domestically? Or, does it see a chance to nail down its Cold War victory by destroying Russia's potential power to be a rival, by turning it into an exporter of oil, gas and other raw materials?*
>
> *Dr. Michael Hudson speaking before the Russian parliament, 15 March 1999.*

> *To make ends meet, professors had to become taxi drivers, nurses became prostitutes and art museums sold paintings right off their walls. Nearly every Russian was cowed and humiliated...*
>
> *Bill Browder, "Red Notice"*

---

[106] (Jeffreys-Jones 2013)

RUSSIA IN THE 1990s: THE MISSING CONTEXT

The transition program engineered by the American deep state and its Wall Street patrons was nothing short of catastrophic for Russia. The perfect storm of sudden price liberalization, drastic curtailment of government spending and bank credit, and opening of domestic markets to unrestricted foreign competition produced a toxic brew that devastated Russian economy, destroyed its currency, and plunged much of the population into poverty and hunger. After 1992, Russian middle class saw their savings evaporate and their real wages halve – if they were fortunate enough to receive them at all.[107] Economic reforms rapidly destroyed the nation's agricultural production and store shelves went almost empty. In 1992 the average Russian consumed 40% less than in 1991.[108] By 1998 some 80% of Russian farms went bankrupt and the nation that was one of the world's leading food producers suddenly became dependent on foreign aid. About 70,000 factories shut down and Russia produced 88% fewer tractors, 77% fewer washing machines, 77% less cotton fabric, 78% fewer TV-sets and so forth.[109] In all, during the transition years, the nation's Gross Domestic Product fell by 50%, which was even worse than during the World War II German occupation.[110]

A huge segment of the population became destitute. In 1989 two million Russians lived in poverty (on $4/day or less). By the mid-1990s, that number soared to 74 million according to World Bank figures. In 1996, fully one in four Russians was living in conditions described as "desperate" poverty.[111] Alcoholism soared and suicide rates doubled making suicide the leading cause of death from external causes. Violent crime also doubled in the early 1990s and during the first six years of reforms, nearly 170 thousand people were murdered. An acute health crisis emerged, resulting in epidemics of curable diseases like measles and diphtheria. Rates of cancer, heart disease and tuberculosis also soared to become the highest for any industrialized country in the world.[112] Life expectancy for males plummeted to 57 years. At the same time abortions skyrocketed and birth rates collapsed: in Moscow they were as low as 8.2 per 1000.[113] In all, Russia's death rates increased by 60% to a level only

---

[107] This is according to statistics maintained by the Geneva-based Economic Commission for Europe (Engdahl, How 'shock therapy' has ruined Russia 1993).
[108] (Klein 2007)
[109] (Lindgren 1999)
[110] (Satter 2007)
[111] (Klein 2007)
[112] (MacDonald 2015)
[113] (MacDonald 2015)

experienced by countries at war.[114] Western and Russian demographers agreed that from 1992 to 2000, Russia sustained between five and six million "surplus deaths" – deaths that couldn't be explained by previous population trends.[115] That corresponds to between 3.4% and 4% of the total population of Russia. To put that number into perspective, consider that during the course of World War II, the United Kingdom lost 0.94% of its population, France lost 1.35%, China lost 1.89% and the U.S. lost 0.32%.[116] Aleksandr Rutskoy was in fact not exaggerating when he called the reforms program an "economic genocide."

Moscow, 1995. Bus-stop advertisement reads, "The world is changing." (Kouprianova 2015)

Russia's plight is difficult to comprehend. I grew up in Croatia, formerly part of Yugoslavia. We also had a one-party communist regime and a socialist, state run economy, so I am intimately familiar with the many failings of that system. With roughly the same timing, Yugoslavia also endured a long drawn-out economic crisis and a traumatic transition to a multiparty democracy and market economy. The transition led to a series of bloody wars of secession that lasted from 1991 to 2000. Croatia was at war for four years, from 1991 to 1995. In spite of all that, Croatia's experience may have been mild compared with what took place in Russia. Throughout these unhappy years, people in Croatia continued to go to work and received their salaries, social services were provided without interruption, shops and pharmacies were always well stocked up, and in

---

[114] Death rates rose from 10 per one thousand in 1989 to 16 per thousand in 1994, an unprecedented level for a country at peace. (Kouprianova 2015)
[115] (Satter 2007)
[116] (Chossudovsky 2010)

spite of a tangible drop in the standard of living the population suffered relatively little poverty and almost no hunger. Apart from those living in active combat zones, the people were able to adjust to the new circumstances and life went on.

For Russia, the dismal economic statistics don't convey the suffering her people endured. Knowing that the average Russian consumed 40% less in 1992 than in 1991, or that the economy operated on only 15% of the currency it required leaves out the human dimension of this experience. What happens to the people when their nation is subjected to a campaign of economic sabotage? A Russian-Canadian blogger Nina Kouprianova published a small collection of personal memories from Russians who lived through the shock therapy reforms:

- Natalia: I remember one particular day from the 1990s: in the morning, really early, we went on a walk to the park with our dogs. We never tried to wake our children up on weekends: the more they sleep, the less they eat. Anyhow, we found several mushrooms in the park and returned home happy, since we had pearl barley at home and could make soup!
- Foma: In my town, all the pigeons were killed [and eaten]. People searched for food dumpster-diving.
- Svetlana: I gave birth to my son in December of 1993. That particular winter was quite cold, and our apartment building barely had any heat. When we returned home from the hospital, it was 10 degrees Celsius inside (50 F), so we lived in a small room without turning off our portable heater for days. I also remember that it was even difficult to buy soap: the stores were empty. My daddy, who was always very organized, came home one day feeling extremely pleased with himself, dragging a three-liter jar with brown stinky goo. The latter turned out to be liquid soap. We used that horrifying substance for bathing for a long time.
- Evgenia: It's scary to remember that to this day I'm afraid to be left alone with an empty fridge, as if I grew up in besieged Leningrad (during World War II—Ed.). To this day, I feel acute shame because I had thoughts about stealing groceries. And, yes, we had to eat food covered with mould.
- Valentina: My friend fainted from hunger making kasha for her two little children. They also did not pay us in money, but in light bulbs, for instance. Then we had to sell the light bulbs in order to buy something to eat.

- Elena: I was happy back then because I was in love. I also had a bag of flour and a bag of potatoes.
- Roman: I remember that my mom bought me a Mars chocolate bar for my birthday. Then there were no more sweets for a long time, because we ran out of money. How many died back then just like that...
- Vladimir: We ate macaroni. For breakfast, lunch, and dinner.
- Marina: I grasped the fact that we have begun to live better when we got the ability to buy fruit for our children on a regular basis. I'm not talking about limes or avocados, but simply apples, pears, and oranges.
- Yana: I was a college student at the beginning of the 1990s. I remember that one winter I kept having dreams about apples. :) Evidently, I lacked vitamins terribly, because apples were a huge luxury for me.
- Olga: I took my little five-year-old child (I had no one to babysit) and traveled to the nearby town (this was embarrassing to do in my own town) and sold worn children's clothing, which my daughter outgrew. If I were lucky, then I used the money I earned to buy food. Then there was barter...
- An anonymous man: For me, the worst thing about the 1990s was not hunger but rather, the constant, tedious, and continuous sense of humiliation.
- Asya: Every recess, I sat at my desk in school because I was exhausted from hunger. I was unable to walk or laugh. Later on, I read that this is how those, who lived in besieged Leningrad, felt. Then I stopped having my period for six months. I also stole bread and tvorog (quark—Ed.) from the grocery store a few times.
- Nina (Kouprianova): [I recall] receiving large, very elongated cans of humanitarian aid at my school with mystery meat inside. Spam, I think. It was very much expired, but we ate it. [I also remember] seemingly endless tank convoys beneath my windows, though it wasn't a parade...

RUSSIA IN THE 1990s: THE MISSING CONTEXT

Did it have to be that way?

Americans, who thought their money was helping a stricken land, have been dishonored; and the Russian people who trusted us are now in debt twice what they were in 1991 and rightly feel themselves betrayed.

Reporter Anne Williamson before the Committee on Banking and Financial Services of the U.S. House of Representatives, 21 September 1999

Was there a better way for Russia to move from communism to capitalism? Was her traumatic experience under Yeltsin regime inevitable, or was the pain intentionally inflicted? To this day many intellectuals in the West maintain that the transition could not have gone otherwise, arguing that Russia had emerged from 70 years of communist rule with a state controlled economy, with private property outlawed and a nonexistent culture of entrepreneurship. The shift between two drastically different economic systems together with the most complex privatization project ever undertaken could never have gone smoothly. The Russians themselves are usually assumed to have been ignorant about the workings of free markets and unprepared for transition's challenges. However, this is simply not true.

Well before the Soviet Union began to unravel it was clear to most of its thinking citizens that their system would capsize unless it drastically changed. In the republics of the former Yugoslavia – having a similar system as the USSR – already in the mid-1980s most people understood that our system was unsustainable and that the only viable alternative was a capitalist market economy based on private property. As in Russia, few favoured the Anglo-American monetary neoliberalism; the preferred model was a capitalist economy with the social state, following the Swedish model. We called this, *"socialism with the human face,"* the very same term that was often invoked in pre-transition Russia.

In Russia, for nearly twenty years numerous economists applied themselves to studying the mechanics of capitalist market economy in anticipation of the coming changes. The school of thought that was particularly popular among them was that of the Swiss economist Wilhelm von Roepke and his disciple Ludwig Erhard, the father of Germany's post-war economic miracle.[117] Unfortunately, when Harvard's advisors arrived in Moscow and started recruiting Russians they would work with, they ignored these learned and prepared economists. One of them was Larisa Piasheva whom Moscow mayor Gavril Popov entrusted with the project of designing and implementing the privatization of Moscow's assets.

In her testimony before the Congressional Committee on Banking and Financial Services, journalist Anne Willamson described Piasheva's program as, *"a fearless and rapid plunge into the market which would have distributed property widely into Russia's many eager hands."* Willamson added: *"When the Administration says it had no choice but to rely upon the bad actors it did select for American largesse, Congress should recall Larisa Piasheva. How different today's' Russia might have been had only the Bush Administration and the many Western advisers ... chosen to champion Ms. Piasheva's vision of a rapid disbursement of property to the people rather than to the 'golden children' of the Soviet nomenklatura."*[118]

Russia's nascent democratic forces did in fact endeavor to effect a more equitable transfer of state properties to Russian citizens: in 1992, based on privatization programs that Piasheva and others had developed, the Congress of People's Deputies approved a scheme that was structured to prevent corruption.[119] At that time however, Boris Yeltsin had already secured the privilege to manage privatization by decree and many of his decrees were drafted by the very coterie of cabinet officials, their American advisors and hand-picked oligarchs who were the main beneficiaries of the process. Any action by Russian lawmakers that obstructed the oligarchs' pillage stood little chance of being realized. But looting the country's wealth was not their only objective – dismembering Russia, destroying its institutions, and inflicting pain on its people was an integral part of that project. The pattern of reformers' conduct on numerous important issues consistently favored destructive, damaging measures over those that might have improved conditions in the country.

To begin with, there was the problem of privatization's timing. If the reformers had any intention of conducting a fair and equitable privatization, they should have completed it *before* the abolition of price controls. In their book, "The Tragedy of Russia's Reforms," Peter Reddaway and Dmitri Glinski point out that, *"The Soviet middle class*

---

[117] (Likoudis 2011)
[118] (Sailer 2014)
[119] (Wedel 1998)

used the relatively prosperous and stable 1960s and 1970s to amass a considerable amount of personal savings in government bank accounts. In the Gorbachev era, when denationalization and deregulation of the economy came on the agenda, these middle-class savings were ripe to be channeled toward productive investment in industry, which in a broader framework of reasonable reform policies could have led to internally generated and sustainable growth along the lines of the postwar Japanese miracle." [120] However, the Russians were deprived of the opportunity to use their savings: the sudden price liberalization unleashed hyperinflation which rapidly destroyed their purchasing power. This was the reformers' elegant solution to make sure Russians couldn't claim their share in the nation's wealth. IMF's insistence on the abolition of energy price subsidies while at the same time drastically curtailing the quantity of currency in circulation predictably destroyed Russia's production of food. Dependency on foreign food aid made Russia and its officials easily compliant with the Western dictate.

Western institutions could have easily alleviated the suffering of Russians in 1993 when a major health care crisis broke out. Jeffrey Sachs reports having met with the head of World Bank's Health Mission at that time, expressly to address the dismal state of health care and social services in Russia and to urge World Bank to take action. To his dismay, he *"discovered that the World Bank planned to take its time to get help to Russia, since there was apparently a need for the bank to study the situation for some years first."* [121] Thus, World Bank purposely withheld the help that was well within its means to provide, contributing to needless suffering and deaths of millions of ordinary Russians.

Intellectual musings of Harvard's historian Richard Pipes showcase the depraved thinking of some of Russia's Western advisors. He contends that it was *"desirable for Russia to keep on disintegrating until nothing remains of her institutional structures."* [122] That same Harvard, which kept the likes of Richard Pipes on its payroll, had since 1987 also accepted CIA funding for their program on intelligence and policy at John F. Kennedy School of Government. [123] The same Harvard that advised the Russian government on shock therapy and privatization also put its employees Andrei Schleifer and Jonathan Hay in charge of HIID to disburse over

---

[120] (Glinski and Reddaway 2001)
[121] (Sachs 2012)
[122] (Klein 2007)
[123] (Lundberg 1995)

$300 million of USAID funds among their cronies in Russia.[124] When Schleifer and Hay were found guilty of fraud and gross corruption, Harvard failed to distance itself from these two criminals, backing Schleifer all the way through nine years of legal proceedings and retaining him on its faculty even after his conviction. The same university's honored alumni Robert Rubin and Lawrence Summers formulated IMF's cruel "aid" policy for Russia from their perch at the US Treasury department. The same Harvard had little compunction about profiting from the misery it had helped inflict on the people of Russia, seeing its endowment balloon from $4 billion in 1992 to $18 billion in 2000.[125]

Bill Browder was right to decry the *"evil foundation,"* and *"dirty dishonesty of Russia."* He failed to explain however, that these were largely the creation of Western financial interests which he too represented. Tens of millions of Russians endured a decade of poverty and humiliation and up to six million of them needlessly met an early death. It is utterly cynical and deceitful for Browder to ignore those Russians as though they were less worthy than Sergei Magnitsky. It is deeply hypocritical of him to pretend to seek justice for Magnitsky while remaining silent about the millions of victims of Western economic assault on Russia. As for the worthy Harvard audiences of Browder's business case presentations, these young men and women would do well not let themselves be misled and emotionally manipulated. Gaining a proper perspective on such important historical events as the fall of the Soviet Union and Russia's subsequent transition should be done through critical thinking rather than misplaced sentimentality. If they ever sought such perspective, they might think to demand their professors and alumni to give them full account of their university's role in the Russian tragedy. But let's not delude ourselves. The whole point of Browder's presentations at Harvard and elsewhere is not to give his audiences an honest account about Russia. It is to sell his story and gain allies and supporters in his relentless crusade against Russia and its new leadership.

---

[124] This was not a case where the well-meaning Cambridge officials lost control over their Moscow-based operatives and remained ignorant of their misdeeds: by December 1993, less than a year after the project began, Alberto Neri, one of HIID's Moscow-based financial officers wrote no less than four memos to the institute's Deputy Director Rosanne Kumins, warning her that Harvard was complicit in financial irregularities and tax evasion and was condoning dissemination of false data, irregularities in employment contracts and misrepresentation of expenditures.

[125] Harvard Endowment was heavily invested in Russia and actively participated in trading of Russian short-term Treasury Bills (Austin Fitts 2002)

4. Enter Vladimir Putin

Something remarkable is taking place in Russia, and it's quite different from what we might expect. Rather than feel humiliated and depressed Russia is undergoing what I would call a kind of renaissance, a rebirth as a nation

F. William Engdahl

In addition to political, social and economic assault it endured during the 1990s, Russia also became the target of radical Islamic terrorist groups, again directed by elements of the American deep state. Deputy Director of CIA's National Council on Intelligence, Graham E. Fuller explicitly stated that their objective was to use Islamist extremists to *"destabilize what remains of Russian power."* [126] The idea in mobilizing Islamic radicals from Afghanistan, Chechnya and other parts against Russia was to "Balkanize" the Federation and break it into smaller sovereign states. The plan almost worked…

Regime change

We Russians make up a people that has never yet worked in freedom, that has never yet had a chance to develop all its powers and its talents.

Maxim Gorky

---

[126] Fuller's statement, cited by F. William Engdahl reads as follows: "*The policy of guiding the evolution of Islam and of helping them against our adversaries worked marvellously well in Afghanistan against the Red Army. The same doctrines can still be used to destabilize what remains of Russian power.*" (Engdahl, What if Putin is Telling the Truth? 2015)

On the 4th of August 1999, a force of around 2,000 Mujahedeen led by Shamil Basayev and Ibn al-Khattab conducted an incursion from Chechnya into Dagestan, killing a number of Russian servicemen and taking control of several towns and villages inside Dagestan. Like much of the rest of Russian institutions, her defense forces were in disarray and offered little resistance. By August 10, the insurgents proclaimed the independent Islamic State of Dagestan and declared war against Russian "occupation" forces.

The crisis prompted President Yeltsin to replace the Prime Minister Sergei Stepashin with an unknown government bureaucrat, Vladimir Vladmirovich Putin. Russia was on the verge of a military defeat in Dagestan and there was a real danger that the republic would break away from the federation, precipitating its irreversible disintegration. Putin immediately took charge of the crisis and quickly turned the situation around. Within a few weeks' time, in mid-September, Russian forces defeated the insurgents and pushed them back into Chechnya. Although the crisis led to a string of terror attacks in Russia and triggered the Second Chechen War, the rapid victory over the insurgency in Dagestan raised Vladimir Putin's reputation and public profile and marked an important turnaround for Russia.

On the last day of the second millennium, less than four months after the Dagestan intervention, Boris Yeltsin unexpectedly stepped down from Russia's presidency and named Vladimir Putin as his replacement. Putin took charge as acting President and was confirmed President of the Russian Federation after the elections in May of 2000. He took over a grievously wounded and dying nation whose population was deeply demoralized and whose institutions barely functioned. Its military and defense industry were eviscerated and its government was infiltrated by the oligarchs and organized crime. The nation's public debt was at 140% of its gross domestic product and just servicing the interest on that debt ate up a third of the government budget.

In spite of all this (or because of it), President Yeltsin was well liked in the West and treated as a friend. Sympathy toward President Putin, who brought a very different management style to the Kremlin, never took hold. With time, as Russia slowly started to heal under his leadership, the West's antipathy toward Putin only grew, escalating over the years to the point where even the leading politicians in the west didn't hesitate to explicitly liken Vladimir Putin to Adolf Hitler. The media in the West invariably characterized Putin as an autocrat, a tyrant, former KGB agent and a thug who was abusing his political power for personal enrichment.

Speaking positively about him or about Russia under his leadership became nearly taboo in any polite society.

Sadly, this demonization proved effective and many people in the west, particularly its intellectual class, can no longer discern the caricature of Russia and of Vladimir Putin painted by their media from reality. Rather than accepting these malicious distortions for truth, we would all do well judge Mr. Putin according to his deeds.

Vladimir Putin's disastrous contribution to Russia's history

> *Beware of the false prophets, who come to you in sheep's clothing, but inwardly are ravenous wolves. You will know them by their fruits. Grapes are not gathered from thorn bushes nor figs from thistles, are they? So every good tree bears good fruit, but the bad tree bears bad fruit*
>
> Matthew 7:16

On 26th July 2014 British magazine *"The Economist"* published an article titled "A web of lies," opening with the following two sentences: "*In 1991, when Soviet Communism collapsed, it seemed as if the Russian people might at last have the chance to become citizens of a normal Western democracy. Vladimir Putin's disastrous contribution to Russia's history has been to set his country on a different path.*" Well, we have already seen how Russia fared in the 1990s after Soviet communism collapsed. For some reason, the bright minds at The Economist thought this path was so promising, it was a real shame – a disaster, no less – that Vladimir Putin took Russia on a different one. Let's take a closer look, shall we, at Mr. Putin's "disastrous contribution."

To start with, Putin played the pivotal role in keeping the country from disintegrating. When he came to power, Russia's regional governors were writing their own laws, disregarded presidential instructions and were not even returning their republics' tax receipts to the Federation's purse. Mikhail Gorbachev stated that Putin "*saved Russia from the beginning of a collapse. A lot of the regions did not recognize our constitution."* [127] But this historical feat was only the starting point of the subsequent renaissance of the nation. Its economy returned to growth and became more vibrant and diverse than it had been perhaps since the reforms of Pyotr Stolypin of the early 1900s.

Economic reforms

In 2000, Russia was one of the most corrupt countries in the world. Without instituting draconian purges Putin took on the oligarchs and steadily curtailed their power, gradually returning Russia to the rule of law. By 2016 his government reduced corruption to about the same level as that of the United States. That was the empirical result of the annual study on corruption published in 2016 by Ernst & Young.[128] The global auditing consultancy asked respondents around the world whether in their experience, corruption is widespread in the business sector. Their survey, which was conducted in 2014, indicated that only 34% of their Russian respondents thought so, the same proportion as in the United States, and below the world average of 39%. Things have probably improved further since then as Vladimir Putin stepped up a high-profile anti-corruption campaign that led to investigations and prosecution of a number of high level politicians around Russia. Even highly ranked members of Putin's own political party were not spared.[129] The unmistakable message of such campaigns was that corruption would not be tolerated and that it would be aggressively investigated and prosecuted. Some of the best evidence that Putin's various anti-corruption measures have had effect can be found in World Bank's Enterprise Surveys which ask businessmen the question, *"was a gift or informal payment expected or requested during a meeting with tax officials?"* In 2005, nearly 60% of respondents answered affirmatively. By 2009 this number was 17.4% and by 2012 it had dropped to only 7.3%.

---

[127] (Gorbachev: Putin saved Russia from disintegration 2014)
[128] (Stulb 2016)
[129] Some of the names arrested in 2016 surprised even the Russian public as they included such high caliber individual as the Mayor of Vladivostok, Igor Pushkarev; Governor of the Kirov region, Nikita Belykh; Governor of the Sakhalin region, Alexander Khoroshavin, Deputy Minister of Culture Grigory Pirumov and Minister for Economic Development, Aleksey Ulyukaev.

ENTER VLADIMIR PUTIN

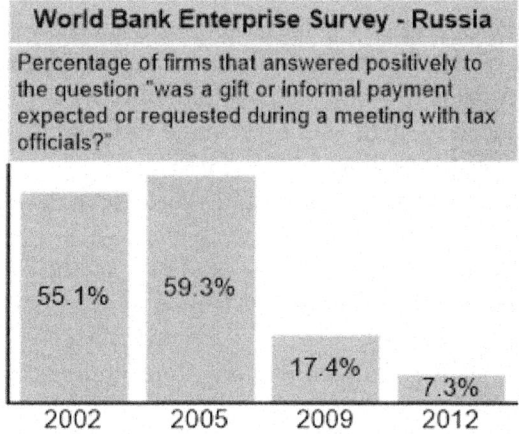

Putin's government also made impressive advances in making it easier for entrepreneurs and small businesses to set up shop, raise capital and operate in Russia.

World Bank's annual "Doing Business" report, ranks 190 world economies on a set of attributes such as the ease of starting a business, obtaining construction permits, obtaining electricity, raising credit, and enforcing contracts. On all the metrics combined, Russia managed to climb from 124th place in the world in 2012 to 40th in 2017.[130] Thus, within only five years, Russia had vaulted an impressive 84 positions in World Bank's ranking. This was not a random achievement but the result of President Putin's explicit 2012 directive that by 2018 Russia should be among the top 20 nations in the world for ease of doing business.

One of the strategically important sectors where Russia has made striking progress is its agricultural industry. After the disastrous 1990s when she found herself dependent on food imports, Russia again became self-sufficient in food production and a net food exporter. By 2014, Russian exports of agricultural products reached nearly $20 billion, almost a full third of her revenues from oil and gas exports. Not only is Russia now producing abundant food for its own needs, the government is explicitly favoring production of healthy foods, a strategy which includes a ban on the cultivation of genetically modified (GMO) crops, introduced by the State Duma in February of 2014. According to official Russian statistics, the share of GMO foods sold in Russia declined from 12% in 2004 to just 0.1% by 2014.

These and many other constructive reforms have had a very substantial impact on Russia's economic aggregates as the following examples show:

---

[130] (Romer 2016)

- Between 1999 and 2013, Russia's gross domestic product (GDP) leaped nearly 12-fold from $1,330 per capita to more than $15,560 in 2013, outpacing even China's remarkable economic growth.
- Russia reduced its debt as a percentage of GDP by over 90%, from 144% in 1998 to less than 14% in 2015!
- Gross national income per capita rose from $1,710 in 2000 to $14,810 in 2013.
- Unemployment fell from 13% in 1999 to below 5% in 2014. Among the working population (those aged 15-64), 69% have a paid job (74% of men).
- Only 0.2% of Russians work very long hours, compared to 13% OECD average
- Poverty rate fell from 40% in the 1990s to 12.5% in 2013 – better than U.S. or German poverty rates (15.6% and 15.7%, respectively)
- Average monthly income rose from around 1,500 rubles in 1999 to nearly 30,000 rubles in 2013.
- Average monthly pensions rose from less than 500 rubles to 10,000 rubles.

Social and demographic improvements

Putin's economic reforms included also a more equitable distribution of wealth. As hopelessness faded and standard of living improved, Russian society started to heal: suicides, homicides, and alcohol poisonings declined dramatically. Over the twenty-year period between 1994 and 2014, suicides declined by 56%, homicide rate by 73%, and alcohol poisonings by 83%!

Incidence per 100,000 residents	1994	2014	Decline
Suicides	42.1	18.4	56%
Homicides	32.6	8.7	73%
Alcohol poisonings	37.8	6.5	83%

The chart below shows the evolution of these improvements over time:

ENTER VLADIMIR PUTIN

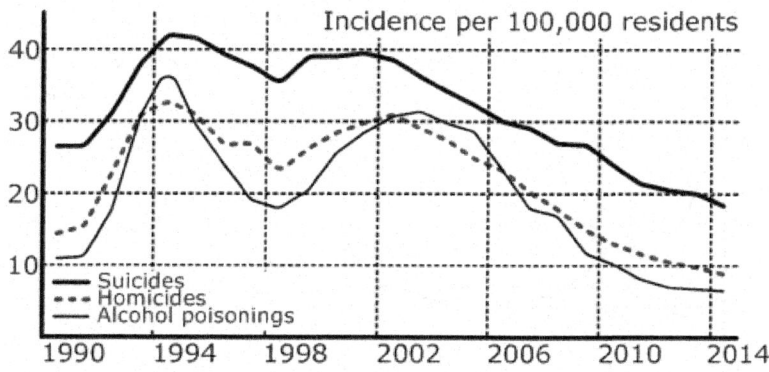

As we can see, these misery statistics rapidly deteriorated with the introduction of shock therapy in 1992, but the trend reversed soon after Putin took charge. By 2014, these figures reached their lowest values since even before 1992. Along with these improvements, the nation's demographic trends also experienced a dramatic turnaround. Russian life expectancy, which sunk to an average of barely 64 years (57 for men), rose steadily from the early 2000s to reach almost 72 in 2016, the highest it has ever been in Russia's history.

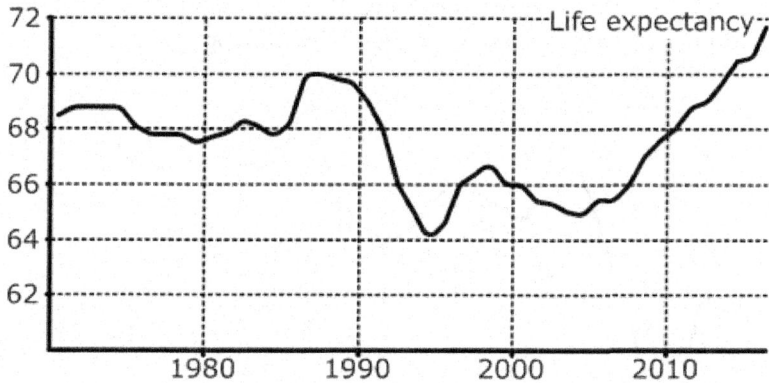

Looking at the way life expectancy in Russia changed over time, we see again that it had collapsed in the early 1990s but the trend turned around sharply under Vladimir Putin's leadership of the country.

Similarly fertility rate, which dropped to 1.16 babies per woman in 1999, increased by almost 50% to 1.7 babies by 2012, comparing favorably to European Union's average of 1.55 babies per woman of childbearing age. Abortions declined 88% from a harrowing 250% of live births in 1993 to 31% in 2013.

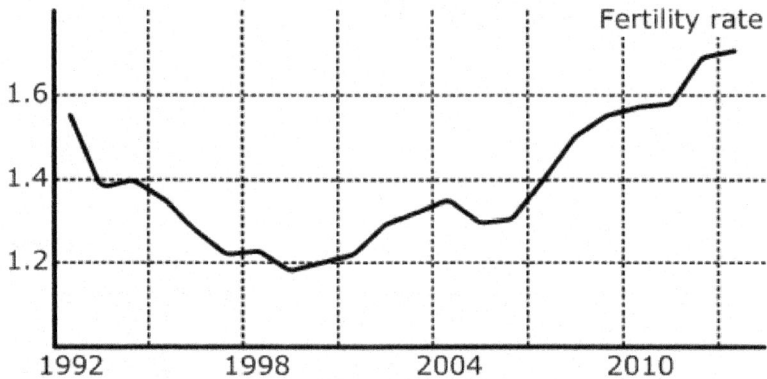

Not only are Russians living longer than ever before and enjoying much better quality of life, they also feel freer and happier. In 2014, Gallup Analytics reported that 65% of Russians, more than ever before, answered "Yes" when asked, "are you satisfied ... with your freedom to choose what you do with your life?" Meanwhile, Russia's happiness index rose more than tenfold, from 6 in 1992 to 70 in 2015. Happiness index, compiled by VCIOM[131] adds the proportion of the respondents reporting that they feel decidedly happy or generally happy and deducts those that report feeling generally unhappy or decidedly unhappy.

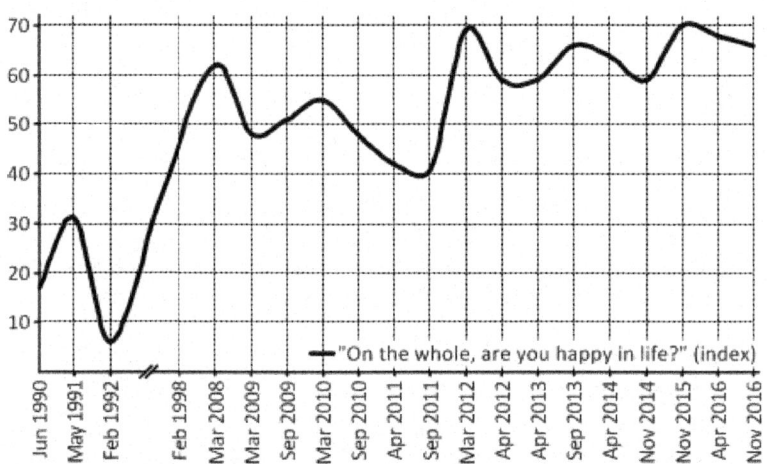

The next chart further corroborates the idea that under Putin's leadership, Russia has been developing as a sane and prosperous society, not only for

---

[131] ВЦИОМ - Russian Center for Research on Public Opinion

the benefit of a narrow ruling class and at everyone else's expense, but for the majority of ordinary Russians.

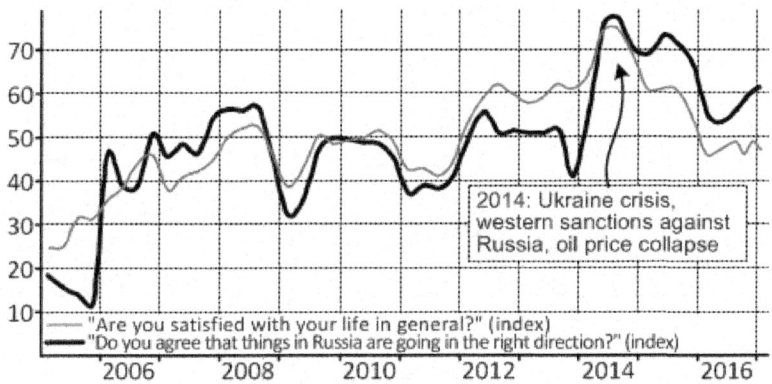

By 2014, the great majority of Russians felt satisfied with their lives and believed that things in Russia were moving in the right direction. These figures only tapered off after the 2014 Western-sponsored coup in Ukraine and the subsequent economic sanctions imposed on Russia. At the same time, the price of oil – still one of Russia's largest export – collapsed from over $100 per barrel to under $40. Economic sanctions and the oil price collapse triggered a significant crisis in Russia's economy. However, in spite of the continuing sanctions regime imposed on the country, its economy started improving again in 2016, thanks to its diverse industrial base that includes a developed commercial and consumer automotive industry, advanced aircraft and helicopter construction based largely on domestic technologies, world's leading aerospace industry building satellites and top class rocket engines, and advanced industries in pharmaceutical, food processing, optical device, machine tools, tractors, software and numerous other branches. Indeed, Russia is far from being just the "Nigeria with missiles," or a "gas station with an army," as many Western leaders like to characterize it.

Insofar as a population's sentiment is a valid measure of its leadership's performance, Russia's development under Vladimir Putin stands in sharp contrast with the weak performance of most other developed nations, including those that most vehemently criticize Russia and its president. According to polls conducted by Ipsos Public Affairs in 25 different countries in November 2016 and published by the World Economic Forum, almost two thirds of the people in the world believed that their countries were moving in the wrong direction. The leading western nations scored just as badly, while some of them did just dismally.

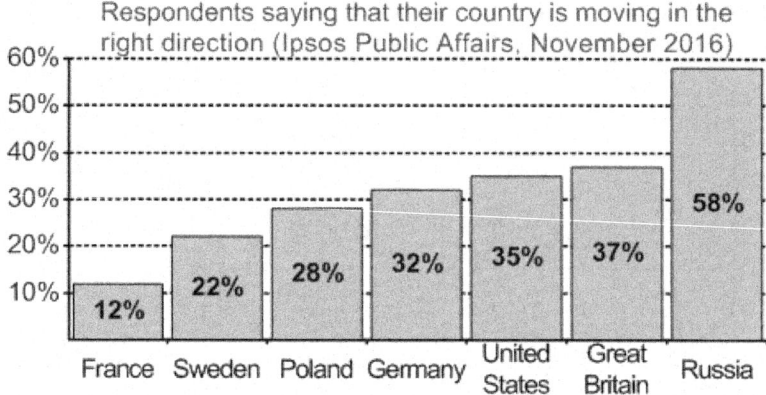

Evidently, Russians feel much better about the way their nation is shaping up than do constituents of many western nations[132] whose sanctimonious leaders like to lecture their Russian counterparts about prosperity, freedom, democracy and other exalted values they purport to cherish.[133]

It may thus only surprise the most credulous consumers of Western propaganda that a high proportion of Russian people trust Vladimir Putin and approve his job performance. In the early 2017, Putin's job approval stood between 80% and 90% and has averaged 74% over the eleven years from 2006. During this period, no western leader has come even close to measuring up with Vladimir Putin.

---

[132] A different, Associated Press – GfK poll in July of 2016 uncovered an even darker public sentiment in the United States: "*A stunning 79 percent of Americans now believe the country is heading in the wrong direction, a 15-point spike in the past year...*" (J. Pace 2016)

[133] VCIOM's figures for November 2016 are somewhat higher than those of Ipsos (62% vs. 58%).

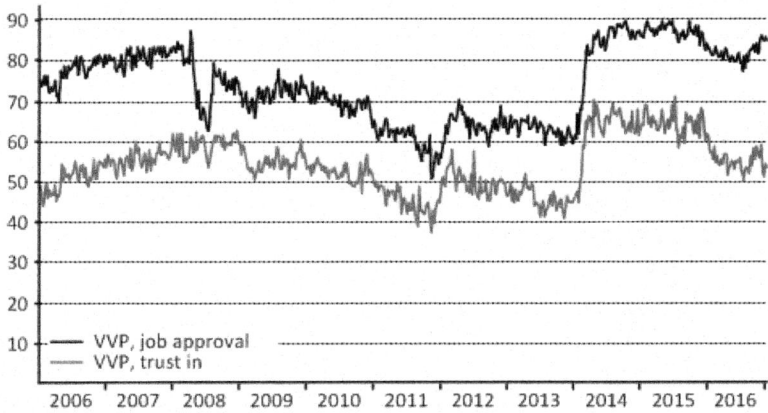

Over the years, I've heard depressingly many intellectuals attempt to dismiss Putin's achievements and Russian people's contentment as the product of Russian government propaganda. Putin the autocrat, you see, keeps such tight control over the media that he can deceive his people into believing that things in the country are much better than they really are. But the idea that government propaganda can influence public opinion in this way is just silly. If the majority of people thought their lives were miserable, state propaganda could not persuade them that everything is great. On the contrary, most people would conclude that the media is deceiving them and might feel even less positive about things as a result.[134] It is sillier still to think that Western intellectuals should have a better appreciation of what it is like to live in Russia than the Russian people themselves. Rather than buying the truth from their media, such intellectuals would do well to take a trip and visit Russia, speak to ordinary people there, and reach their own conclusions. My own travels in Russia, as well as reports from other visitors largely agree with the positive picture that emerges from the statistics we've just examined.

Impressions of modern Russia

In the summer of 2015 I spent two weeks in St. Petersburg. This was not my first visit to Russia, but it was the first time I went there alone to experience the ordinary life in the country. I enrolled in an intensive course of Russian language and rented a room in a Soviet-era apartment where my host was a retired woman named Lyudmila. For the following

---

[134] This, for instance, was the situation in the late 1990s when only 5 to 10 percent of Russians thought that the country was heading in the right direction in spite of the ruling elite's nearly total control of the media.

two weeks I commuted mornings and evenings from the periphery to the center of St. Petersburg and back, attended my lessons and spent my free time socializing with other students and exploring the city and its surroundings. My impressions of St. Petersburg were very positive – I might have been in any major European city. I did however, notice a few things about St. Petersburg that were different from what I would expect in the cities of western Europe.

For one thing, I saw no homeless people. While I expect that there are *some* homeless people in Russia, during my two weeks in St. Petersburg I did not see a single one. I also did not see anyone looking through trash to find food. Sadly, this has become an increasingly frequent spectacle in many cities in the west where pensioners in particular need to supplement their diets with their neighbors' leftovers. Russian people in general seemed rather fit and the only obese people I saw were foreign tourists. To be sure, there *are* fat and overweight people among Russians, but I saw none that were morbidly obese and the proportion of overweight population seems nowhere near what you find in the US, UK or my native Croatia where obesity rates have exploded over the last two decades.

An increasingly frequent site in many cities in Europe.

In all of my interactions with Russians I found them invariably polite and courteous, although not quite as outwardly engaging as the "new world" people like the Americans, Australians or New Zealanders. Most of the Russians I encountered also gave me the impression that they are generally well informed and educated, again in contrast with typical westerners.[135] Walking into a Russian bookstore for me was a different experience: when a young man working there saw me looking at the English section of Russian classics, he walked up asking if I needed any help and took time to tell me his thoughts and impressions about nearly every author and every book in the section – in almost perfect English. I walked away with Dostoevsky's "The Idiot," and Bulgakov's "Master and Margarita." In the west, I typically find rushed and overworked employees rarely willing or able to offer any thoughts or recommendations about books in their store.

I have also noticed something curious in St. Petersburg, which I'd only seen in the German parts of Switzerland before that: pedestrians in the street wait patiently for the green light before crossing the road even when there are no cars passing in the vicinity. To a habitual jaywalker,[136] this is always a startling observation, as when you think it's OK to cross the road at the red light because there's no traffic, only to realize that you were the only one breaking ranks with other pedestrians. That makes for a bit of an embarrassment, but on the serious note I believe that this shows a relatively high level of civility and discipline in the local culture.

My one slightly unpleasant experience happened one day as I walked through a random part of town and a young man walked up to me and asked me for money. While he was visibly drunk, he was neither aggressive nor disagreeable and when I made a hand gesture meaning "no," he said nothing and continued on his way.

In contrast to Bill Browder's portrayal of the country, I found Russia to be a healthy and well-ordered society. If the people there lived despondent lives in fear of their government, they certainly hid it well. To be fair, Browder lived in Russia from 1996 to 2005 and at that time he had experienced a very different environment. My first visit to Russia was in April of 2006 and Russia really was a different place back then – it *did* feel a bit sad, dark and rusty. Still, the fact that it no longer is that way only underscores the positive transformation that took place under Vladimir Putin's leadership.

---

[135] This impression reflects the actual level of education of Russiains. According to the Organization for Economic Cooperation and Development (OECD), Russians are the most highly educated nation in the world with 95% of all adults aged 25 to 64 having completed a secondary degree – a much higher figure compared with OECD average at 76%. More than half of all Russian adults also have completed a university degree.

[136] In American slang, jaywalking means crossing the street randomly or when the traffic light is red.

My own experiences of Russia may be too small a sample from which to draw any strong conclusions, but in recent years, many other travelers reported similarly positive impressions from their own recent visits in Russia. One of them was Sharon Tennison, an American who has worked in Russia (and USSR) for 30 years from the mid-1980s. During the early 2000s, she travelled throughout Russia several times every year, and described the gradual changes she could observe: "*Taxes were lowered, inflation lessened, and laws slowly put in place. Schools and hospitals began improving. Small businesses were growing, agriculture was showing improvement, and stores were becoming stocked with food. Alcohol challenges were less obvious, smoking was banned from buildings, and life expectancy began increasing. Highways were being laid across the country, new rails and modern trains appeared even in far out places, and the banking industry was becoming dependable. Russia was beginning to look like a decent country.*" During more recent years, in 2013 and 2014, Tennison travelled by rail and car around the Urals, and visited the cities of Ekaterinburg, Chelyabinsk and Perm: "*the fields and forests look healthy, small towns sport new paint and construction. Today's Russians look like Americans (we get the same clothing from China). Old concrete Khrushchev block houses are giving way to new multi-story private residential complexes which are lovely. High-rise business centers, fine hotels and great restaurants are now common place—and ordinary Russians frequent these places. Two and three story private homes rim these Russian cities far from Moscow. We visited new museums, municipal buildings and huge super markets. Streets are in good repair, highways are new and well-marked now, service stations looks like those dotting American highways. In January I went to Novosibirsk out in Siberia where similar new architecture was noted. Streets were kept navigable with constant snowplowing, modern lighting kept the city bright all night, lots of new traffic lights (with seconds counting down to light change) have appeared. It is astounding to me,*" concludes Tennison, "*how much progress Russia has made in the past 14 years since an unknown man with no experience walked into Russia's presidency and took over a country that was flat on its belly.*" [137]

Another American visitor, Merlin Miller, summed up his experience visiting Russia in 2015: "*In Moscow, we were greeted with an impressive mix of grand architecture and modern facilities. The city, now numbering nearly 14 million people was vibrant. Their subway system was impeccable, with a palace-like decor, including crystal chandeliers...and their trains ran on time! The Russian people were physically fit and better*

---

[137] (Tennison 2014)

dressed than contemporary Americans. We found no hostility among them and they were uniformly helpful. As Americans, we were probably perceived as loud and obnoxious, while they were quiet and cautiously respectful. ... It appeared to me that our nations are going through bizarre role-reversals. They have expectations of greater freedom and prosperity, while we are experiencing a loss of liberty and wealth, and a sense of uncertain desperation. ... We saw no obvious poverty and, since the Putin era, renovations have accelerated. Corruption has been significantly reduced, and there is also a growing sense of fiscal responsibility." Merlin's wife, Susan Miller wrote that, *"Everywhere ... I see reflected a country that has energy, and that is rising above its past history to become a land of new hope and opportunity. Most important, Russia is a place where people are finding their roots - in family, faith, values, and communities."* [138]

The long-time Russia analyst F. William Engdahl summed up his impressions of Russia in rather stronger prose: *"Something remarkable is taking place in Russia... Russia is discovering positive attributes about her culture, her people, her land that had long been forgotten or suppressed. ... My first of many visits to Russia was more than twenty years ago, in May, 1994. I was invited by a Moscow economics think-tank to deliver critical remarks about the IMF. My impressions then were of a once-great people who were being humiliated to the last ounce of their life energy. Mafia gangsters sped along the wide boulevards of Moscow in sparkling new Mercedes 600 limousines with dark windows and without license plates. Lawlessness was the order of the day. ... Rather than feel humiliated and depressed Russia is undergoing what I would call a kind of renaissance, a rebirth as a nation... in my recent visits to Russia in the past year as well as in numerous discussions with a variety of Russian acquaintances, I sense a new feeling of pride, of determination, a kind of rebirth of something long buried ..."*

A particularly interesting testimonial came from a commenter under an article about Russia's improving business environment. The gentleman going under the pseudonym "SF Expat," wrote as follows (please excuse the grammar, I'm quoting the comment word-for-word): *"...my own direct experience of doing business for decades in the US and then 15 years in Russia, I have seen distinct changes in both environments. In the late 60s and 70s it was remarkably easy to start a business and moderately likely to succeed in US business. By 2000 the US had become much more difficult and cost of overhead that had increased so much for startups, and essentially wiped out small business, with a lower percent of business*

---

[138] (Miller 2015)

being smaller in relation to the total. In the 90s Russia it was very hard to run a legal business without using bribes and influence. By 2003-2004 the atmosphere changed a lot and it became a liability to use influence and bribes. Since that time the number of small business has increased a lot and think corruption has greatly diminished. In my business, never was there a hint a bribe was needed to get something done.

My most recent registration for a corporation was just last spring and it was amazing how streamlined the process was. A LLC registered from start to finish at one central document center for the city administration for a very modest fee, most of the process automated with terminals, took less than 3 hours, including going to the bank to create an account and make the initial deposit as required. No lawyer was required. Russia, at least in the cities I know, I can say, it is easier to start and operate a business than the US.

The most significant factor is employees. Russia is the most educated country and the quality of applicants would shock western employers, with the degree of competence, dependability, education and attitude being at such a higher level than in the US. in 15 years I have never had an applicant without a university degree even though none was required for the job. The weakest part that needs additional improvement is importing and dealing with customs." [139]

At the time of this writing (in early 2017), Vladimir Putin has led Russia, either as President or as Prime Minister (May 2008 – May 2012) for full 17 years and the country's transformation during that time has been nothing short of spectacular. It has changed from a failed state on the verge of collapse, to a rising power. Its impoverished and demoralized population is today in many ways living better than it has ever done in its nation's long history. For the first time in generations, Russian people have been shedding their fatalism and embracing the future with hope and optimism. Increasingly, Russian people have been rediscovering their sense of national pride, something that has been largely absent during much of Russia's difficult history.

If we should judge Mr. Putin by his deeds, it would be entirely unreasonable and unfair to defame him with all the ugly labels like thug, tyrant, killer, autocrat, or Hitler, which are so casually thrown his way from the west. And if we should judge him on his character as a man, we should at least take a closer look at who he is.

---

[139] (Expat 2016)

ENTER VLADIMIR PUTIN

So, who is Vladimir Putin

> *... the current efforts of our President, his heroic deeds will not be fully appreciated any time soon. His mission – to extricate the country every year millimeter by millimeter from the national, financial, economical and other types of traps we got caught in since 1917.*
>
> *Lieutenant General Leonid Petrovich Reshetnikov*

For a long time, even after Bill Browder alerted me to the fact that Putin might actually be a force for good in Russia, I had little interest in understanding Putin as a man. I thought of him as a politician and I generally subscribe to the idea that political power attracts precisely the sort of people who should not have it. I also believe that power corrupts even otherwise decent men and women, and I expected that Vladimir Putin was no different. It was not difficult for me to believe that he probably *was* corrupt and that he used his position to enrich himself, his family members and his associates. That, at any rate, is what everyone else in the west knew about Mr. Putin.

It was only as a consequence of the shrill and constant demonization of Vladimir Putin in the aftermath of the 2014 coup in Ukraine that I felt compelled to try and find out more about who Mr. Putin's was as a person. I started by watching many of his speeches and interviews, listening carefully at what he was saying, as well as the way he was speaking. I also watched a number of documentaries about him – a few flattering films and many unflattering ones. I also searched online for testimonials from people who knew him personally and worked with him. The portrait of the man that emerged from many such testimonials as well as his own actions seems to be in a complete discord with the reputation Vladimir Putin had gained in the west. Here are some of the incidences that impacted my own perception of him.

Working for the people...
In the aftermath of the 2008 financial crisis Vladimir Putin declared publically that he bore responsibility to ensure that the 1998 crisis would not repeat itself on his watch. His government also took proactive steps to limit the fallout from the crisis. In July 2008, Putin personally went to the town of Pikalyevo in Leningrad Oblast to confront the directors and

owners of a large metallurgical factory. This was not long after the owners had shut the facility down, suspending without pay thousands of their workers. Addressing the gathering, Putin excoriated them, saying that because of their unprofessional conduct and greed, thousands of families would find themselves destitute. This was unacceptable to his government and he ordered the owners to restart the facility, else the government would do it without them. He further ordered the management to immediately ("*deadline today*") pay all workers' salary arrears, amounting to more than 41 million rubles. This particular video was obviously part of a Russian news report and almost certainly served a public relations purpose, but even so, its intent and message was to alert the oligarch class not to treat the lives of their employees as a disposable resource.

Putin took similar action protecting the ordinary people in another crisis situation. During his first winter as president, entire towns and villages across the far east of the country counting as many as 400,000 inhabitants, lost heating for the lack of coal. A serious crisis emerged with mines shutting down, workers out in the streets and even hospitals ceasing to function because of the cold. But the coal for heating was available in Russia, only most of it was already allotted for export. Vladimir Putin didn't think that Russian people should suffer freezing conditions all winter in order for that coal to be exchanged for American dollars. He decreed that export of coal be stopped immediately and that all available quantities be sent back to Siberia to fuel the boiler stations.

What these examples show is that in Putin's world, well-being of the people takes precedence over financial profits of the investor class. This concept may seem exotic and alien to Westerners who for a generation had been brainwashed with neoliberal economics where profits trump any and every other concern, including health and well-being of the people. Nonetheless, I believe that beyond the brainwash, every normal person – even western-educated economists – would agree that in a crisis, the decent thing to do would be to take care of the people and let the oligarchs cope with one quarter or a year of impaired profitability of their enterprises.

A hard working leader

According to his chief of security, Alexander Korzhakov, Boris Yeltsin worked about two hours per day. The rest he spent eating, drinking, playing tennis, hunting or enjoying some other pastime. Vladimir Putin reportedly works exceptionally long hours and several of his advisors and ministers have testified to working with him until very late into the night and then receiving a call from him early in the morning the next day.

ENTER VLADIMIR PUTIN

Exiled banker and former oligarch Sergei Pugachev described his experience: *"...we hardly parted company, we met on a daily basis – from early morning to late evening until 3, until 4 AM, every day, every day. We naturally discussed matters of state business development, the state of the economy and so on. Putin needed someone who understood and knew those matters well."* [140]

Some of his advisors and ministers reported meeting with him to discuss some matter within their own domain of specialty only to be startled in realizing that Putin commanded a more detailed understanding of that very matter than they themselves had. Being that immersed in and devoted to his occupation enables Vladimir Putin to hold his famous marathon press conferences when he speaks for three or four hours answering journalists' questions with accurate and detailed information and without teleprompters. His 14th annual call-in marathon in 2016 lasted 3 and a half hours during which he took and answered 80 questions! Most western politicians no longer dare to face any public forums without pre-packaged and rehearsed speeches, which they read off teleprompters, taking only a handful of questions from friendly reporters before their handlers usher them away from any potential embarrassment.

Fight against terrorism

Russia and the United States have had one major thing in common in the 21st century: their respective wars against terrorism. As the United States took its war on terror to Afghanistan and Iraq, Russia had been fighting her own war on terror in Chechnya which went on for nearly ten years, from August 1999 to April 2009. In the Summer of 2015, only six years after the hostilities had ceased Time magazine's correspondent Simon Shuster visited Chechnya. He reported that, *"Chechnya has undergone a striking transformation. Its cities have been rebuilt with money from Moscow. All traces of its separatist rebellion have been suppressed."* [141]

Indeed, Chechnya under Putin has attained the highest levels of prosperity it's *ever* had. The video clip embedded with Shuster's article related how, *"The kids growing up in Chechnya these days are a lot luckier than their parents and grandparents. At least the youngest ones have only known their homeland to be a peaceful and even quite beautiful place, full of enormous mosques and skyscrapers and shopping districts and fast food joints."*

By contrast, American war on terror has left chaos and disorder in all nations it has touched, from Afghanistan and Iraq, to Lybia, Syria, Yemen,

---

[140] (Harding, Smith and Maynard 2015)
[141] (Shuster and Martinelli 2015)

Somalia and Sudan. Kosovo, which has been a de-facto American protectorate since the year 2000, is today the poorest and most corrupt nation in Europe with massive population exodus and unemployment in excess of 35%. Ever sanctimonious West has frequently accused Vladimir Putin of heavy handedness in his fight against Chechen terrorists (whom they usually call "rebels" or "separatists"), but this is an arbitrary and meaningless reproach. Western analysts may know what distinguishes a gentle war on terror from the ruthless kind, but this is a pointless debate that I would propose to settle by "judging them by their fruits."

Forgiving Cuba's debts

When Vladimir Putin visited Cuba in 2014, he wrote off 90 percent of the Cuba's $32 billion debt owed to Russia from the Soviet times. Conceivably, this may have been a calculated gesture made with some ulterior motive favorable to Russia's interests. Even so, the gesture was remarkable because at that time, Western creditors led by the IMF had been pushing a cruel and inhumane austerity program on Greece for full repayment of her own debts. The same IMF that had raided Russia twenty years prior was now forcing an economic strangulation on Greece with similar effects on that country as it had on Russia in the 1990s.

The deranged mindset of Greece's creditors was on display during the Brussels Group meeting in March of 2015. As Greece was coming dangerously close to defaulting on her debt obligations, the delegation representing her creditors suggested to Greek finance minister Yanis Varoufakis that his government would be able to service its debts by withholding the payment of public employee salaries and pensions for two months.[142] Recommending outright theft of money from ordinary Greeks did not seem to faze or embarrass Greece's enterprising creditors.

One and a half years later, in November of 2016, the "leader of the free world," US President Barack Obama came to Greece on his last official visit. On that occasion, he offered neither help nor debt relief. Instead, he rubbed more salt into the country's wounds by reiterating that Greece had to continue to press on with austerity, which had already pushed its economy into a crushing depression.

Regardless of motives and national interests, Vladimir Putin's gesture in Cuba stood in sharp contrast to that of Greece's creditors and U.S. President Obama. In essence, Vladimir Putin's gesture toward Cuba was generous and humane. At the same time, West's treatment of Greece has been inhumane and cruel.

---

[142] (Durden 2015)

ENTER VLADIMIR PUTIN

Edward Snowden asylum

In June of 2013, U.S. National Security Agency (NSA) contractor Edward Snowden unveiled the massive extent of NSA's global surveillance program that illegally collected nearly all electronic and telephone communications of ordinary, law abiding Americans and foreign nationals. Exposing the secrets of the American (and British) surveillance state turned Edward Snowden into a wanted man overnight and the CIA mounted one of their most massive manhunts ever. To evade capture, on Sunday, 23rd Jun 2013, Snowden boarded an Aeroflot flight from Hong Kong to Moscow. His plan was to fly on to Cuba and from there further to another South American country, possibly Venezuela or Ecuador. U.S. government charged him with espionage and began immediately to pressure various governments around the world to apprehend Snowden and extradite him. By the time his flight from Hong Kong landed at Moscow's Sheremetyevo airport, American authorities revoked his passport and he was unable to continue his trip from Moscow, at which point his whereabouts became unclear.

Two days later, on 25th June, Vladimir Putin confirmed that Snowden was still at Sheremetyevo, that he was a free man, that he may choose his own final destination and that Russia would not arrest or extradite him. Through various channels, the U.S. government spent the following days trying to persuade their Russian counter parts to seize Snowden and turn him over. So keen were the Americans on getting Snowden that when they thought that he might attempt to flee Russia on the presidential jet belonging to the Bolivian President Evo Morales, they ordered the French, Spanish, Italian and Portuguese authorities to breach international law and deny Bolivian President's flight access to their airspace, forcing his aircraft to land in Vienna where President Morales and his crew were detained for 14 hours.

CIA's information that Snowden was on the plane turned out to be false so the whole diplomatic incident only succeeded in unmasking the nature of the relationship between the empire and its European vassals as well as their cavalier attitude toward international law. Apparently laws are there to be broken when the hegemon's expediency obliges. The incident also showed Edward Snowden that it would have been futile for him to seek asylum with any western nation allied with the U.S. since they would have been likely to violate their own laws to comply with an American extradition request. As a result, Snowden had little choice but to stay put and request asylum in Russia. On the 1st July, Putin stated that Edward Snowden might be granted asylum in Russia on condition that he desists in causing further damage to *"our American partners."*

Watching these events unfold through late June and July of 2013, I wondered if the Russians wouldn't in the end get Edward Snowden and trade him for some big concession from their "American partners" who were clearly extremely keen on getting the renegade whistle-blower. I remember thinking that the outcome of that incident would give us an important indication of what Vladimir Putin was made of: would he do the right thing and offer Snowden asylum and protection, or would he end up trading him off? My gut feeling was that Putin would indeed do the right thing, but at the same time I cringed at the thought that I might end up disappointed. After several weeks of legal procedures, on July 31st 2013, Snowden was granted asylum in Russia.

Today (it's late March 2017), Edward Snowden has been living as a free man in Russia for nearly four years, thanks largely to Vladimir Putin's principled stand and courage in defying American pressure. If not for his asylum in Russia, Snowden would today most likely be serving a very long prison sentence. For me, this episode very significantly bolstered the conviction that Vladimir Putin was not a thug but a decent, principled man.

The corruption thing

One of the main themes used to demonize Putin in the west are the incessant insinuations that he is corrupt and that his corruption enabled him to build up massive personal wealth. But while these allegations are invariably presented with zero evidence, we do have *some* evidence that Putin is in fact *not* corrupt. I found the testimony from Sharon Tennison very interesting in this regard as well. Tennison was the founder and president of Center for Citizen Initiatives (CCI) and had worked in Russia (and the USSR) for 30 years. In the course of her activities, she has had at least one personal encounter with Putin and had over the years came to know many other American officials and businessmen who had worked with him. According to Tennison, none of those officials *"would describe* [Putin] *as 'brual,' or 'thuggish,' or other slanderous adjectives and nouns that are repeatedly used in western media."*

Tennison first met Vladimir Putin in 1992 and described the experience in one of her blog articles: *"I met Putin years before he ever dreamed of being president of Russia, as did many of us working in St.Petersburg during the 1990s. ... For years I had been creating programs to open up relations between the two countries ... A new program possibility emerged in my head. Since I expected it might require a signature from the Marienskii City Hall, an appointment was made. My friend Volodya Shestakov and I showed up at a side door entrance to the Marienskii* building. We found ourselves in a small, dull brown office, facing a rather trim nondescript man in a brown suit. He inquired about my reason for coming in. After scanning the proposal I provided he began asking intelligent questions. After each of my answers, he asked the next relevant question. I became aware that this interviewer was different from other Soviet bureaucrats who always seemed to fall into chummy conversations with foreigners with hopes of obtaining bribes in exchange for the Americans' requests... This bureaucrat was open, inquiring, and impersonal in demeanor. After more than an hour of careful questions and answers, he quietly explained that he had tried hard to determine if the proposal was legal, then said that unfortunately at the time it was not. A few good words about the proposal were uttered. That was all. He simply and kindly showed us to the door. Out on the sidewalk, I said to my colleague, 'Volodya, this is the first time we have ever dealt with a Soviet bureaucrat who didn't ask us for a trip to the US or something valuable!' I remember looking at his business card in the sunlight—it read Vladimir Vladimirovich Putin."[143] At least in this 1992 encounter with Tennison Vladimir Putin seemed to fulfil his duties in a professional manner without seeking kickbacks or favors from Tennison who was obviously well accustomed to that exact behavior from other government bureaucrats.

In the course of her work in Russia through 2000s, Tennison had interviewed many of her organization's alumni about their work experiences. In those interviews, her last question was always about Vladimir Putin: "*So what do you think of your new president?*" She reported that, "*None responded negatively, even though at that time entrepreneurs hated Russia's bureaucrats. Most answered similarly, 'Putin registered my business a few years ago'. Next question, 'So, how much did it cost you?' To a person they replied, 'Putin didn't charge anything'. One said, 'we went to Putin's desk because the others providing registrations at the Marienskii were getting rich on their seats.'*"

Next, Tennison tells the story involving Vladimir Putin and the former U.S. Consul General, Jack Gosnell. Gosnell had worked closely with Putin on various projects. In 2001, Putin's wife, Ludmila had a severe auto accident and Gosnell took the initiative, without telling Putin, to arrange an airlift and hospitalization for her in Finland because medical care in Russia at the time was quite dismal. When he informed Putin about these arrangements, Putin was overcome with his thoughtful offer but insisted that he could not accept and that like other Russians, his wife would have to be treated in a Russian hospital.

---

[143] (Tennison, Putin, by Sharon Tennison 2014)

Tennison then goes on to share another handful of testimonies from various American officials who knew Putin. One of them, a senior officer of the Center for Strategic and International Studies (CSIS) had worked closely with Putin and told Tennison that none of his dealings with Putin were questionable and that the reputation he was getting from the U.S. media was unfair and undeserved. Another official who also worked closely with Putin equally reported that, "*... there was never any hint of bribery, pressuring, nothing but respectable behavior and helpfulness.*" Then there was an official from the U.S. State Department whom she had met as they were both invited to a radio interview about Russia. As they were chatting together after the interview, Tennison remarked, "*You might be interested to know that I've collected experiences of Putin from numerous people, some over a period of years, and they all say they had no negative experiences with Putin and there was no evidence of taking bribes.*" The State Department man unhesitatingly replied that, "*No one has ever been able to come up with a bribery charge against Putin.*"

Tennison also shares an interesting detail about Putin which she learned from one of her Russian friends, a certain psychologist named Lena, who went to school with him. Lena described Putin as a quiet youngster who was, "*poor, fond of martial arts, who stood up for kids being bullied on the playgrounds.*" Lena also explained to Tennison why Putin went to serve in the KGB: "*She remembered him as a patriotic youth who applied for the KGB prematurely after graduating secondary school (they sent him away and told him to get an education). He went to law school, later reapplied and was accepted. At that time,*" explained Lena, "*... we all admired the KGB and believed that those who worked there were patriots and were keeping the country safe. We thought it was natural ... to choose this career.*" Thus, Vladimir Putin might have joined the KGB with the same essential motivation that induced many young Americans to join the American military after the September 11, 2001 terror attacks: a sense of patriotism and the desire to serve his country.

When I came across Tennison's article I was still inclined to believe that Putin *was* corrupt in some way so her testimony came as a surprise to me. Tennison's article painted a portrait of a man who is quite the opposite of a thug: Putin stood up to schoolyard bullies; Putin went to the KGB for similar reasons why many young Americans joined the US Army after the terror attacks of September 11, 2001; Putin took no bribes; Putin was curteous and helpful as a public official; Putin turned down privileged treatment for his wife after her car accident... The way Tennison portrayed Vladimir Putin was at odds with my stereotype of a typical politician. Still, her account seemed credible; perhaps Vladimir Putin really *is* a very highly unusual politician. Author Catherine Brown wrote of him as follows: *"nothing which is known about Putin's history and proud, workaholic character suggests someone to whom the things that money can buy have a strong appeal; a sybaritic Goering he is not."* [144] I had my remaining scepticism largely dispelled when I came across another, nearly forgotten detail from Putin's public service.

Kursk submarine tragedy

On the 12th August 2000, in the course of the first major exercise of Russian naval forces in more than ten years, Russian submarine "Kursk" sank, taking its crew of 118 sailors to the bottom of the Barents Sea. After the navy's confused and ineffective rescue efforts and a series of misleading communications, on 22nd August Putin went personally to Vidayevo village in the Murmansk oblast to face the families of Kursk sailors. The meeting was organized in a large auditorium where the President faced a packed crowd of hundreds of desperate and angry people from the podium. Some of the journalists there were surprised that Putin dared to come face to face with these people, most of whom were still hoping against hope to hear good news that the sailors could be rescued. Putin however, knew otherwise: the sailors were doomed and there was no theoretical chance of their lives being saved.

Rather than deceiving the gathering with false hope, Vladimir Putin chose to tell them the truth: *"... None of our or foreign specialists can reach the 8th compartment in order to ... lift it up. I am taking responsibility for my words, I could tell you a lot of things and run away. I am telling you things the way they are. This is the bitter truth, but it is the truth."* This episode revealed an important measure of the man's integrity and courage. As president of the Russian Federation, he could have done what a typical politician would: avoid the unpleasant gathering with some excuse, send a deputy along with president's message of his profound concern, prayers for the brave heroes, and so on, and hide until the rage blows over. Instead, Putin chose to come face to face with the families of the sailors while their emotions were still red hot, in order to personally report to them the dismal truth.

The image of Putin, the man that emerges from these episodes is that of a principled and decent man. The character he conveys in public very significantly contrasts with the image of a typical politician. Putin in fact seems to hold a certain disdain for politics and has preferred to describe himself as a bureaucrat. In one interview, he expressed his distaste for

---

[144] (Brown, Deconstructing Russophobia 2016)

political campaigning as a way to attain power: *"One has to be insincere and promise something which you cannot fulfil... So you either have to be a fool who does not understand what you are promising, or deliberately be lying."* [145] This struck me as an earnest statement that happens to agree with my own view of politics and most politicians. In a broader sense, Putin's political philosophy espouses a very circumspect view of state power. In a speech to the Federal Assembly in 2005, Putin drew on the philosophy of Ivan Ilyin to outline the limitations of state power: *"State power cannot oversee and dictate the creative states of the soul and mind, the inner states of love, freedom and goodwill. The state cannot demand from its citizens faith, prayer, love, goodness and conviction. It cannot regulate scientific, religious and artistic creation... It should not intervene in moral, family and daily private life, and only when extremely necessary should it impinge on people's economic initiative and creativity."* [146]

It is unusual for a politician to speak of such things as states of the soul and mind or the "inner states of love" to a gathering of other politicians but these ideas do appear to run as a theme in Putin's conception of political leadership. At the 15th Congress of the Russian Geographical Society, he ventured the following statement: *"In general, love is the whole meaning of life, of being. Love of family, of children, and of the motherland. It is such a multifaceted phenomenon that is the basis of all our actions."* [147] To a Westerner, exposed to a relentless defamation of Vladimir Putin, this may be difficult to believe. After all, we know that he was a KGB agent, that he routinely ordered assassinations of his critics and political opponents, that he has made himself the wealthiest man in the world, and many other similarly negative "facts" about him. Most Westerners, particularly the intellectuals among them, have trouble conceiving of the possibility that their media reporting on Russia is distorted and that their views are mistaken and wrong. The notion that majority of Westerners could have a mistaken view about a country and its President who are subject to news coverage and commentary on a daily basis, indicates that this coverage is presented with a strong and persisting bias. If this is the case, and on balance of evidence it *does* appear so, we ought to examine the sources and the causes of this bias. But before we delve into this fascinating subject, we should return to Mr. Browder who has made it his life's work to perpetuate and enhance this bias.

---

[145] (Atkisson 2016)
[146] (Grenier 2015)
[147] (Holodny 2014)

5. Bill Browder, the great pretender

> *For those who don't know, the sensation of finding a 'ten bagger' must be the financial equivalent of smoking crack cocaine. Once you've done it, you want to repeat it over and over and over as many times as you can.*
>
> Bill Browder

> *I was never driven by money... when I went into finance, my goal was to be the best in that field.*
>
> Bill Browder[148]

In Red Notice, Browder presents himself as an entrepreneurial hedge fund manager. He went to Russia as he learned about the enormous, once in a lifetime investment opportunities that were available there. Supposedly, this was his own discovery, which had led him to build up a successful hedge fund business, all on his own bold initiative. As any start-up hedge fund manager, Browder needed adequate seed capital to launch the business. As he pitched his story to numerous prospective investors, he ultimately secured $25 million investment from Edmond Safra and took things forward from there. This, in essence, is how Browder describes his path to success.

---
[148] (Rashty 2015)

The superentrepreneur

At first blush, Browder's story appears as credible as it is fascinating, but on closer scrutiny, there are many reasons to doubt Browder's self-portrayal as a larger-than-life, self-made entrepreneur. I do not necessarily doubt his achievements as he describes them. Rather, I believe that he had helpers and handlers who paved his way to success but whose role he omits from his story, making himself appear as something of a super-entrepreneur.

The Murmansk asylum

To begin with, I found certain aspects of Browder's Murmansk Trawler Fleet story extremely hard to believe. This was where Browder purportedly got his first taste of investment opportunities available in Russian privatization programs. The management of the Murmansk Trawler Fleet had hired him *"to advise them on whether they should exercise their right under the Russian privatization program to purchase 51% of the fleet for $2.5 million."* The firm's book value was roughly $1 billion and its management thought it was a great idea to pay $50,000 to a young consultant from London to tell them whether they should buy their own company for $2.5 million, a 99.5% discount on the book value!

To swallow this story you'd have to believe not only that this firm's managers were fantastically unsophisticated, but also that they lacked any measure of common sense. As someone who's grown up in the communist block and was a young adult when our own privatization programs started, I can tell you that Browder's story does not even begin to add up. It is true that we didn't have stock markets and that private property was extremely limited, but most people understood perfectly well that their firms owned assets and that these assets had a certain economic value. The management of Murmansk Trawler Fleet, who were sophisticated enough to read Browder's consulting proposal in English, could not make up their minds to buy $20 million trawlers for $50,000 apiece. Such a decision only requires a minimum of common sense, not a $50,000 consulting engagement with some London slick who'd never seen a trawler in his life.

Again, the fact that Russia was in transition does not explain this away; as someone who has experienced the transition from socialism to capitalism I can say that, unless the management of the Murmansk Trawler Fleet collectively lived inside a loony asylum, Browder's story seems entirely incredible. This in turn leaves open the question of *how* and *why* Browder became involved with the Russian privatization program in the first place. As we'll see further on, this question is not of minor significance with respect to Bill Browder's role in Russia.

BILL BROWDER, THE GREAT PRETENDER

Thirty meetings in four days

Browder's first fact-finding visit in Moscow is also suspect. Namely, after his stint in Murmansk, rather than flying back to London, Browder changed his itinerary and flew straight to Moscow where over the next four days he arranged a total of 30 meetings through which he "*pieced together the full story of what was going on with the Russian privatizations.*" Thirty meetings in four days corresponds to an average of nearly eight meetings per day. Somehow he was able to arrange these thirty meetings last minute with next to no pre-advice. Unless Browder was counting every taxi ride as a meeting, this hardly seems credible, particularly as these meetings were not related to Salomon Brothers business nor did his employer have anything to do with arranging them. Browder tells us that he simply checked into the Metropol Hotel in Moscow and without speaking a word of Russian or knowing anyone in the city, he went through the phone directory and started cold-calling people at the U.S. Embassy, Ernst & Young, American Express, Russian privatization ministry and other organizations where he managed to find thirty individuals available to squeeze in a meeting at his convenience.

It may seem fastidious on my part to take issue with Browder's 30 meetings in 4 days, but as a hedge fund manager I have some experience of working promotion campaigns in major cities like Moscow and trying to arrange as many meetings with prospective investors as possible over a few days' time. Invariably, such trips are carefully planned months in advance, working with paid local consultants who help to arrange and schedule many of the meetings. In spite of all the work that goes into preparation of these visits, I have *never* managed more than six meetings in a single day and *never* even came close to stacking up thirty in a single week. Again, I am not taking issue with the supposed fact that Browder *did* actually have thirty meetings in four days in Moscow. I *am* however, highly skeptical that he could have pulled that off all on his own by cold calling people, having just parachuted into Moscow unannounced.

Browder's excellent adventure in Davos

Sometime in January of 1996, as Browder was busy working to secure the $25 million seed investment from Edmond Safra, his friend Marc Holtzman rang him up: "*Hey, Bill, I'm going to go to Davos – you want to come with me?*" Browder presents Holtzman as an investment banker who ran a boutique bank focused on Eastern Europe and Russia. Browder had met him five years before while he was working for Robert Maxwell. In the winter of 1996 Holtzman was organizing a dinner reception at the World Economic Forum in Davos for Gennady Zyuganov, head of the

Russian communist party and Boris Yeltsin's main rival in the 1996 presidential elections. Browder accepted Holtzman's invitation and a short few weeks later[149] he was in Davos, where he and Holtzman shared a room with a single bed and poor Browder had to sleep on the floor.

Holtzman's dinner event was held at one of the two five star hotels in Davos and was that evening's *"hottest ticket in town,"* attended by *"a couple of dozen billionaires and CEOs."* After Holtzman had finished saying how honored he was to be hosting the event for Zyuganov and thanking his guests for attending, he turned toward Browder and added: *"And I'd like to also thank my co-host Bill Browder, who helped to make all this possible."* Browder thought that was a *"nice gesture"* on Holtzman's part.

So there we had Bill Browder, an unknown thirty something entrepreneur who had not even launched his Moscow business, co-hosting one of the major events at the World Economic Forum in Davos, all through the inexplicable largesse of a random acquaintance he had met five years earlier. For a simple entrepreneur, such a stroke of luck would have to count as a real miracle – the equivalent of winning a lottery without even having bought a ticket. Else, perhaps Browder was not just a self-made maverick entrepreneur as he pretends he was but part of a well-connected network of powerful players.

If Browder in fact did have secret helpers in his ascent as the big time Russia investor, Marc Holtzman was probably one of them. Another amazing detail related to Browder's adventure in Davos was that at that point he already knew Russia's former Finance Minister Boris Fyodorov with whom he was apparently on the first name basis. When Holtzman and Browder came to the Davos hotel where *"all the Russians convened,"* Browder spotted Fyodorov who, in their ensuing conversation about the upcoming presidential elections told him, *"Don't worry about the election, Bill. Yeltsin is going to win for sure."* I thought it would be odd for Russia's former finance minister to engage some completely unknown yet-to-start up businessman in a friendly conversation and to spill such extraordinarily sensitive and confidential information to him, addressing him as Bill.

As for Marc Holtzman, he vanishes from Browder's story but for a small detail in the following chapter. Namely, several weeks after his Davos trip when Browder arrived in Moscow to set up his business, he rented an office just down the hall from Holtzman's office. Probably just a coincidence.

---

[149] The 1996 World Economic Forum in Davos was held from the 1st through 6th of February.

Protection in high places

During the years he spent in Russia, as well as thereafter, Browder seems to have enjoyed remarkable protection in high places. The first example of this happened when he got himself into a dangerous conflict with Vladimir Potanin, one of Russia's most powerful oligarchs. At that time, people who opposed the oligarchs frequently turned up dead so when Browder challenged Potanin over an illegal stock issue that would have been adverse to Browder and his investors, in only a few hours' time Edmond Safra arranged for Browder's protection a team of 15 heavily armed bodyguards led by a former Mossad agent. Even in the 1990s Russia, getting a small private army unit with four armoured cars overnight is very impressive indeed.

In 2006, after Browder already got thrown out of Russia, it would be none other than Britain's Prime Minister Tony Blair who was due to intervene personally with Vladimir Putin on Browder's behalf during the St. Petersburg G8 summit. This intervention was even announced by the British newspapers, "The Observer" in a headline, "*Blair to Raise Fund Manager's Case with Putin.*" The intervention did not actually happen because shortly before Blair was to meet with Putin, Israel launched a military campaign against Lebanon, overshadowing many of the summit's issues with a new high priority development. The fact that British Prime Minister's agenda would include an intervention on behalf of a hedge fund manager and that one of British major dailies would announce this in a news headline was very unusual. To be sure, Browder *was* a successful hedge fund manager by then, but the idea that his status in Russia was a high priority matter for the British government seemed truly extraordinary. Even at its peak size, Browder's fund was still only a mid-sized fund with no major economic or political consequence for either nation.

Even after his star as a hedge fund manager had faded, Browder still seemed to enjoy a notable degree of protection from international law enforcement mechanisms. In mid-May 2013 Russian authorities went to the Interpol to request Browder's arrest. Although such requests are routinely honored and almost never disputed, not only did the Interpol reject Russia's application, Interpol's General Secretariat promptly deleted all information in relation to William Browder. Russian authorities subsequently reapplied for the arrest warrant against Browder but were snubbed by the Interpol yet again. Their request directly to the British government for Browder's extradition was also rejected.

However, the most astonishing aspect of Browder's extraordinary leverage was his ability to successfully lobby the U.S. Senate and the

House of Representatives into passing the Magnitsky Act,[150] a piece of legislation that was highly adversarial to Russia and damaging to the two nations' bilateral relations. The American Congress passed the bill essentially on the basis of Browder's own version of events. For a has-been hedge fund manager who was not even a U.S. citizen, this is an amazing accomplishment. It is more amazing still if we consider that many elements of Browder's story couldn't withstand an impartial review. Indeed, one would expect that before passing such a consequential new law American lawmakers might at least have conducted minimal due diligence. For some reason however, they collectively abdicated their responsibility and accepted Browder's story as truth worthy of sacrificing their own reputation as well as damaging the relationship between the U.S. and Russia. After mobilizing U.S. Congress in his "fight for justice," Browder managed almost unchallenged to achieve similar feats in Canadian and European Parliaments: while the Europeans decided to deny visas to Russian individuals involved in mistreatment of Sergei Magnitsky, Canadian Parliament went a step further announcing their intention to freeze any Canadian assets belonging to them.

Such extraordinary accomplishments can be understood in one of two ways: either American, Canadian and European lawmakers are a bunch of witless, incompetent and sentimental dupes the likes of which have never occupied the chambers of government in the history of mankind, or Bill Browder has powerful helpers capable of making sure these lawmakers only ask the right questions and reach the right decisions. All things considered, both cases sound compelling but to my mind, the second one is slightly more plausible.

Bill's tall tale unravels

Red Notice is a very well written book and upon casual reading, it seems convincing. As such it leaves the reader with the *impression* that Browder was the victim of an aggressive legal persecution by corrupt elements of Russia's security apparatus whose main purpose was theft of money from its victims and from the state, and that this criminal organization operated under Vladimir Putin's command. In part, Browder creates this impression through a subtle blurring of the story's timeline so that his expulsion from Russia appears related to the police raids on his firm's offices which led to a massive tax fraud and ultimately to Sergei Magnitsky's tragic death. But those raids took place more than 18 months *after* Browder's expulsion and

---

[150] The full title of the act was, "Russia and Moldova Jackson-Vanik Repeal and Sergei Magnitsky Rule of Law Accountability Act of 2012."

were conducted in pursuit of long-standing investigations of Browder for tax evasion, which he forgets to mention. The link between the police raids and the subsequent tax fraud was Browder's own invention. A more careful deconstruction of this plot may strain the reader's attention at this point, but this is essential for us to detect Browder's brazen deception.

After his expulsion from Russia, Browder pursued various routes to try to have his visa reinstated and to regain entry into Russia. One of the abortive efforts was Tony Blair's intervention with Vladimir Putin during the St. Petersburg G8 Summit in July 2006. As we've already seen, this intervention never took place because of the breakout of a new crisis in the Middle East. At this point in his book, Browder ambushes the reader with a verbal three-card monte, and it goes like this: at a press conference after the G8 Summit, Moscow Times journalist Catherine Belton asked Vladimir Putin why Bill Browder was expelled from Russia. Putin gave audience the impression that he wasn't aware of this issue and responded that he wouldn't know why any particular person might get expulsed from the country but he imagined that they may have broken the nation's laws. Browder then takes it upon himself to illuminate us about what Putin's coded response *really* meant: *"We never mention enemies by name, and that includes Bill Browder. I am now instructing my law-enforcement agencies to open up as many criminal cases against him as possible."* The fact that Browder felt qualified to decode Putin's words and turn them into something very different from what was actually spoken is so very odd that he had to add, speaking in his own behalf: *"If you think this interpretation is paranoid or an exaggeration, it wasn't. If anything, I wasn't being paranoid enough."*

Putin's statement about Browder's expulsion and Browder's paranoid interpretation of it made up the last two paragraphs of the chapter titled "The G8." The very next chapter, titled "The Raids," introduces the story of Russian police investigations against Browder and his company. By putting his own words into Putin's mouth, Browder made it appear that the investigations were launched on Putin's orders just to attack poor Bill Browder who was merely trying to get his visa to return to Russia. Thus, Browder would have us believe that Ms. Belton inadvertently provoked Vladimir Putin's rage by mentioning his enemy by name, and so the heavy-handed legal persecution of Bill Browder began, all on a whim of a vicious tyrant.

Some six months later, in January of 2007, Browder went to the World Economic Forum in Davos. There, he approached Russia's Deputy Prime Minister Dmitry Medvedev to solicit his help in regaining his Russian visa. Medvedev responded that he'd be happy to help and asked Browder to provide him his visa application which he would pass on to the Federal

Border Service with his personal recommendation to approve it. Around three weeks later, on the 17th February, Hermitage Capital received a call from an Interior Ministry's investigator, Lieutenant Colonel Artem Kuznetsov who wanted to drop by for some clarifications, suggesting that the sooner Hermitage answered his questions, the sooner their problems would go away. Kuznetsov spoke to Vadim Kleiner and according to Browder, the precise transcript of the call went as follows:

> *"We were notified by the Immigration Service that the CEO of your company wishes to visit our country and asked if we had any response. Before I reply, I wanted to come by your office and talk, show you some papers, ask a few questions. I can't tell you my questions over the phone –unfortunately it's not so simple as that. My answer will depend upon how you behave, what you provide, et cetera. If you are interested in meeting, that's fine. If not, no problem. It's up to you. The sooner we meet and you provide what is necessary, the sooner your problems will disappear."* [151]

For his part, Browder decided that this wasn't a *"normal inquiry,"* and that Kuznetsov was probably trying to extort a bribe so he simply ignored the request. Just over three months later, on the 4th of June 2007, 25 police officers under Kuznetsov's command raided Hermitage Capital and Firestone Duncan offices, seizing the firms' computers and large amounts of paperwork relating to certain Russian companies through which Hermitage Capital conducted their Russian investments. Of particular interest were three firms called Kameya, Makhaon and Parfenion.

According to Browder, the tax crimes department of the Moscow Interior Ministry had opened a criminal case against Hermitage's Ivan Cherkasov for tax evasion amouting to $44 million. It was at this point that Browder *"retained"* Sergei Magnitsky, the *"best tax lawyer,"* who was *"rumoured never to have lost a case."* [152] Browder asked Magnitsky to analyze whether they had done anything wrong because they *"needed to be absolutely sure."* Magnitsky worked until late into the night and called the next morning with his analysis: *"Guys, I've looked at every aspect of Kameya's tax situation. Ivan [Cherkasov] has done nothing wrong."* In September 2007 Magnitsky allegedly received a letter from the Moscow Tax Office where Kameya had submitted its returns, stating that Kameya had even overpaid taxes by $140,000. For Browder, that letter *"completely exonerated Ivan"* and constituted *"ironclad proof,"* that the charges

---

[151] (Browder 2009)

[152] Please bear with me, soon you'll see *why* Magnitsky never lost a case

against him were *"utterly bogus."* However, this part of the story revolves only around Kameya and Browder fails to mention whether Magnitsky or Moscow tax office had anything to say about Makhaon's and Parfenion's tax situation.

Only a few weeks later, in mid-October 2007, a major new development took place: a court in St. Petersburg issued a judgment against Makhaon in the amount of $71 million. This was a complete surprise to Browder since these companies were inactive. As it turned out, *someone* had stolen Hermitage's three companies and loaded them up with a total of $973 million in liabilities through bogus court cases in St. Petersburg, Kazan and Moscow. This *someone* was able to do this using these firms' original seals, certificates of ownership and registration files,[153] – the very documents that had been seized by the police during the June 4 police raids. In this way, Browder's tale makes it obvious *who* stole the companies and fraudulently loaded them up with legal liabilities.

To bolster his case, Browder performs another three-card monte to implicate Interior Ministry's investigators Pavel Karpov and Artem Kuznetsov in the theft of Hermitage's companies. Namely, on 29th November 2007 Karpov gave Hermitage's lawyer Eduard Khayretdinov access to certain documents that Khayretdinov had been requesting. But when he came to see Karpov, Khayretdinov became incensed at Karpov's arrogant demeanor and burst out that he knew what they were up to, and knew *"everything about what happened in St. Petersburg."* At this point, Mr. Karpov allegedly soiled his $3,000 suit and tried to defend himself saying, *"It wasn't me. This is Kuznetsov's project."* Thus, if we are to believe Browder's story, not only did Karpov admit to being privy to the theft of Hermitage's companies and the bogus court rulings against them, but he also voluntarily implicated his colleague Kuznetsov as the mastermind behind the crime.

It took Browder and his team another few months to work out *why* their companies were stolen. Browder pegs their *eureka* moment to one Saturday morning in late May 2008 as they went through all the documents they had and realized that the court rulings against their firms corresponded almost exactly to the stolen firms' 2006 profits. With the newly created liabilities, Kameya's, Makhaon's and Parfenion's 2006 profits became zero, so their (new) owners could petition the tax authorities for reimbursement of the $230 million in taxes that were previously paid. Indeed, on the Christmas Eve in 2007 Russian tax office

---

[153] Such company thefts were known as "Russian raider attacks," where raiders stole entre companies from their rightful owners, stripping them of assets and loading them up with liabilities.

paid out the $230 million refund, which was the single payout of this kind in Russia's history.

Thus, through his convoluted tale, Browder tries hard to convince us that the same people from the Interior Ministry who were after him for tax evasion also perpetrated a large-scale financial fraud against the Russian tax authorities using the companies they stole from him. Furthermore, this plot was uncovered by Sergei Magnitsky who alerted the authorities about it. As a result, he was tortured and killed in prison in order to silence him and cover up the crime. Although Browder himself sustained no loss from this crime – the $230 were stolen from Russian taxpayers – he was so shattered by Sergei Magnitsky's plight that ever after he died, Browder devoted his life completely to fighting for justice and unmasking of those responsible for Magnitsky's death.

In this way, Browder's tale shapes up as an appealing story about the struggle of good against evil, about a lone maverick taking on a powerful network of dangerous criminals and corrupt government officials in selfless pursuit of justice... This would be a beautiful story – if only it were true. Already on the face of it, much about Browder's story seems fishy. However, tracing the exact shape of his deception only became possible as later developments shed new light upon it.

U.K. High Court of Justice: Pavel Karpov v. William Browder

Since Magnitsky's death, Browder and his team have worked hard to destroy the reputations of Interior Ministry's investigators Karpov and Kuznetsov, publishing documents and videos that implicated them with corruption, torture and murder. This compelled Karpov in 2013 to file a lawsuit for libel against Bill Browder in the U.K. High Court of Justice in London. [154] The reaction from Browder and his defense team was interesting. While they ostensibly relished the opportunity to *"submit to the jurisdiction of English courts which will, for the first time, be able to provide an impartial and independent investigation of these matters,"* [155] in reality they made sure no such impartial investigation could take place. They petitioned the court to strike out Karpov's suit as an abuse of the court system, inexplicably depriving Browder of the perfect opportunity to face and humiliate his Russian nemesis in an English court.

The judge, Mr. Justice Simon did in fact strike out Mr. Karpov's suit, ruling that the U.K. High Court was not the right jurisdiction for it. However having carefully considered Karpov's complaint, Mr. Justice

---

[154] Pavel Karpov v William Browder & Ors in the U.K. High Court of Justice, Queen's Bench Division Case No. HQ12D03133
[155] (Mercouris 2016)

Simon concluded that Browder had failed to substantiate his allegation that Karpov was involved in Magnitsky's death, since he presented no evidence that he had any role in Magnitsky's torture or mistreatment. Browder based his accusation of Karpov on two dubious premises: the claim that he had a *motive* to cause Magnitsky's death, and the presumption that *because* he played a role in Magnitsky's arrest, he *should have* foreseen the likelihood of Magnitsky's dying in detention.

Although Karpov's lawsuit inflicted only minimal damage to Browder's carefully contrived story, the real trouble for Browder was brewing on the other side of the Atlantic.

U.S. District Court – Southern District of New York: USA v. Prevezon Holdings

In September 2013, U.S. Government filed a civil forfeiture case against Prevezon Holdings owned by a Russian citizen Denis Katsyv on allegations that he was linked to the $230 million Russian tax fraud. Although Browder was not a party to the case, he persuaded the U.S. Attorneys and provided most of the information they used to launch the case against Prevezon.[156] As Prevezon's defense attorneys wanted to cross-examine Browder, the court issued a subpoena for him to appear for questioning and provide the defense with a set of relevant documents. Browder proved extremely reluctant to give any testimony under oath. While his lawyers fought for nearly two years to keep him from being cross-examined, Browder himself did everything he could to avoid being served the court subpoena. After several abortive attempts to track him down, one process server attempted to serve Browder in Aspen Colorado. Browder literally ran away from him and the judge ruled that the subpoena was not served properly. Six months later, in February 2015 process server Nicholas Casale caught up with him in New York as he sat in a limousine after a TV appearance. As Casale approached him, Browder escaped again by opening the limo door on the opposite side and running away through traffic on foot. Unfortunately for Browder, the judge ruled that the subpoena was served properly that time and the date for his deposition was set for Wednesday, 15th April 2015. On that day, Browder was obliged to appear in New York at the offices of Baker Botts, LLP, where he would spend fully seven hours of the day being questioned by attorneys Mark Cymrot, Esq; Paul Levine, Esq; and Moritz Abramovitz, Esq.

The 386-page transcript of the deposition proved to be a very illuminating reading. It reveals Browder's tale to be a far cry from the

---

[156] The government itself confirmed as much. (Sputnik 2016)

compelling version he had laid out in his book and in countless interviews, speeches, and presentations which he tirelessly promotes around the world.

The tax fraud thing

Browder's tale centers on his three stolen companies – Kameya, Makhaon and Parfenion.[157] However, Browder never mentions two other companies through which Hermitage conducted its investment activities: Saturn and Dalnaya Step. Both of these companies were founded in the Republic of Kalmykia which offered a low tax rate plus a further reduction of taxes for firms that hired at least 50% of employees with handicaps. Many details about those two firms emerged on record during his deposition.

Browder was Saturn's general director and was personally responsible for filing its tax returns. And while Saturn used Kalmykia's favorable tax regime, a court ruling in 2003 found that employees whom Saturn listed as handicapped had nothing to do with the company and that they were only used to obtain income tax relief. As a result, Saturn owed an additional 4.9 million rubles in taxes plus penalties amounting to some 1.6 million rubles. Later, the court waived most of the penalties, but the outstanding tax bill still had to be paid. As Prevezon's lawyers questioned him about Saturn, they alleged that Browder put the firm into bankruptcy in order to avoid paying its tax bill. Browder denied this, claiming that Russian federal tax service audited Saturn in 2003 and gave it a clean audit. Furthermore, he claimed that this audit overrides court rulings. But when Prevezon's attorney Mark Cymrot asks Browder to produce a copy of the tax audit, which he was required to provide under the subpoena, it seems that Browder's dog ate his audit report.

Mr. Cymrot then proceeds to question Browder about Dalnaya Step, the other Kalmykia company where he was the general director. In 2005, an arbitration court ruled that Dalnaya owed 551 million rubles in taxes (about $20 million), and again rather than paying the tax, Dalnaya was put into bankruptcy for which Mr. Cymrot produces documentary evidence. Browder claimed that he knew nothing about any of this: he had no knowledge that Dalnaya Step owed any taxes, or that there were court rulings against it, or that it was put into bankruptcy.

---

[157] In his deposition however there is no mention of Kameya; instead, the three companies mentioned are Makhaon, Parfenion and Rilend. It is unclear why there is no mention of Kameya or whether it may have been renamed as Rilend. Also, it appears that Parfenion was the new name of Saturn but this remains unclear because Browder could not confirm it.

Mr. Cymrot: *So in other words there were taxes due. Is that the way you would understand that?*
Browder: *Yes*
Mr. Cymrot: *And you were totally unaware of these events? You weren't aware of this decree, aware of the appeal, aware of the fact that Dalnaya Step was placed in bankruptcy, and that taxes were owed?*
Browder: *Totally unaware.*

Browder then explains that in 2004 Hermitage had transferred Dalnaya to the firm Visao Risk Management to be liquidated. Visao was run by one Jakir Shaashoua, who turned out to be the very Israeli ex-Mossad agent in charge of the 15-men security team whom Edmond Safra had sent to Browder for protection in 1998 during his showdown with Vladimir Potanin. Except that in Red Notice Browder presents Jakir Shaashoua under a false name, Ariel Bouzada. When Mr. Cymrot asks Browder why he changed Shaashoua's name in his book, Browder answers, "*I don't recall.*"

Mr. Cymrot then recapitulates the situation that existed in 2007 when police raids on Hermitage's Moscow offices took place:

Mr. Cymrot: *So at the time that the search warrant was executed in June of 2007, the situation was that the courts had found that you had taken advantage of the tax regime in Kalmykia, had taxes due, they were unpaid, the company was bankrupt. You say that's not grounds to conduct an investigation?*
Bill Browder: *I don't – I don't know what you're – you're trying to say here.*
Mr. Cymrot: *What I'm trying to say is, you've said that the investigative authorities had absolutely no basis for conducting an investigation for Hermitage Fund in 2007. ... And what these decisions show is there were false statements on tax returns, there were taxes due, they went unpaid and the company was placed in bankruptcy.*

Browder defends himself by claiming that in 2006, after he'd been expelled from Russia, the Interior Ministry sent a letter to Hermitage informing them that there were no open criminal investigations against them. But when asked to produce a copy of this letter, Browder does not have it – a strange thing since that letter would have been a critical piece of evidence supporting his story.

Mr. Cymrot: *But -- so the Ministry of Interior was investigating Hermitage for tax fraud from 2004 and finally searched its offices with a search warrant in 2007, correct?*
Browder: *No.*
Mr. Cymrot: *What happened?*
Browder: *The Interior Ministry was investigating Hermitage in 2004; closed the case in 2005.*
Mr. Cymrot: *Who told you that?*
Browder: *I got information in 2000 – some recent year.*
Mr. Cymrot: *From whom?*
Browder: *I can't remember where it came from.*

Browder got the information that investigations against him were closed in 2005, but he could neither produce any evidence to back up his claim, nor could he recall when, how, or from whom he got that information. Still, he continued to stick to his claim because he was, "*pretty sure it's true.*" But later during his deposition, Mr. Cymrot produced a document proving that it most certainly wasn't true. The document in question was a record of examination of Sergei Magnitsky dated 18th October 2006 with the heading, "Investigator for Particularly Important Cases of Tax Crimes Investigation Department." It shows that Magnitsky was questioned about Saturn Investments and about Mr. Shaashoua's role in it, proving that the investigation against Browder *was* indeed ongoing in late 2006.

Browder also sought to delegitimize investigations against him by claiming that they were politically motivated. Mr. Cymrot however, reminded Browder that at the time when the investigations began, he was an outspoken supporter of Vladimir Putin so there would have been no grounds for politically motivated persecution. Browder acknowledged as much but still insisted that his persecution was politically motivated because back then he was going after corruption at Gazprom.

Misrepresenting Sergei Magnitsky

In Red Notice, Browder is careful to give us the *impression* that he only hired Sergei Magnitsky after the 2007 police raids on his offices. He forgets to mention that Magnitsky was involved in the management of Hermitage's Kalmykia companies at least since 2002 and possibly as early as 1999 and he played an important role in setting up the whole scheme that led to Browder's tax fraud and his ultimate conviction for it in 2013. Browder dedicates several pages of his book to disqualifying and ridiculing the 2013 trial in Moscow where he was convicted in absentia. "*Putting me on trial when I wasn't in Russia was highly unusual. It would be only the second time in post-Soviet history that Russia would try a Westerner in absentia. But that wasn't the worst part. Their truly unbelievable move was to also try Sergei Magnitsky."*

Browder suggests that Putin was creating legal history through this process. The last time, *"a dead person had been prosecuted in Europe,"* explains Browder, *"was in AD 897, when the Catholic Church convicted Pope Formosus posthumously, cut of his papal fingers and threw his body into the River Tiber."* You see, Putin's prosecution of Browder and Magnitsky was just *that* insanely scandalous and medieval. Browder again ventures to interpret for us the evil tyrant's twisted logic: *"In Putin's mind, if he had a court judgment against Sergei and me, his officials could then visit all the European governments who were considering their own version of the Magnitsky Act and say, 'How can you put a piece of legislation in place that is named after a criminal convicted in our court? And how can you listen to his advocate, who has been convicted of the same crime?'"*

"... Sergei and me," cries Browder... the evil Russians convicted two innocent lambs of *"the same crime..."* Except this is not exactly what happened: the only person convicted of the crime was Bill Browder.[158] Hiding behind the deceased Magnitsky and pretending to be "his advocate," was just another one of Browder's deceptive three-card montes. When Mr. Cymrot produced a copy of his conviction with an English translation, the following exchange ensued:

Mr. Cymrot: *You have said many times that Mr. Magnitsky was convicted posthumously. You've said that?*
Browder: *Yes*
Mr. Cymrot: *And on the first page it appears that it's dismissed against Mr. Magnitsky, correct?*
Browder: *No.*
Mr. Cymrot: *Under paragraph 4 of Article 24 of the Code of Criminal Procedure of the Russian Federation. Do you see that?*
Browder: *Yes.*
Mr. Cymrot: *So he wasn't convicted posthumously, right? You were wrong about that?*

---

[158] Russian law does not permit prosecution of deceased individuals. They can only be tried in court for the purpose of their exoneration of wrongdoing, not for the purpose of conviction. It appears that Sergei Magnitsky's mother brought her son's case to trial but failed to exonerate him. In this sense, it is technically true that the court found him guilty and declined to rehabilitate him, but it is not true that he was "convicted" of any crime.

Browder: *No. I don't – I don't read it as such.*

Mr. Cymrot: *... It says "sentenced." ... The sentence only refers to you, correct?*

Browder: *I see my name here.*

Mr. Cymrot: *"William Felix Browder found guilty of committing two crimes" and – and then it goes on, right?*

Browder: *Correct.*

Mr. Cymrot: *And there's nothing about Mr. Magnitsky being convicted of anything, correct?*

Browder: *I'm not a Russian criminal lawyer, so I couldn't make a judgment about this – about this conviction.*

Mr. Cymrot: *Well, it appears from these two entries that you were wrong. That he was never convicted posthumously, right?*

This exchange goes on another few pages in the transcript as Mr. Cymrot presses Browder to explain what exactly substantiates his claim that Mr. Magnitsky was convicted of anything. Browder can't substantiate it because he is "*not a Russian criminal lawyer*," but he insists nevertheless, that Magnitsky *was* in fact posthumously convicted and refuses to acknowledge that he could be wrong. Mr. Cymrot then changes tack, continuing to challenge Browder's credibility from a different angle:

Mr. Cymrot: *... When you told people Mr. Magnitsky's a lawyer, did you also tell them he never went to law school and never had a law license?*

Browder: *I'm sorry. I...*

Mr. Cymrot: *When you tell – how many times have you said, "Mr. Magnitsky is a lawyer?"*

Browder: *I don't know.*

Mr. Cymrot: *50? 100? 200?*

Browder: *I don't know.*

Mr. Cymrot: *Many, many times, right?*

Browder: *Yes*

Mr. Cymrot: *Have you ever told anybody that he didn't go to law school and didn't have a law degree?*

Browder: *No.*

Thus, it turns out that Sergei Magnitsky was not a lawyer at all. Why Browder insisted on misrepresenting him as such is not clear but at least this helps us understand Browder's claim in Red Notice that Sergei Magnitsky was rumored never to have lost a case... It was for the same reason why Maya, my Golden Retriever also never lost one.

BILL BROWDER, THE GREAT PRETENDER

Framing the Russians for the $230 million tax fraud

Browder's questioning then turns to June 2007 police raids on Hermitage and Firestone Duncan offices. Browder had alleged that Russian Interior Ministry seized corporate stamps, the original charters, tax certificates, registration certificates and seals of the three Russian firms [159] through which Hermitage ran investment transactions. The fact that these documents were in the Interior Ministry's possession when the firms were stolen is extremely important to Browder's story because they represent the key link between the Ministry officials and the $230 million tax fraud effected through these firms. But in Browder's deposition we find out that the seals that were seized by the Interior Ministry were *not* the same ones that were used to steal his companies. This was established through a forensic analysis of the seals. Browder's right hand man, Vadim Kleiner, was apparently well aware of that fact. If Vadim was aware of it, Browder probably was too, but he claims ignorance.

>Mr. Cymrot: ... *Mr. Kleiner never informed you that he was aware of a forensic analysis that showed that the same seals were not used?*
>Browder: *Correct.*

When Mr. Cymrot points out that those seals represent the key link tying the Interior Ministry with the fraud, Browder claims there are many other links, except he can't actually point to any specific one and falls back on claiming incompetence: *"I'm not a lawyer here..."*

>Mr. Cymrot: *If the $230 million fraud were done with other documents, there is no tie between the $230 million fraud and the criminal investigation of you; isn't that correct?*
>Browder: *No, no.*
>Mr. Cymrot: *Why not?*
>Browder: *You're mischaracterizing the whole – you're simplifying and mischaracterizing the – the whole story.*

Browder then proceeds to read the text of his complaint where he implicates Interior Ministry's Artem Kuznetsov in the fraud by claiming that *"on or about 28 April 2007,"* he flew to Cyprus on a private jet together with one Dmitry Klyuev, a convicted fraudster and owner of the Universal Savings Bank (through which part of the $230 million tax

---

[159] The three firms were Makhaon, Parfenion and Rilend. For whatever reason, there is no mention at all of Kameya, the one firm for which Browder claims they paid all taxes in full and possibly even overpaid.

refund was recycled). Klyuev supposedly was the mastermind of the network that carried out the fraud. While in Cyprus, they also met with Pavel Karpov and two Russian lawyers, and some ten days later Klyuev met Olga Stepanova, the head of the Moscow Tax Office No. 28 (which paid out a major part of the $230 million refund).

So there you have it, the whole merry bunch of fraudsters met in Cyprus where they must have forged their evil plans. But when Mr. Cymrot asks Browder *how* he knew that Kuznetsov went to Cyprus with Klyuev, Browder replies that he'd seen copies of travel records, only he can't remember how he got those records or from whom, only that this person (whom he couldn't remember) was a *whistle-blower*.[160]

> Mr. Cymrot: *I see. But that's just a label* [whistle-blower]. *We don't know the name, we don't know the address ... and we don't know whether the documents are real, right?*
> Browder: *I don't know.*
> Mr. Cymrot: *But you relied upon it?*
> Browder: *My team did.*
> Mr. Cymrot: *And you ultimately went to the U.S. Attorney's office and said, 'This happened'?*

As his deposition continued, Browder presented the same sterling quality of evidence about the meeting between Dmitiry Klyuev and Olga Stepanova: some anonymous someone told his team that this meeting took place. That was it. The fact that they couldn't prove that the meeting actually took place or what Klyuev and Stepanova may have discussed didn't seem to bother Browder. His further supporting evidence, consisting of money transfers that allegedly ended up in different individuals' accounts or their purchases of expensive cars and apartments also turned out to be entirely useless. In Browder's mind however, all these trips to Cyprus, meetings between the alleged fraudsters and their supposed wealth prove their involvement in the fraud conclusively enough to justify his making public accusations against them, destroying their reputations, and having them placed on the list of sanctioned individuals under the Magnitsky Act. However, none of his allegations could stand up in a court of law. As Browder's depositions shows, Olga Stepanova was almost certainly innocent of Browder's malicious accusations against her. So, probably, was Major Pavel Karpov.

---

[160] Whistleblower: an honorable truth teller and therefore his information must be true and beyond any reasonable doubt.

Browder's complaint against the Interior Ministry omits another important detail in the story. Namely, in November and December of 2007, Pavel Karpov invited Firestone Duncan employee V. Y. Yelin to his office to retrieve documents and seals impounded during the June raids. Among these were the documents pertaining to Hermitage's stolen firms. But rather than getting their materials back, Browder's employees Vadim Kleiner and Ivan Cherkasov instructed Firestone & Duncan *not* to retrieve them, as though they *wanted* the documents and seals to remain at the Interior Ministry. At the very least, this little trick made it possible for Browder to continue to claim in his numerous speeches that the documents and the seals were *still* in the possession of the evil Interior Ministry.

Browder's deposition covered further issues as Prevezon's defense attorneys probed various aspects of Browder's tale which he craftily arranged to implicate his accusers as the real criminals, to claim victimhood and exonerate himself of any wrongdoing. One by one, each of his claims proved to be highly problematic on closer analysis: many are based on his own say-so or information obtained from anonymous sources, dubious documents or testimony from various dodgy characters whose credibility Browder attempts to bolster by calling them whistle-blowers or human rights activists.

Browder himself comes across as the dodgiest character of them all. He claims that he can't remember important details about his story at least 50 times and answers "*I don't know*" fully 211 times. Moreover, he appears to lack expertise in just about every relevant subject: twenty six times he declined to concede straightforward assertions because he was not an expert on the subject matter, like a man who refused to confirm that $1 + 1 = 2$ because he wasn't a mathematician. In fact, Browder comes across as the diametrical opposite of the character he projects in the countless speeches he delivers around the world. On such occasions, and I've had the privilege to witness two of them, Browder comes across as a highly competent man with remarkable command of detail and nuance with which he builds up his gripping tales.

During his deposition however, bungling Browder did not hesitate to flaunt his expertise in one particular domain: geopolitics. When Mr. Cymrot asked him why he called the U.S. Secretary of State John Kerry "Putin's lapdog," Browder explained that, "*... in my opinion he's following a policy of appeasement towards Russia.*" How exactly was Kerry appeasing Russia? To begin with, Kerry wasn't a big fan of the Magnitsky Act, and after the Act was signed into law, Kerry blocked Browder's efforts to keep adding more names to the list of sanctioned persons. He was also quite unhappy with Kerry's lukewarm support of expanding the *"sanctions policy* [against Russia], *more generally, arms to Ukraine, Syria, Iran etcetera."*

Apparently, Browder favors any measure that is adverse or hostile toward Russia, regardless of whether or not it has anything at all to do with the plight of Sergei Magnitsky or with the Interior Ministry supposed tax fraud. All this seems a bit perplexing coming from a man who claims to be merely fighting for "justice for Sergei."

Edmond Safra's lieutenant

... money laundering may go down in history as one of the worst plagues of all time.

Robert Walsh[161]

When Browder came to Moscow in 1994 to participate in the voucher privatization program, he was able to pick up $25 million in crisp $100 bills from a bank owned by a relative of some colleague of his at Salomon Brothers. This may seem like an inconsequential detail in the story but it is an interesting detail. Large amounts U.S. dollar-denominated bank notes don't just spontaneously materialize in a foreign country. How they got there adds another dimension in our understanding of Russia's transition in the 1990s, its massive wealth giveaway and Bill Browder's role in this sordid enterprise.

Republic National Bank's money planes

In 1993, agents of the Criminal Investigation Bureau of the New York State Banking Department learned that the Republic National Bank of New York was selling tens of billions in U.S. dollar notes to as many as 50 corrupt Russian banks.[162] Although they raised alarm about this, neither the FBI nor the CIA were inclined to launch an investigation. Instead, it would be the journalist Robert Friedman who investigated the story and exposed it in a January 1996 *"New York"* Magazine article titled "The Money Plane." The article's title referred to the Delta Airlines flight 30 that flew direct from New York to Moscow five times a week transporting dozens of large white canvas bags full of new $100 bills. It usually carried

---

[161] (Walsh 2017)
[162] (Friedman, The Money Plane 1996)

no less than $100 million and at times more than $1 billion. From 1994 to 1996 these money planes had dispatched *at least* $40 billion in uncirculated $100 bills. This amount far exceeded the total value of all rubles in circulation in Russia and even all the funds loaned to Russia throughout the 1990s by the IMF.

Republic National Bank of New York (RNB), which was the principal conduit of this operation, was owned by none other than Bill Browder's business partner, Edmond Safra. RNB distributed these bills to numerous Russian banks which would buy the dollars on behalf of their clients who paid for them with wire transfers from London bank accounts. Many of those banks were known fronts for Russian organized crime. A 1994 CIA report cited by Friedman identified ten of the largest Russian banks as mobbed-up fronts. Report's authors ask, "*So why are the Repulic National Bank and the Federal Reserve continuing to supply ... bills to banks that so many money-laundering experts agree are tainted?*"

An official from the Federal Comptroller of the Currency, which regulated Safra's bank, stated that, "*That money is used to support organized crime; it is used to support black market operations. ... In my personal opinion, it is an absolute abomination. It should not exist. Yet it appears that at least part of the federal government sees nothing wrong with it.*" He added: "*What I understand is that they are aiding in organized crime activities out of the former Soviet Union through their so-called correspondent bank relationships.*" Russian Central Bank official Viktor Melnikov corroborated this view noting that much of the imported U.S. dollars were being used for illegal purposes, including narcotics, trafficking and currency smuggling.

According to a U.S. State Department cable cited by Freedman, an estimated 50% to 80% of all Russian banks were under control of organized crime groups. The reason why Russian banking system turned so toxic was because when the USSR collapsed, its government controlled banking system collapsed as well. Government banks were replaced by thousands of private ones, chartered and regulated by the new Russian Central Bank.[163] However, the regulatory regime was practically non-existent and anyone who could pay a $100,000 bribe to a banking official could set up a new private bank. As a result, thousands of new, private banks sprang up in a short period of time. The system lacked any money-laundering laws, regulatory agencies, depositor insurance or control over

---

[163] As a matter of fact, an alternative banking system started to emerge already in 1988. A reorganization of USSR's banking industry was initiated in January of that year and by August there began a wave of creation of cooperative and commercial banks. (Fedorov 1989, vol. 1, no. 4)

proprietorship. Now even convicted felons could own banks, and the financial industry that emerged was perfectly suited for illegal black market operations and money laundering.

The way this massive industry typically worked was as follows: Russian assets like weaponry, gold, oil or other commodities stolen by the mob would be sold on the spot markets in Western Europe. The proceeds of these sales were wired through European front companies and deposited in London banks. This money was then used to order large amounts of U.S. dollar banknotes to be delivered in Russia through Moscow mob banks. The notes were supplied by the Federal Reserve Bank of New York and delivered to Russia through Safra's Republic National Bank.

The reason why Russian mob needed U.S. dollar notes is perfectly straightforward but it is not always well understood. Namely, money in London bank accounts was of little use to mobsters operating on the streets of Russia. What they needed was physical cash: with the economy in freefall collapse and the ruble becoming more worthless with each passing day, people who could deal in physical U.S. currency became the rainmakers in Russia's burgeoning gray economy. With the dollar notes, they could buy valuable assets at steep discounts,[164] bribe plant managers, law enforcement officers, military generals, judges, politicians and journalists, and finance their own private armed gangs.

Naturally, much of the money was also spent on narcotics and luxuries like real estate, yachts and expensive cars. Another important aspect of trading with physical dollar bills was that such transactions could not be traced back along the supply chain, enabling the parties to transactions to remain invisible to law enforcement and difficult to investigate, especially beyond Russia's borders.

In the first two years after Soviet Union's collapse, an estimated $60 to $70 billion worth of material assets including weapons, oil, gold and artwork were stolen out of the country by organized crime networks. While the mob did the dirty work on the ground, Russia's new banking system was the centerpiece in the conveyor belt that exchanged the nation's wealth for the bits of paper printed by the U.S. Federal Reserve Bank. Edmond Safra was the key middle man in this exchange, but the masterminds of the operation were individuals in the very top echelons of power at the Federal Reserve and U.S. Treasury Department.

It would not have been possible for one relatively small bank to obtain over $40 billion in brand new notes without the knowledge and full cooperation of the Federal Reserve System. That amount was massive for the economy of Russia, but it wasn't exactly small change for the

---

[164] This included even military hardware in arms depots of the Russian Army.

American economy either. According to data from the St. Louis Federal Reserve Bank, the total currency in circulation in the U.S. in 1994 was around $325 billion. The $40 billion printed up to distribute in Russia corresponded to about 13% of all the currency in circulation in the U.S., a very substantial amount that could not have been just smuggled out under the counters at the Fed.[165] The operation was carefully planned and organized with cooperation and approval of high level officials at the Federal Reserve Bank of New York, the U.S. Treasury and U.S. State Departments. Robert Friedman mentions a high level meeting of US Treasury and Federal Reserve officials which was convened in 1995 specifically to discuss RNB's massive US dollar sales to Russia.

Since an operation of this magnitude could not be kept secret, Federal Reserve officials produced a palatable justification for it, saying it was the best way to bulk up the sagging ruble and help Russia integrate into global free markets. Edmond Safra was the choice middleman in this operation because this type of activity was exactly his specialty. Although Safra grew up in Syria, when he was only 21 years old, he set up a bank in Brazil (Banco Safra) which became a magnet for Jewish flight capital from Middle East and South America. Early on in his career, Safra specialized in money laundering, trading gold and physical cash and working with organized crime networks.

To facilitate his trade he also cultivated close relationships with various central banks around the world. Occasionally, his activities triggered alarms with regulatory agencies and law enforcement, as in the mid-1980s when U.S. Customs and the Drug Enforcement Agency (DEA) together with the Swiss police investigated RNB for laundering more than $800 million in Colombian and Turkish drug money.

Another of his banks, the Trade Development Bank was implicated in money laundering activity that facilitated Oliver North's operations in the Iran-Contras scandal, which included running drugs out of Columbia and bringing it back into the United States. What emerged from these cases was that wherever American deep state ran covert operations, Edmond Safra was among their choice providers of financial logistics. This helps explain why neither Safra nor his bank were ever convicted of any crimes and why RNB could continue to operate largely unmolested by regulators until 1999 when it was bought by HSBC.

---

[165] When U.S. banks purchase dollars to resell abroad, they have to file reports on each transaction with the Federal Reserve System, the U.S. Treasury Department, U.S. Customs and with the Comptroller of the Currency.

For he's a jolly good felon... and so say all of us!

When Friedman's article came out, it clearly touched a raw nerve among American financial and government circles. The prospect of possibly having to investigate Safra's bank induced a near panic among New York's banking regulators and law enforcement agencies. To preempt this, they scrambled to dismiss the substance of Friedman's revelations and distance themselves from any potential controversy. Within three weeks from the article's publication, New York Congressman Charles E. Schumer raised the issue of Friedman's article in the House of Representatives and submitted for Congressional Record a set of letters from New York law enforcement agencies and bank regulatory bodies. Along with his own remarks, these materials amounted to a collection of sycophantic assurances that New York legal establishment saw no evil, heard no evil, and would certainly speak no evil on account of Safra's bank which the Honorable Schumer described as a *"well-respected institution serving the New York community and employing thousands of its residents."*[166]

Among the materials Schumer submitted was a letter from the Comptroller of the Currency, Eugene A. Ludwig to RNB's CEO Walter H. Weiner in which Ludwig assures Weiner that whatever information Friedman obtained from his office was unauthorized and that, *"these statements do not reflect the OCC's position concerning Republic Bank's bank note dealings with Russian banks."* He made sure to clarify OCC's position: *"We are satisfied that Republic's bank note activities are conducted in a manner consistent with the applicable laws we administer."* Michael Shaheen of the U.S. Department of Justice also took pains to soothe Mr. Weiner. Referring to statements in "The Money Plane" attributed to an Assistant United States Attorney (AUSA) Shaheen wrote: *"I wish to assure you that the statements attributed to the AUSA do not represent the views of the Department of Justice. More specifically, the attributed statements do not reflect any position of the Department of Justice on the Republic National Bank's banknote transactions with Russian banks."*

A letter from the Banking Department of the State of New York added more comforting words to poor Mr. Weiner: *"You can be assured that if, and to the extent that, such statements may have been made by former employees of this Department, they have not been authorized to be made by this Department, were made without our awareness and do not constitute, in any manner, statements or positions of the New York state*

---

[166] (Schumer 1996)

Banking Department in respect of Republic or with regard to banknotes dealings with Russian banks by Republic and other banks." Perhaps the most groveling of all the letters was the one sent to Anne T. Vitale, Republic's Deputy General Counsel by Stanley E. Morris, Director of the Financial Crimes Enforcement Effort. Morris assures Vitale that, *"Banks such as Republic, with a history of strong compliance programs and valuable cooperation with law enforcement authorities in this country, can be expected to recognize the risks of particular transactions in their efforts to avoid becoming ensnared in wrongdoing. ... Our program of partnership with the financial community relies on highly experienced officials such as you and banks such as Republic to carry out our law enforcement mission. I look forward to continuing to work with you in the fight against money laundering."*

This spectacle of bank regulators and law enforcement officials genuflecting before a bank they're supposed to regulate and investigate was something of a revelation all in itself. Where banking officials should operate in respectful compliance with law enforcement agencies, it seems that in New York it is the law enforcement community that operates with reverence to the banks they are supposed to regulate. But in this whole parade of servility one element was conspicuously absent: any denials of Robert Friedman's allegations about RNB's cash transactions with Russia's mob banks. Rather, Republic's activities were defended as not only within the law but also done for a higher cause and therefore not be questioned by the lowly regulators. In a letter to the Editor of the New York Magazine, New York County District Attorney Robert M. Morgenthau wrote that, *"under current law, banks which buy dollars in New York and resell them to Russian banks are not required to and, indeed are unable to know, the identity of the Russian banks' customers. Republic, in fact, sells only to banks licensed by the Russian Central Bank."*

Robert S. Strauss, former U.S. Ambassador to Russia also wrote to the editor lecturing him about the virtues of flooding the Russian economy with U.S. dollar banknotes: *"As former Ambassador to Russia, I have seen firsthand the importance of selling dollars to Russian banks: U.S. currency helps to stabilize the Russian economy ... in the best interests of the U.S. and the free world. The circulation of the U.S. currency in Russia is an important element of U.S. trade and foreign policy."* Further on, Strauss added that, *"Providing a steady supply of U.S. currency to Russian banks is perhaps the single most efficient form of support the U.S. can offer any country in a position as delicate as Russia's."*

Of course, the ultimate objective of all this correspondence was to preempt any future investigation of Safra's bank by declaring officially and on the record that its activities were conducted in compliance with all applicable laws and regulations and in accordance with U.S. trade and foreign policy so as to ensure that no further details about this operation would come unveiled in the future.

Browder and the West's criminal plunder of Russia

How does Bill Browder fit into all this? In his tale, he presents himself as an independent entrepreneur who pulled himself by his own bootstraps and made a big success of his hedge fund business. Edmond Safra's $25 million seed investment was merely one of the stepping stones in his path. But as we already discussed, Browder's whole story about his consulting engagement with the Murmansk Trawler Fleet and his subsequent trip to Moscow where he held 30 meetings in four days to work out the great investing opportunity in Russian privatization doesn't quite add up. Neither does the idea that he was the one who alerted Edmond Safra about the investment opportunities in Russia and that Safra invested in Hermitage Fund, simply following Browder's lead. As one of the key financiers behind Russia's transition process, Safra certainly knew fully well what was going on there and was already earning huge profits from his Russian operations before he ever met Browder. The idea that Safra would make a $25 million investment with an inexperienced start-up fund manager seems hardly credible. The meeting between Safra and Browder *might* have happened as Browder described it, but the arrangement that they struck up was perobably very different from what he suggested.

While Safra's bank profited enormously by financing the criminal plunder of Russia, the real prize was not in plundering the nation's wealth cargo by cargo, bar of gold by bar of gold... The real prize in Russia was to take ownership of the facilities that produced such assets. To do that, you needed more sophisticated operatives working within the Russian legal system. Robert Friedman alludes to this in "The Money Plane" article: *"More savvy Russian hoods have hired sophisticated money managers and international lawyers to move their dirty money."* Edmond Safra certainly counted among those "more savvy" hands in Russia and Bill Browder and Jamison Firestone took on the roles of those sophisticated money managers and international lawyers he could rely upon to move his dirty money.

In all likelihood, Edmond Safra simply hired Browder as his own agent, helped him set up shop in Moscow and defended him when necessary in order to take possession of as large a chunk of the Russian economy as possible. Hermitage Capital was merely the legitimate front of an operation that included a wider variety of activities than just buying Russian stocks. We may not know the entire scope of these operations until the completion of a comprehensive investigation, not only within Russia but also in all major western money centers. Obstructing and delegitimizing such an investigation defines the objectives of Browder's present day endeavors and explains his motives much more credibly than does his destructive obsession with "justice for Sergei."

The $230 million tax fraud: whodunit?

> *"Browder and his agents engaged in a series of misrepresentations to execute the fraud, to distance themselves from it, and to pin it on the Russian officials investigating Browder for a separate tax fraud his companies committed."*
>
> *Prevezon court filing, Southern District Court of New York*[167]

With a more complete perspective on Bill Browder and his employer in Russia, we can now revisit the mystery of the Russian $230 million tax fraud. As we have seen, *someone* stole three of Hermitage's Russian investment firms and used them to fraudulently claim $230 million in tax rebates from the Federal Tax Service. According to Browder, this was done using the original corporate documents and seals, all of which were in possession of the Interior Ministry where Lieutenant Colonel Artem Kuznetsov was conducting an investigation against Browder and Hermitage. But as it turned out, the operation was done using forgeries of the documents and seals, which opens the possibility that Kuznetsov and the Interior Ministry officials aren't the only suspects in the case. Whoever carried out this fraud had access to the original corporate documents and seals of the stolen companies, was able to manipulate court proceedings, had strong connections high in the tax office hierarchy, was capable of performing sophisticated banking operations including money laundering and even setting up and liquidating entire banks. A network of corrupt state officials connected with the Interior Ministry *might* have had these capabilities.

---

[167] (Hollingsworth and Bow 2015)

But so did people connected with Bill Browder and his *goodfellas*. Before the key documents and seals were confiscated by the Interior Ministry they were kept at Firestone Duncan offices in Moscow. Both Hermitage and Firestone Duncan had detailed understanding of the structure and functioning of the Russian administrative, judicial and tax bureaucracies. During their ten odd years of operation Hermitage and its lawyers have litigated some 40 court cases gaining valuable experience and connections in Russian judiciary. As Browder used to boast in his speeches, Hermitage invested a great deal of time and effort in cultivating relationships through the state bureaucracy including the tax service. Finally, through their association with Edmond Safra and later with HSBC bank who both ran extensive money laundering operations, Browder and his *goodfellas* were easily capable of laundering the stolen money and disappearing it from Russia. Even if Bill Browder himself was not involved in the fraud, it is possible that some of his business associates in Russia were.

Working a lot with Renaissance Capital

This is all the more likely given that this same tax fraud was perpetrated in the case of another large investment fund. Using firms stolen from Renaissance Capital, a network of fraudsters perpetrated the same scheme to obtain a $106 million tax refund from Russian tax authorities. Apparently, some of the same individuals took part in both Renaissance and Hermitage tax fraud operations. The main difference was that Renaissance Capital kept quiet about the affair.[168] Renaissance Capital and its founder Boris Jordan appear in Red Notice as Browder's adversaries in his conflict with Vladimir Potanin. Like Browder, Jordan came to Russia to take part in her transition. His various entanglements with George Soros earned him the moniker, "right hand of George Soros" in Russia.[169] In a similar way as Browder worked for Safra, Jordan managed Russian operations for Soros in their common mission to extract as much profit from Russia and take control of as much of its economy as possible.

On many occasions during the 1990s privatization feeding frenzy, various oligarchs and their financial backers clashed amongst themselves

---

[168] (Stooge 2011)

[169] In 1992, at the tender age of 26, Jordan became the Managing Director of the Moscow office of Credit Suisse First Boston. During his tenure, Credit Suisse First Boston became the leading investment bank in Russia. In 1995 he cofounded Renaissance Capital. Jordan also headed the investment group Mustcom with George Soros as one of his principal investors. In 1998 he set up a private equity fund Sputnik Group again backed by Soros.

and one such clash was between Browder's Hermitage and Jordan's Renaissance over Sidanco share issue in 1997. Although Safra's and Soros's respective teams stepped on each other's toes on that occasion, they worked together on other affairs. Browder himself suggests as much in Chapter 25 of his book. The chapter titled "High-pitched Jamming Equipment," recounts the story of Browder's meeting with Igor Sagyrian, President of Renaissance Capital. In December of 2007, Sagyrian called up Browder to arrange a meeting in person: "*... I just wanted to discuss with you what other steps we can make because we are working a lot with you...*" Browder's story provides no details about how exactly Renaissance worked *a lot* with Hermitage, but on this occasion Sagyrian wanted to obtain Browder's consent for Renaissance to liquidate Hermitage's stolen companies. Sagyrian also reached out to Jamie Firestone with the same proposal which apparently greatly agitated Firestone. Browder finds himself thoroughly perplexed because, "*... how could Sagyrian liquidate something he doesn't control?*" and wondered "*Where did Sagyrian get this information?*" Still, Browder chose *not* to ignore this particular request and even hastened to finish his business in the Middle East to return to London and prepare for the meeting with Renaissance's Sagyrian.

Part of his preparations involved hiring a former British Special Forces security specialist who brought in two other surveillance specialists in order to record his conversation with Sagyrian, "*so that we could analyse every word he said.*" Unfortunately, we only have Browder's own account of what was said during the meeting because Sagyrian apparently used some kind of evil Russian space technology jammer so that Browder's Boy Scout recording equipment only captured white noise for the whole duration of the meeting. Even his security specialist was puzzled: "*He frowned, turning the recorder over in his hand. 'I don't know, it could either be that this thing is faulty or that Sagyrian was using some kind of high-pitched jamming equipment.'*"

"*Jesus Christ,*" gasped poor Browder, too innocent to conceive of such foul play: "*Jamming equipment? Where do you even get that?*" His security specialist assured him that it's not easy, but "*... it's commonly used by special services like FSB.*" Apparently it was not used by the British Special Forces whose lame surveillance specialists never considered the possibility that the equipment they provided might not correctly record Browder's conversation with Sagyrian. And if the implication of this gripping story is too subtle for the readers of Browder's tale, he is kind enough to elucidate us: "*... I might just have sat down with an actual spy.*"

For all we know, it is possible that Browder's story about this meeting was true. If so, we have a ready-made explanation of why the recording of this particular meeting doesn't exist and can't be provided should any future investigators request to examine it. On the other hand, it could be that the conversation between Browder and Sagyrian contained incriminating evidence against one or both of them, so Browder and his *goodfellas* made sure to disappear it. In that case, Browder's account of the meeting is merely a smokescreen, misrepresenting the business relationship between Hermitage and Renaissance behind a contrived, thriller-like suspense.

Nevertheless, Browder's account of the episode does yield a few interesting details: that Hermitage and Renaissance were *"working a lot together,"* that Sagyrian knew everything about the case of Hermitage's stolen companies, that he insisted on having a discussion with Browder in person and that their discussion was related to this case. For some reason Sagyrian thought that Renaissance Capital would be able to liquidate Hermitage's stolen companies if Browder agreed to this, which was the whole point of arranging the meeting in London. In his tale however, Browder maintains that he had no control over the companies since someone connected with the Interior Ministry stole them from him. But if that were the case, it would have been easy enough for Browder to inform Sagyrian that the companies were stolen and that he could therefore be of no further help in the matter. This would have saved them both the waste of time and effort in hastily arranging the pointless meeting in London and involving security specialists with their voice recording and evil jamming devices. But instead, for some odd reason, Browder thought it was so important for him to turn up for that meeting that he hurried up his Middle East business to return to London and prepare for it.

Another important detail about this encounter was its timing: it took place in December of 2007, only days before the massive $230 million tax rebate was paid out by the Russian tax service.

Browder's defector lawyers

Browder continues with his suspect storytelling in chapter 27. The chapter titled "DHL" recounts how on 21st August 2008, a mysterious DHL parcel from London arrived at Eduard Khayretdinov's office in Moscow. Less than an hour later, the office was raided by the police who promptly seized the parcel. Browder's story gets a bit comical as he tries hard to convince us that this parcel wasn't sent by Hermitage at all but by some "Eastern European" looking men who flew in from Russia to send the parcel from a DHL depot close to Hermitage's London offices. Maybe. In any case, three days after these raids, Browder's lawyers Khayretdinov and Vladimir Pashtukov both received the summons to appear in court in Kazan for questioning on the 30th August. Seemingly confident that they had done nothing wrong and had nothing to hide, both Khayretdinov and Pashtukov promptly fled the country to join Bill Browder in London where they continued to work in his employment. This hardly befits a party of upstanding professionals innocent of any illegal acts.

Laundering AVISMA's profits

One of the subtle ways Browder deflects suspicion from himself in his book is by consistently representing himself as a principled and highly moral character: he runs a world class business, pays and overpays his taxes, puts his personal safety at risk to serve his investors, actively fights corruption, works to make Russia a better place, fights for justice and saves lives. At the same time, he repeatedly denounces corruption in Russia and the oligarchs who, *"engaged in asset stripping, dilutions, transfer pricing and embezzlement, to name but a few of their tricks."* Morally upright Browder expresses utter dismay that terrible things like that could be *"done without the slightest sense of shame."*

With such profuse virtue-signaling on Browder's part, the last thing a reader might expect would be that he himself had anything to do with any of that *"dirty dishonesty of Russia."* Yet this is exactly what emerged from little known court case related to the Russian company AVISMA.

AVISMA, or Aviation Special Materials, was the producer of titanium products used in the production of aircraft. Mikhail Khodorkovsky's bank Menatep and its industry group Rosprom purchased AVISMA through the infamous loans-for-shares program. AVISMA controlled about a third of the global titanium sponge market with sales of around $100 million and profits of about $15 million a year.[170] Khodorkovsky drained most of AVISMA's profits offshore through so-called transfer pricing: he used TMC Holdings, an Isle of Man company to buy AVISMA's output at artificially low prices, reselling it subsequently at market prices and booking the bulk of profits offshore. In this way, Khodorkovsky deprived AVISMA of profits, its minority shareholders of dividends, and Russian tax authorities of the revenues they would otherwise collect. In 1997 Bill Browder and his partners Kenneth Dart and Francis Baker bought a 60% stake in AVISMA from Khodorkovsky for $85 million. When they took over AVISMA, they knowingly continued the transfer pricing scheme Khodorkovsky had used. In a later interview, Francis Baker stated that the

---

[170] (Komisar, Russian Sanctions Highlight Role of Western Enablers 2014)

scheme was part of their business plan which made the investment attractive in the first place.[171]

The arrangement got derailed when TMC's owner Peter Bond declined to turn over the profits Browder and his partners expected from sales of AVISMA's products. After much acrimonious discussions and negotiations, Browder and partners decided to take Bond to court in the Isle of Man. The transfer pricing scam and the large money laundering operation associated with it came to light thanks to the legal documents that emerged through the litigation. In a January 1999 letter, Francis Baker wrote that, *"... we appear to have run into an immense Russian bank money-laundering scheme in the Isle of Man – clearly a criminal matter. However, not being social reformers, our objective is to get the money due us, clear the AVISMA accounts and proceed to other matters."* [172]

The money laundering operation involved offshore firms and bank accounts at Barclays Bank and Bank of New York. The banks ran the money through about twenty different entities so that according to Baker, *"the monies put in one end of the machine came out totally clean at the other end of the machine."* [173] Referring to the Bank of New York, Baker stated explicitly that, *"The bank was very complicit with that."*

Dirty dishonesty of Bill Browder

President Vladimir Putin has made it his single most important national policy to cover up the murder of Sergei Magnitsky

Bill Browder[174]

Browder's business associations suggest that while he was in Russia – and probably thereafter – he operated within an organization serving the interests of high-caliber western financiers. As such he almost certainly

---

[171] In a court affidavit, their lawyer stated that the transfer pricing scheme was what made the Avisma transaction profitable for Browder, Dart and Baker. (Komisar, Russian Sanctions Highlight Role of Western Enablers 2014)
[172] (Komisar, Russian Sanctions Highlight Role of Western Enablers 2014)
[173] Idem.
[174] (Campbell 2013)

networked with shady figures and well-connected individuals in high finance who played their part in the sustained pirate raid against Russia that included laundering of the raid's proceeds through "well respected" western financial institutions. Moreover, the AVISMA case shows that Browder didn't mind using these associations to appropriate a piece of the action for himself, in what his partner Francis Baker described as *"clearly a criminal matter."* Together with his subsequent deposition in the U.S.A. vs. Prevezon case, AVISMA case unmasked Browder's manufactured image of a morally upright corruption fighter as false. It also proved his crusade for justice and human rights as a cynical, self-serving deception. Behind his fake veneer of respectability, Browder's deeds show him to be every bit as greedy, unscrupulous and dishonest as the crooks he saw around every corner in Russia.

Monopolizing "truth"

Keeping up appearances is hard work: lies are fragile and like those inflatable wavers, they start to collapse if you stop pumping a lot of hot air through them.

Constant pumping of hot air required!

To maintain his deceit, Browder has had to keep travelling the world making speeches and presentations for many years now. But in addition to telling his story, Browder has had to aggressively suppress any voices that might call him on his lies. This included banning certain people from attending his speeches and preventing others from presenting their own, alternative versions of events. When in December of 2016, the Institute for Advanced Studies[175] in Princeton hosted one of Browder's performances, investigative reporter Lucy Komisar registered to attend. Unlike most members of his typically ill-informed and credulous audiences, Komisar was well informed about Browder's activities in Russia and had written a number of articles on him. It was she, in fact, who exposed the story about his AVISMA deal. Even though Browder's Princeton presentation was open to the public, Komisar was disinvited from the event at the last moment. Chris Ferrara, the media director of the Institute for Advanced Studies wrote a note to Komisar explaining that "*all press must be vetted and approved by Mr. Browder's London office.*" [176] Komisar did not obtain the approval to attend from Browder's office and was therefore removed from the list of attendees.[177]

Browder displayed an even more egregious intolerance for freedom of expression some six months earlier when the documentary film maker Andrei Nekrasov ran a promotion campaign for his film, "The Magnitsky Act – Behind the Scenes." Over the years, Nekrasov had built a reputation for producing documentaries that were critical of the Russian government, and with the Magnitsky affair, he initially followed Browder's narrative of the events and even envisioned Browder as the film's narrator. But his research into the subject turned up a number of problems with Browder's story. Nekrasov reached out to him for an explanation, but was unable to get in touch with Browder for several months. Nekrasov finally tracked down Browder at a book signing event where he tried and failed to get clarifications from him. Ultimately however, Nekrasov managed to meet

---

[175] The Institute for Advanced Study in Princeton, has no relation with Princeton University.

[176] (Komisar, Institute for Advanced Study in Princeton bans Lucy Komisar from Wm Browder speech 2016)

[177] By allowing Browder's office to vet who may or may not attend public events, Western institutions of higher learning make themselves complicit with his campaign of deception. If a guest speaker isn't willing or able to defend his story before an informed audience that's allowed to question him, organizations like the Princeton Institute, whose motto is "*truth and beauty,*" should not offer a platform for such guests. *Perhaps* the rule should be: you are welcome to tell us your story but you must allow the audiences to question you. If that's not acceptable, perhaps there's something wrong with your story.

with Browder and with the cameras rolling, he began to lay out his findings. As he did so, Browder became visibly vexed until at one moment he stood up and abruptly interrupted Nekrasov with an accusation that he was spreading Russian propaganda. He also threatened Nekrasov that his "*FSB tactics,*" would not go well for him.[178]

When Nekrasov's film was completed, Browder sought to block its screenings. With threats of lawsuits, he and his lawyers were able to prevent an already scheduled screening in Brussels to a group of Members of the European Parliament. He did the same with another screening in Norway, and even managed to pressure the Franco-German television network "Arte" to cancel the showing of Nekrasov's film on its channel. Two months later, in June 2016, Browder tried to force The Newseum in Washington DC also to call off the screening of Nekrasov's film.[179]

Open, civilized societies seek resolution of contentious issues by allowing proponents of different sides in any dispute to present their respective points of view. An informed, open debate is by far the best mechanism of conflict resolution because we can only arrive at constructive solutions to problems by taking different stakeholders' points of view into consideration. Browder's approach is contrary to that of civilized societies: he seeks to silence all points of view but his own. He seeks to persuade not by initiating an informed debate, but by suppressing all debate. He defends his story by excluding from his audiences individuals that are capable of challenging his version of events. This is not the conduct of a truth teller pursuing elevated objectives like human rights, justice, and truth. Truth does not need such aggressive defense. As Oliver Wendell Holmes wrote, "*Truth is tough. It will not break, like a bubble, at a touch. Nay, you may kick it about all day, and it will be round and full at evening.*" Browder is clearly anxious that his story cannot take any kicking at all.

Desecrating Sergei Magnitsky

The most significant point about Andrei Nekrasov's film was that it contradicted Browder's story about how and why Sergei Magnitsky ended up in prison and how he died. Having reviewed Magnitsky's original testimony, Nekrasov found no references in it to Pavel Karpov, nor any accusations suggesting that he was the original whistleblower in the $230

---

[178] (Carden 2016)

[179] Thankfully, The Newseum, whose laudable mission is to promote freedom of expression and "the five freedoms of the First Amendment to the U.S. Consitution," refused to be cowed by Browder's intimidation and showed the film to a Washington audience. (Landler 2016)

million tax fraud case. For his part, Karpov also stated that, *"there was no sign of [Magnitsky] exposing us."* In fact, Magnitsky's testimony was not about him accusing the Interior Ministry of anything – he was simply being questioned by the police in their investigation of Browder's tax evasion. The accusatory bits were apparently slipped into the English language translation of Magnitsky's testimony which Browder himself provided to the Council of Europe and other organizations. Magnitsky's accusation of the Interior Ministry officials is critical to Browder's story because it is supposedly the very reason why Magnitsky's was arrested. Nekrasov's doubts about Browder's version were validated by Michael McFaul, former U.S. Ambassador to Russia who stated that, *"When I was in the Government, we studied closely [Magnitsky's] tragic case and had radically different assessment."* [180]

Another detail about the way Browder used Magnitsky to garnish his story emerged during his deposition in the U.S.A. vs. Prevezon case. At one point, Prevezon's attorneys brought up the name of Oleg Lurie, a controversial Russian journalist who had spent many years investigating the story of how IMF money that went into Republic National Bank in 1998 ended up stolen. Lurie, who had met with Magnitsky in prison claimed that Magnitsky was asked to take the fall for the Saturn and Dalnaya Step tax returns and that he had turned down Browder's offer of legal assistance. Lurie also alleged that someone using Browder's name had contacted him and offered him $160,000 to change his story about Sergei Magnitsky. Apparently, he had recorded those conversations and produced the recordings in support of his claim. When Mr. Cymrot questions Browder about this, Browder does not deny it:

Mr. Cymrot: *Did you ever have somebody suggest to Mr. Magnitsky that he should take responsibility for the Saturn and Dalnaya Step tax returns?*
Browder: *I don't remember.*

I would have expected Browder to reply, *"absolutely not"* to that question. Instead, Browder's *"I don't remember,"* suggests that Magnitsky may indeed have been asked to take the fall for Saturn and Dalnaya Step. This might also explains Browder's weirdly contorted story about Magnitsky's arrest which gave me the suspicion that Magnitsky's coworkers were warned to avoid arrest while Magnitsky was left hanging as the proverbial

---

[180] Sadly the New York Times article citing Ambassador McFaul did not detail what assessment he *did* reach about this case, leaving his statement in this case somewhat ambiguous. (Landler 2016)

head to roll. Recall, when Magnitsky was arrested, the police also attempted to arrest his assistants Irina Perikhina and Boris Samolov who somehow managed to avoid arrest.

If Magnitsky was indeed left as the fall guy, then Browder and his *goodfellas* share responsibility for his death. After he died they cynically desacrated his name to cover their criminality and con the whole world into erecting legal and administrative barriers that will hamper further investigation of their embezzlement and money laundering operations.

Escaping American gestapo

Although it is unrelated to Magnitsky's death and the $230 million tax fraud, the story about Browder's change of citizenship from U.S. to U.K. and his varying explanations of this act, add another shining exhibit of the quality of Browder's character. He became UK citizen in 1998. In a 2011 interview for Institutional Investor's Alpha magazine, Browder explained that he didn't give up his U.S. citizenship for tax reasons but because his then wife was English and because he liked the UK. "*I did not do it for tax reasons,*" he insisted: "*My tax bill was roughly the same either way.*" [181] Four years later, Browder thought up a better explanation. During his deposition in the U.S.A. vs. Prevezon lawsuit it turned out that Browder gave up his U.S. citizenship just as the laws about reporting foreign income came into effect. Browder pretended that he was not aware of this and explained instead that he gave up U.S. citizenship because his family had been persecuted in the United States during the McCarthy era:

Mr. Cymrot: *You gave up your U.S. citizenship in 1998, right?*
Browder: *Correct.*
Mr. Cymrot: *Just as the laws about reporting foreign income came into effect; is that right?*
Browder: *I don't know.*
Mr. Cymrot: *Why did you give up your U.S. citizenship in 1998?*
Browder: *I immigrated to the U.K. ten years earlier.*
Mr. Cymrot: *So the U.K. required you to give up your U.S. citizenship?*
Browder: *No.*
Mr. Cymrot: *So why did you give up your U.S. citizenship?*
Browder: *Personal reasons.*
Mr. Cymrot: *And what are those personal reasons?*
Browder: *My family was persecuted during the McCarthy era.*
Mr Cymrot: *And your father is the head of the economics department where, what university?*

---

[181] (Osipovich 2011)

Browder: *He's not –*
Mr. Cymrot: *Where was he?*
Browder: *My father was a professor of mathematics at the University of Chicago.*
Mr. Cymrot: *Was he the head of the department at some point?*
Browder: *Yes*
Mr. Cymrot: *And your uncle, what position did he have?*
Browder: *He was a mathematician at Princeton.*
Mr. Cymrot: *Head of the department at one point?*
Browder: *Yes.*
Mr. Cymrot: *But your concern that your family was persecuted, but they made it to the head of the department of two prestigious universities and that's why you gave up your U.S. citizenship?*
Browder: *Yes*
Mr. Cymrot: *What kind of persecution did you face?*
Browder: *My grandmother was sick with cancer and the U.S. Government tried to deport her to Russia when she was dying.*
Mr. Cymrot: *What year was that?*
Browder: *In 1950 something.*
Mr. Cymrot: *I see. And so in 1998, this all came back as a rush of emotion and you decided to give up your U.S. citizenship?*

Apparently, after Bill Browder gave up his U.S. citizenship, the U.S. Internal Revenue Service reinstated the great American tradition of persecuting the Browder family by placing Bill on a "name and shame" list of Americans who renounced their citizenship to avoid paying their taxes. Thankfully for him, he was by then living between Moscow and London, travelling on a British passport, safely out of reach of the American Gestapo.

All things considered Bill Browder, his staff, and other associates may well be the prime suspects in the $230 million tax fraud case. Browder's conduct betrays not a righteous man fighting for justice, but a devious man anxious to cover his track. He takes great pains to avoid exposing himself to questioning in a court of law and instead, he takes his supposed fight for justice to the court of public opinion where he relentlessly promotes his own version of events while aggressively denying others the opportunity to present theirs. Whatever Browder is actually fighting for, his preferred method consists of a nonstop, indiscriminate demonization of Russia, its President and all those seeking to bring him to account for his various violations of law. The day I picked up his book, I thought highly of Bill Browder. I suppose I fell for his tall tales. Today I see him as a rather sinister and dangerous conman – someone who is prepared to set the world on fire rather than concede any wrongdoing and submit himself to the course of justice. In his youth, when his parents sent him to *"a string of psychiatrists, counsellors and doctors,"* perhaps they recognized that they were raising a troubled young man who needed help.

6. War and peace

Whoever wins Eurasia, rules the world.

Zbigniew Brzezinski

Understanding Bill Browder's professional affiliations brings us a step closer to understanding some of the most powerful forces that shape the West's adversarial relationship toward Russia as well as her negative image in the West. As we discussed earlier, this image did not emerge spontaneously through truthful media reports. It emerged through a concerted effort to distort Russia by many of the most outspoken Western public officials, intellectuals, journalists, media groups and think tanks.[182] Ever since her leaders began to assert the nation's sovereignty and resist Western dictate, Russia has been treated with a marked negative bias. These changes started to take shape already in the later years of Boris Yeltsin's presidency, but with Vladimir Putin's more assertive leadership, the negative bias turned to open hostility. As early as 2004, a group of 114 top ranking Western intellectuals and public officials drafted "An Open Letter to the Heads of State and Government Of the European Union and NATO," in which they warn ominously that, *"President Putin's foreign policy is increasingly marked by a threatening attitude towards Russia's*

---

[182] According to the Moscow-based reporter John Helmer, some 450 of these think tanks, based in the U.S. and Europe, focus on matters of war, peace, international relations, and economic security. About 100 of them regularly analyze Russian affairs and all but ten of them are *"committed antagonists of Russia."* Among the leading think-tanks producing Russophobic rhetoric are the Brookings Institution, American Enterprise Institute, Freedom House, Hudson Institute, Progressive Policy Institute, Aspen Institute, Council on Foreign Relations, and Trilateral Commission. (Helmer 2015)

neighbors and Europe's energy security, the return of rhetoric of militarism and empire..."[183]

With few exceptions, Western media have insisted on representing Russia as a backward, aggressive autocracy posing a grave threat to Western democracies, their liberal social order and their way of life in general. In 2014, in the wake of the Western-sponsored coup d'état in Ukraine, unfavourable treatment of Russia and especially of Vladimir Putin have escalated to a relentless campaign of unhinged demonization. For the vast majority of mainstream media outlets, positive – or even neutral – bias in reporting on Russia has become a taboo. Even more disconcertingly, when a positive report about Russia does slip through, it seems to get *memory-holed*, just like in George Orwell's "1984." A handful of examples of this came to my attention while researching for this book. In March of 2015, Forbes Magazine contributor Mark Adomanis wrote an article titled, "10 Charts that Explain Russia." Adomanis wrote a few short paragraphs and presented a set of ten charts showing economic, social and demographic improvements in Russia since the early 2000s. I've saved a copy of the article at the time, but when I later looked it up to record the bibliographic reference, it was no longer available and in its place I found the following page:

It appears that Mark Adomanis sinned by honestly presenting a set of statistics showing that under Putin's leadership Russia was improving. He

---

[183] This letter was published by the Journal of Democracy, a publication of the International Forum for Democratic Studies supported by the U.S. National Endowment for Democracy. Signatories of the letter include former U.S. State Secretary Madeleine Albright, U.S. Senator John McCain, former Swedish Prime Minister Carl Bildt and Professor Anders Aslund, one of the leading architects of Russia's "shock therapy" economic transition. (Aslund et al. 2004)

wrote: *"Russia is not some unknowable mystery. With surprising ease one can find an enormous amount of statistical information on its demographic, economic, and social trends. And what does this data say? Well, in general the past decade has seen an improvement in a lot of basic social indicators. Compared to the not-too-distant past Russians live longer, drink less, make more money, work more frequently, have more children, and kill themselves less often. That's not my 'opinion,' it is what the data says."* Mindful of the established taboos against reporting positively on Russia, Adomanis added that, *"Some people find this impossible to accept. They 'know' that Putin's malevolence, corruption, and incompetence have spilled over into every corner of Russian society, and that no progress of any kind is possible when a country is run by such a man."* More defensively still, he concludes his article with the following two sentences: *"But my goal in this post isn't to convince anyone of a particular narrative or interpretation. All I want to do is bring to light some data that I consider important and allow readers to make up their own minds as to what (if anything) it really means."*

Adomanis' timid prose reflects the personal risk a reporter must take to present a dissenting point of view anywhere in the Western mainstream media. In spite of offering what he termed, "data journalism," some faceless someone determined that his article had to be memory-holed. Clearly, some part of the Western establishment has a valuable stake in the entrenched "truth" that Russia is bad, that Vladimir Putin is evil, and that it's not worth confusing the delicate minds of people in our liberal democracies by spoiling that message with needless nuance.

Just how hard Western press works to avoid making *any* positive references to Russia came to light again when on March 1, 2017 U.S. National Reconaissance Office launched a spy satellite aboard an Atlas V rocket powered by the Russian-made RD-180 engine. The 1,500 word official press-release about this launch mentioned RD-180 engine three times but never once mentioned where it was made. Media reports about this event followed suit, entirely omitting any mention of Russia. [184] Obviously, an "Upper Volta with missiles," or a "gas station with an army," shouldn't be capable of making advanced technological products.

---

[184] (Cloughley, The Beneficiaries of Conflict With Russia 2017)

The dangers of demonization

It's 100% permissible – bordering on obligatory – to spout the most insane, evidence-free conspiracy theories if they involve Russia & Putin

Glenn Greenwald (25 Nov. 2016)

Propagandizing the Western mind to fear and loathe Russia has been effective in convincing a large segment of the Western public that Russia is indeed our enemy in spite of the absence of an even remotely clear and present danger of Russia attacking any other nation, Western or otherwise. Every year, polling organization Gallup surveys a large sample of American adults on foreign policy issues asking them, among other things, "What one country anywhere in the world do you consider to be the United States' greatest enemy today?" In 2012, only 2% of Americans thought that country was Russia, but by 2015 a full 18% of Americans thought Russia was their country's greatest enemy, more than any other nation in the world. At the same time, 49% of Americans thought Russia's military power was a "critical threat to the U.S." [185] Similar results would probably have been obtained in many European nations where population had been treated to an equally frenzied anti-Russian propaganda.

It is important to recognize the full extent of risk involved with singling out one nation and systematically demonizing it before domestic audiences. Typically this is done to prepare the population to accept a military confrontation. In the run-up to World War I, Lord Nordcliffe remarked that, *"To create an atmosphere for war, you have to introduce in the populace the hatred of 'the other'."* Accordingly, the defamation of Russia has been used to rationalize the needless hostility in West's dealing with her and to justify NATO's ongoing and ever more dangerous military encirclement of Russia. That encirclement has included *very* significant deployments of troops and weaponry as well as large and frequent military exercises along Russia's borders.

In a 2016 radio-interview with John Bachelor, the longtime analyst of Russian affairs, professor Stephen Cohen noted that, *"NATO has decided to quadruple its military forces on Russia's borders or near Russia's borders... The last time there was this kind of Western hostile military*

---

[185] (Jones 2015)

force on Russia's borders was when Nazis invaded Russia in 1941. There has never been anything like this. During the 40-year Cold War there was this vast buffer zone that ran from the Soviet borders all the way to Berlin. There were no NATO or American troops there. This is a very radical departure on the part of the [Barack Obama] administration. ... Russia is not threatening any country on its border." Since that interview, NATO has continued stockpiling heavy weaponry, building up permanent logistics infrastructure, and deploying additional troops along Russian borders. The U.S. has built missile "defense" bases[186] in Romania and Poland, deployed nuclear bomb-capable aircraft close to Russia and allocated $8 billion of U.S. taxpayers' money to upgrade their arsenal of B-61 nuclear bombs kept in the United States and five other NATO-member nations.[187]

Nobody in the West should feel reassured about these extensive preparations as just posturing by Western liberal democracies or believe that we don't launch aggressive wars against other nations except as a measure of last resort. History does not warrant such reassurance. In June of 2014, a group of American researchers published an article in the American Journal of Public Health, pointing out that, *"Since the end of World War II, there have been 248 armed conflicts in 153 locations around the world. The United States launched 201 overseas military operations between the end of World War II and 2001, and since then, others, including Afghanistan and Iraq."* [188] To be sure, each of these wars was duly explained and justified to the American public and for all those Americans who believe that their government would never deceive them, each war was defensible and fought for a good reason. Nonetheless, the fact that one country has initiated more than 80% of all wars in the last seventy years does require an explanation.

---

[186] These bases, costing some $800 million each can, in only a few hours' time, be converted into ballistic missile launch platforms for aggressive attacks.
[187] (Cloughley, Make No Mistake: Russia Remains the Only Target Country of NATO's Nuclear Weapons 2016)
[188] (Wiist, et al. 2014)

WAR AND PEACE

Rise of the military industrial complex

Every gun that is made, every warship launched, every rocket fired signifies, in the final sense, a theft from those who hunger and are not fed, those who are cold and not clothed. This world in arms ... is spending the sweat of its laborers, the genius of its scientists, the hopes of its children. This is not a way of life at all in any true sense. Under the cloud of threatening war, it is humanity hanging from a cross of iron.

Dwight D. Eisenhower

In the most extreme circumstances we have made it very clear that you can't rule out the use of nuclear weapons as a first strike.

Michael Fallon, British Defense Minister

War is so very repugnant to the vast majority of people in any nation that we must pause and ask ourselves how we came to accept the dystopian state of permanent war in the 21st century? The systemic causes of this propensity for war are deeply rooted in modern monetary and economic system. Explanation of these causes would require a rather involved argument, and to avoid making too much of a digression here I have included this discussion in Appendix I to this book. For now however, we should note one significant manifestation of these forces: the large and powerful military industrial complex (MIC) that arose in the U.S. and NATO member states in the aftermath of World War II. MIC is an alliance of government, military, Wall Street banks and private, for-profit defense corporations. U.S. President Dwight Eisenhower singled out this association as one of the greatest threats to the nation's security and liberty. Today, more than half a century after his presidency, it is worth pondering the message of Eisenhower's January 1961 farewell address:

"... we have been compelled to create a permanent armaments industry of vast proportions. Added to this, three and a half million men and women are directly engaged in the defense establishment. We annually spend on military security more than the net income of all United States corporations.

This conjunction of an immense military establishment and a large arms industry is new in the American experience. The total influence – economic, political, even spiritual – is felt in every city, every Statehouse, every office of the Federal government. We recognize the imperative need for this development. Yet we must not fail to comprehend its grave implications. Our toil, resources and livelihood are all involved; so is the very structure of our society.

In the councils of government, we must guard against the acquisition of unwarranted influence, whether sought or unsought, by the military-industrial complex. The potential for the disastrous rise of misplaced power exists and will persist.

We must never let the weight of this combination endanger our liberties or democratic processes. We should take nothing for granted. Only an alert and knowledgeable citizenry can compel the proper meshing of the huge industrial and military machinery of defense with our peaceful methods and goals, so that security and liberty may prosper together."

Unfortunately, it seems that Eisenhower's words went unheeded and the disastrous rise of misplaced power has indeed come to displace the democratic processes and liberties in the United States and its allied nations. MIC has been able to metastasize through a constant arms buildup and frequent warfare. According to a J.P. Morgan study, *"shares in the major US arms manufacturers have risen 27,699% over the past fifty years versus 6,777% for the broader market."* [189]

---

[189] (Petras 2014)

The endless cast of enemies and threats

It is part of the general pattern of misguided policy that our country is now geared to an arms economy which was bred in an artificially induced psychosis of war hysteria and nurtured upon an incessant propaganda of fear.

General Douglas MacArthur in a 1951 speech

To continue to prosper the military-industrial complex and their financiers depended on a steady supply of enemies, existential threats and fear. During most of the second half of last century the designated enemy No. 1 has been the international Communism in general and Soviet Union in particular. Douglas MacEachin, director of CIA's Office of Soviet Analysis described in the 1980s the importance USSR's role as the America's enemy No. 1: "*The Soviet Union is so fundamental to our outlook on the world, to our concept of what is right and wrong in politics, to our sense of security, that major change in the USSR is as significant as some major change in the sociological fabric of the United States itself.*"

When the USSR finally collapsed, the American security designated international terrorism as the replacement enemy to justify further increases in military spending and a series of limited wars in the Middle East and parts of Africa. But as the American public grew weary of the multiple, never-ending, unwinnable terror wars in the Middle East, the emergent thinking among Western think tanks shifted in favor of a great war against a major power.

The RAND Corporation, an influential member of the military industrial complex, published a report in 2008 advocating war against a major power as a way to stimulate the U.S. economy.[190] The report did not specify the target, but at the time the main candidates were thought to be Iran, Russia, or China. Accordingly, the media and public relations industry close to the MIC launched a subtle marketing campaign to generate public consent for this new and improved idea.

---

[190] (Watson and Dai 2008)

In October 2010, Washington Post columnist David Broder wrote how a war (with Iran) would help solve the economic crisis in the U.S. In 2012, Council on Foreign Relations, another powerful pro-war think tank published an article by Matthew Kroenig, titled "Time to Attack Iran." [191] Plans to attack Iran seem to have been shelved for a time, but Russia has meanwhile graduated to the spot of the new greatest enemy and most existential threat to the United States. In April 2014, historian Ian Morris penned an article in Washington Post with the preposterous title, "In the long run, wars make us safer and richer." The article was featured on the Post's web site with a picture of a nuclear bomb blast with the caption, *"War is brutal. The alternative is worse."*[192]

Amazingly, Washington Post would have its readers believe that while going to war would be awful, *not* going to war would be even worse! Not to be outdone, the New York Times gave its own contribution to the worthy cause in June of that year, publishing Tyler Cowen's article, "The Lack of Major Wars May Be Hurting Economic Growth." Cowen strained to convince his readers that warfare isn't as bad as it used to be, including in his article a chart showing how much battle-related death rates have fallen since the 1950s:

---

[191] (Kroenig 2012)
[192] (Morris 2014)

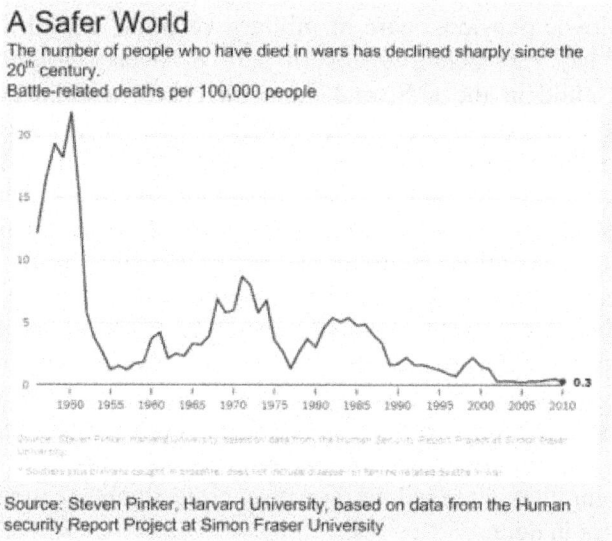

Source: Steven Pinker, Harvard University, based on data from the Human security Report Project at Simon Fraser University

As you can see, by 2010 battle related deaths – soldiers plus civilians caught in crossfire – fell to only three persons per million. These compelling figures prove that waging war is now safer than driving cars, giving birth or inhaling secondary smoke. Undeterred, Cowen carries on intellectualizing how, *"It may seem repugnant to find a positive side to war in this regard, but a look at American history suggests we cannot dismiss the idea so easily."* Yes, please let's not dismiss this splendid *idea* quite so easily.[193] George Orwell was certainly correct in pointing out that *"political speech and writing are largely the defense of the indefensible."*

Understanding why Western elites long for another World War is not complicated. The U.S. is the world's greatest debtor nation. Presently,[194] federal Government's debt is well over 100% of the gross domestic product (GDP) with additionally some $200 trillion in so-called unfunded

---

[193] What Cowen and his fellow war advocates fail to mention is that since "battle-related" death rates only count combatants and civilians caught in the cross fire, they do not include civilians killed under missiles and bombing raids, terror attacks, unexploded ordnance and land mines and indirect deaths from war's consequences like hunger, disease, homelessness, exposure, lack of clean water, lack of health care, etc. Cowen omits another fun fact about modern warfare: that civilian deaths constitute 85% to 90% of casualties of war with about 10 civilians dying for every combatant killed in battle. Cowen also forgets to mention the 110 million land mines planted in 70 countries since 1960… These continue to maim and kill for decades.

[194] Writing in mid-2017

liabilities. These liabilities are related to government's obligations like federal employee pensions, care of military veterans, Social Security and Medicare. They represent the absurd sum of over $640,000 per man, woman and child in the U.S. and more than $1.7 million per taxpayer. These obligations could never be honored even if the economy was registering solid growth. But since the 2008 financial crisis and the resulting economic recession, U.S. economic recovery has been the weakest on record in spite of unprecedented fiscal and monetary stimulation that has raised the total credit market debt to 360% of the GDP. These levels of debt have become an impediment to economic growth and made the nation vulnerable to grave social tensions on multiple fronts. Public and private pensions across the U.S. are severely underfunded and hundreds of thousands of retirees are already discovering that they need to continue working in order to sustain themselves in their "retirement" years. Meanwhile, the younger generations are facing a weak jobs market and those of them that attended universities collectively accumulated $1.4 trillion dollars in debt.

A major war would help the government paper over all these problems while preserving the established order of society. Your pension is gone? We're at war, we must share sacrifices. Your health care is unaffordable? Blame the Russians. There are no jobs? No worries, the military has plenty of opportunities if you aspire to become cannon fodder somewhere overseas. War would be the perfect smokescreen for the ruling establishment to usurp the mantle of patriotism, take the whole nation hostage, silence dissent, oppress all genuine political opposition and even do away with the Bill of Rights. It is therefore understandable why they have so much invested in fixating Russia as America's greatest enemy in the people's collective consciousness. If one day a nuclear bomb exploded over one of the U.S. cities, a frightened and misinformed population might be easily convinced that it was a Russian attack and rallied to support a major military escalation. This is why President Eisenhower underscored the importance of an alert and knowledgeable citizenry in preserving security and liberty.

Our American friends and partners

The issue which has swept down the centuries and which will have to be fought sooner or later is the people versus the banks.

Lord Acton (1834-1902)

Given the pervasive and deep-rooted hostility of the American establishment toward Russia and the role American advisors played during Russia's transition in the 1990s, it may seem odd that Vladimir Putin remained consistently open for friendly dialogue with his American counterparts, always referring to them as *our partners* and even *our American friends*. On important occasions, Putin backed his friendly disposition toward the U.S. with real action. As Soviet defector Lev Alburt wrote, *"Putin was the first to call Bush on September 11, and he offered what America needed: the Northern Alliance to help the US to defeat the Taliban and capture Bin Laden; transit for US and US-allied forces over Russian territory; Russian bases in Central Asia; intelligence; supplies; indeed everything America might need to fight terrorism. All of this and more Putin delivered, ignoring grumbling among his military and intelligence chiefs."* [195] Trusting in the commonality of Russian and American interests, Putin has indeed maintained this attitude even in the face of disapproval on the part of many Russians. One Russian diplomat told Lev Alburt that, *"In our government, there is only one man who still believes that Russo-American partnership is possible, and worth aiming for. Because that man is Vladimir Putin the rest of us follow."*

One possible reason why Vladimir Putin might believe in the commonality of U.S. and Russian interest is because he understood that the enemy that has had Russia in its crosshairs for over two centuries now, is the same system, or structure of power that has taken the American people and their government captive, squandering America's wealth and destroying her prosperity in their drive to build a global empire. This enemy is the global financial oligarchy that has been able to impose control over most nations of the world through their system of money and

---
[195] (Alburt 2015)

credit and their central banking franchise. In biblical times they might have been called *money-changers*. We culd also call them, *empire builders*.

Because their franchise is global and distributed across many nations and capitals, even when any given country managed to curtail their power, the money-changers always managed to burrow their way back, subverting their governments and reversing their independence. Perhaps the most epic political battle against the bankers was that waged by the U.S. President Andrew Jackson. In 1832, Jackson managed to rout out the bankers by vetoing the renewal of the 20-year charter of The Second Bank of the United States. In his veto, Jackson wrote that a bank that would control the nation's currency, receive its public moneys, and hold thousands of its citizens in dependence, *"would be more formidable and dangerous than a military power of the enemy."* At the end of his political career, Jackson thought that destroying the central bank was the single most important accomplishment of his presidency.

After Jackson's presidency, the United States prospered for nearly 80 years without a central bank. By 1913 however, the money changers established another central bank with a 100-year charter, the Federal Reserve System. This very same financial oligarchy that took control of the Bank of England and set up the Federal Reserve System in the U.S., has today spawned a global central banking franchise that controls most of the world's central banks. The ultimate owners of this system belong to the same dynastic oligarchy that has over the centuries supported multiple attacks on Russia, from Napoleonic Wars (1803-1815), Crimean War (1853-1856), the Bolshevik Coup (1917), Hitler's 1941 invasion, as well as the 1990s raid conducted under the guise of Shock Therapy transition.

I believe that Vladimir Putin has understood – he certainly is sophisticated enough a thinker – that he could not vanquish this global oligarchy by confronting them head-on and throwing them out of Russia. That would only set them back temporarily as they would use their system of money and credit to claw their way back into Russia's institutions and subvert her independence once more. Perhaps he has resolved instead to build bridges of understanding and cooperation with Russia's American friends and work together to rid both nations, and perhaps all of humanity, of the money changers for good. If this truly is Mr. Putin's game plan, and if he finds in the United States true partners and allies in this struggle, we may be so fortunate to witness a new U.S.-Russian alliance that could turn the tide of history away from the dystopian state of disenfranchisement, debt servitude and permanent war, toward a new era of peace, cooperation and prosperity.

The first U.S. – Russian alliance

The division of the United States into federations of equal force was decided long before the Civil War by the high financial powers of Europe. These bankers were afraid that the United States, if they remained in one block and as one nation, would attain economic and financial independence, which would upset their financial domination over the world. The voice of the Rothschilds prevailed... Therefore they sent their emissaries into the field to exploit the question of slavery and to open an abyss between the two sections of the Union.

Otto Von Bismarck (1815-1898)

I have two great enemies, the Southern army in front of me and the bankers in the rear. Of the two, the one at my rear is my greatest foe.

Abraham Lincoln

As a student, I spent three years of my life in the U.S., both in high school and university. I took several history classes, which included a whole semester of U.S. history. Through all the coursework, I have never heard or read anywhere that the U.S. ever had an alliance with Russia, other than during the World War II. I have only come across this forgotten bit of history through my research on matters related to banking and finance.

The United States and Russia began cultivating friendly relations from 1809 when U.S. President James Madison appointed John Quincy Adams, the eldest son of the second U.S. President John Adams, as U.S. Ambassador to the court of Russian Emperor Alexander I. During the six years of his Ambassadorship, John Quincy Adams recorded 33 encounters with the Emperor, many of them informal, through which they developed a cordial relationship of mutual respect.[196] This relationship helped foster positive relations between Russia and the U.S. over many decades. Historian Thomas Bailey wrote that, "*since 1809, the fixed policy of the Czar's government had been to encourage the growth of the United States as a potentially strong commercial and naval make weight against the foes of the Empire.*" [197] The two nations' friendship was solidified during the Crimean War (1853-1856) which broke out when France, Britain and the Ottoman Empire attacked Russia. The United States, its press and its public supported the Russian side, so much so that there was some likelihood that the U.S. would join the war on Russia's side. While that intervention did not happen, friendly relations between Russia and the United States remained the constant of both nations' respective foreign policies through most of the 19th century.

The British saw the rising power of the United States[198] as a potential threat to their control of the world's key naval trade routes. In the mid-19th century (1848-1863), the Empire was at its most aggressive in asserting its hegemony, waging major wars in China, India and Russia to preserve it. An important part of this project included also breaking the power of the United States by dividing the nation into two smaller states and turning them into vassals of the empire. The polarization between the predominantly agricultural economy of the Southern states and the more prosperous industrial economy of the North led to political disputes that gave the British the perfect opportunity to implement their favored *divide and rule* strategy of global conquest. France under Napoleon III actively supported the British agenda. By encouraging the Southern states to secede from the Union, Britain and France helped precipitate U.S. Civil War. They were on the verge of succeeding in their designs when Russia intervened on the side of the Union and played the decisive role in preserving it.

---

[196] (Claffey and Sikes 2008)
[197] (Tarpley, U.S. Civil War: The US-Russian Alliance that Saved the Union 2011)
[198] The rise of the United States was something of a historical wonder of that time; Russian Foreign Minister, Prince Gorchakov wrote in 1861 that the U.S. "*has exhibited to the world the spectacle of a prosperity without example in the annals of history.*"

WAR AND PEACE

Russian intervention in U.S. Civil War (1861-1865)[199]

My high school and university history classes left me with the impression that U.S. Civil War was fought over the issue of slavery: the "North" (good guys) was against slavery and wanted it abolished; the "South" (bad guys) wanted to keep the slaves, so they all went to war. Good guys won, bad guys lost, slaves got their freedom, and the world was made a better place. That, in a nutshell, is what I thought I knew about the Civil War. I'm not sure why I had that idea so, to make sure I wasn't mistaken I conducted an informal survey among my American friends and acquaintances, all university educated people, some of them with advanced degrees. I asked about a dozen of them what *they* thought U.S. Civil War was about. To a person, *all* of them unhesitatingly answered that it was about the abolition of slavery. Furthermore, none of them were aware that Russia played any role at all in the Civil War. It struck me that maybe my friends and I all had the same basic idea about that event because we were *meant* to have that idea, which is now pretty much part of the popular culture. However, the popular interpretation is oversimplified, omitting some critical aspects of history.

While slavery *was* one of Civil War's pivotal issues, the notion that the war was fought over slavery alone is simply wrong. The main issue on the opposing sides' agendas was the secession of the southern Confederacy vs. the preservation of the Union. The issue of slavery was a distant second on President Lincoln's agenda and he showed no intention to force the southern states to free their slaves. In his inaugural address he said: *"I have no purpose, directly or indirectly to interfere with the institution of slavery in the states where it now exists. I believe I have no lawful right to do so, and I have no inclination to do so."* Lincoln did not change his position even well into the war. In his August 22, 1862 letter to Horace Greely, he wrote, *"My paramount objective is to save the union, and it is not either to save or destroy slavery. If I could save the union without freeing any slave, I would do it."* [200]

Far from being a domestic affair about the human rights of slaves, the Civil War was a momentous geopolitical event with massive international implications. In his 1960 book "War for the Union," historian Allan Nevins wrote that, *"It is hardly too much to say that the future of the world as we know it was at stake. ... Anglo-French intervention in the*

---

[199] For my grossly condensed summary of this important historical event I am indebted to Dr. Webster Tarpley who, in addition to bringing this episode to public attention, also provides a thorough and invaluable review of numerous other historians' works on this subject.

[200] (S. Jones 2017)

American conflict would probably have confirmed the splitting and consequent weakening of the United States; might have given French power in Mexico a long lease, with the ruin of the Monroe Doctrine; and would perhaps have led to the Northern conquest of Canada. ... The popular conception of this contest is at some points erroneous, and at a few grossly fallacious..." [201]

Behind the veil of overt neutrality, British and French governments both worked to bring about the breakup of the Union, covertly siding with the Confederation. A powerful faction in the British cabinet, which included the Prime Minster Lord Palmerston, Chancellor of the Exchequer William Gladstone, and Foreign Minister Lord John Russell, strongly advocated British intervention on the side of the Confederation. However, for a variety of reasons, Britain had to be extremely cautious about taking any strong actions. For one thing, Britain was dependent on the U.S. and Russia for over 50% of all of her wheat imports. Any serious interruption to that trade risked bringing about famine and a social uprising at home. Another recurrent British worry was the risk that their troops might defect to the American side. After years of fighting multiple wars on three continents, the Empire already suffered a growing intervention fatigue. As a result, much of the British public and even Palmerston's War Minister George Lewis opposed the prospect of yet another military adventure.[202] While extensive plans were made for the Royal Navy to bomb and burn the cities of New York and Boston, help the Confederation break the Union's naval blockade, and even to foment a secession of Maine, war hawks in the British government needed a good pretext to overcome the dovish faction's opposition to war.

Illustration of the U.S. – Russian alliance published in the British magazine, "Punch." President Lincoln is portrayed as a troglodyte.

---

[201] (Tarpley, U.S. Civil War: The US-Russian Alliance that Saved the Union 2011)
[202] Idem

WAR AND PEACE

On October 23, 1862, Foreign Minister Lord Russell convened a cabinet meeting to discuss his plan of intervention between the Union and the Confederacy. France's Napoleon III offered his own support in carrying out this plan and even invited Russia's Czar Alexander II into the alliance. The idea was to pose an ultimatum to the warring sides to agree to an armistice, followed by a lifting of the Union's blockade of Confederacy's ports. The objective of Britain and France was to organize negotiations during which they would pressure Washington to accept Confederacy's secession and recognize its status as an independent nation. Washington's refusal would give Britain and France the needed justification to recognize the Confederacy's independence and provide it with military assistance against the North. On 29th October 1862, only six days after the British cabinet meeting, Russian Foreign Minister, Prince Gorchakov received Washington's envoy Bayard Taylor in a very cordial meeting. Gorchakov informed Taylor that France and Britain asked Russia to back their armistice ultimatum, assured him that Russia would *not* support their plan and that Washington could rely upon Russia's commitment. In the following days, *"Journal de St. Petersbourg,"* the official publication of Czar's government, published Russia's official position on the issue, denouncing the French-British plan against the U.S. In effect, Russia formally sided with Abraham Lincoln's government, opposing the British, French and the Vatican which also supported the Confederacy.

Meanwhile, on the American continent things were not going too well for Washington. In spite successful battlefield campaigns at Antietam and Gettysburg, the Confederacy proved very resilient and scored a major reverse against the Union at Chickamauga. By autumn of 1863 the Union had grown exhausted from warfare. Facing the widely expected French-British military intervention and persisting reports that the British were about to deliver critical armaments for the Confederacy to break the naval blockade, an ominous mood overcame the Union and the morale sank to its low point. At that juncture precisely, on September 24, 1863 Russian Imperial fleet arrived to New York while another contingent sailed to San Francisco. The fleet remained anchored at these two key port cities for over six months, through April 1864. On the 26th September 1863, the New York Times jubilantly wrote: *"The presence of a Russian fleet in the harbor of New York is welcomed by all persons with the greatest pleasure. Five splendid men-of-war, fully manned and in perfect trim, are now lying at anchor in the North River, in full view of our noble harbor..."* [203] Russian Admirals had been instructed that, should the U.S. and Russia

---

[203] (New York Times 1863)

find themselves at war against Britain or France, Russian fleet was to submit to President Lincoln's command to operate together with the U.S. Navy against their common enemies. This move by Czar Alexander II was the clearest possible signal to the British and the French to desist in their plans to intervene militarily in the American war.

God bless the Russians

A number of historians judged Russia's role in the preservation of the United States as decisive. Webster Tarpley stated that, "*During the American Civil War, the Russian attitude was the most powerful outside factor deterring Anglo-French interference.*" [204] American historian and Lincoln biographer Benjamin P. Thomas wrote that, "*in the first two years of the war, when its outcome was still highly uncertain, the attitude of Russia was a potent factor in preventing Great Britain and France from adopting a policy of aggressive intervention.*" [205] In his 1992 book "Union in Peril," American historian Howard Jones wrote that, "*Russia's pro-Union sentiment prevented participation in any policy alien to the Lincoln Administration's wishes.*" Philip Van Doren-Stern pointed out that, "*The Russian visit ... ended the last chance of European intervention. And it was now practically impossible for the South to be recognized as an independent nation...*" [206]

The arrival of the Russian fleet to New York and San Francisco "*unleashed an immense wave of euphoria in the North.*" [207] Shortly after their arrival, Russian sailors and officers were led in a parade down Broadway under American and Russian flags, cheered by thousands of New Yorkers. On November 5, a ball in the honor of the Russian guests was organized in New York at the Academy of Music. A Harper's Weekly reporter wrote that, "*the Russian guests from the fleet were worn out by the expressions of friendship and affection extended to them.*" [208] In a very overt display of appreciation for the Russian fleet's arrival, President Lincoln sent his wife to visit with the Russians in New York where she drank a toast to the Czar. The New York Herald pointed out that, "*Mrs. Lincoln knew what she was doing,*" as her action would generate, "*a hearty response throughout the country.*" [209] The New York Sun wrote

---

[204] (Tarpley, U.S. Civil War: The US-Russian Alliance that Saved the Union 2011)
[205] Idem
[206] Idem
[207] (Tarpley, U.S. Civil War: The US-Russian Alliance that Saved the Union 2011)
[208] (Delahaye 1983-1984)
[209] Idem

that Russia was, *"the only European power that has maintained a hearty sympathy with the United States during our present troubles."* [210]

Lincoln's Secretary of the Navy Gideon Welles wrote in his journal, *"In sending them [the fleet] to this country there is something significant. What will be its effect on France and the French policy we shall learn in due time. It may be moderate; it may exasperate. God bless the Russians."* Oliver Wendell Holmes, one of America's most popular authors at that time, wrote in 1871 the following tribute to Russia, referring to the Civil War episode: *"Thrilling and warm are the hearts that remember; Who was our friend when the world was our foe."*

But beyond the euphoria of the moment, Russian intervention of 1863 had long-lasting impact, further reinforcing the friendship between the two nations. Historian E.D. Adams spoke of the *"special relationship,"* and even *"extreme friendship"* between the U.S. and Russia, noting that in the North, Russia was widely regarded as a *"true friend"* in contrast to the resentment felt toward London and Paris and their *"unfriendly neutrality."* Another historian, Thomas Bailey wrote that the *"curious and incongruous friendship,"* between the U.S. and Russia had become *"an indestructible part of our folklore."*

---

[210] Idem

The bankers' revenge

For the first time in its history, Western Civilization is in danger of being destroyed internally by a corrupt, criminal ruling cabal which is centered around the Rockefeller interests, which include elements from the Morgan, Brown, Rothschild, Du Pont, Harriman, Kuhn-Loeb, and other groupings as well. This junta took control of the political, financial, and cultural life of America in the first two decades of the twentieth century.

Carroll Quigley, Tragedy and Hope

We are opposed around the world by a monolithic and ruthless conspiracy that relies primarily on covert means for expanding its sphere of influence — on infiltration instead of invasion, on subversion instead of elections, on intimidation instead of free choice, on guerrillas by night instead of armies by day

John F. Kennedy

It may seem strange from today's perspective that there ever was a time when friendship between Russia and the U.S. was a part of the American folklore but during most of the 19th century, that was the case. I find it curious that not only did this friendship give way to a persisting, and at times obsessive hostility, but that it has also almost completely faded from memory. How should we account for that? To venture an explanation, we have to return to the devious scheming of the money changers.

During the Civil War, the bankers were able to take advantage of the Union's dire financial straits to push through the National Banking Act of 1863. That act established the U.S. National Banking System, a form of central banking arrangement for the United States and the money changers' Trojan horse at the heart of the United States economic and political system. Abraham Lincoln resented the power of the bankers and would probably have used his authority to oppose them after his reelection and the conclusion of the Civil War. Just before the passage of the Act, in a letter to Wiliam Elkin, Lincoln wrote: *"I see in the near future a crisis approaching. It unnerves me and causes me to tremble for the safety of my country... The money power of the country will endeavor to prolong its reign by working upon the prejudices of the people, until the wealth is aggregated in a few hands and the Republic is destroyed."* [211] Lincoln's former Treasury Secretary, Salmon P. Chase expressed remorse about the passage of the National Banking Act, naming his agency's role in promoting it as, *"the greatest financial mistake in my life. It has built up a monopoly which affects every interest in the country."*

Unfortunately, Lincoln would never have a chance to push back against the bankers: almost as soon as the Civil War ended, a mercenary named John Wilkes Booth assassinated President Lincoln.[212] During his trial, some evidence emerged that Booth had been hired by, or on behalf of a group of international bankers. While that evidence had apparently been deleted from the public record,[213] the well-informed German Chancellor Otto Von Bismarck also cast the money changers as prime suspects in Lincoln's assassination: *"The death of Lincoln was a disaster for Christendom... I fear that foreign bankers with their craftiness and tortuous tricks will entirely control the exuberant riches of America and use it systematically to corrupt modern civilization. They will not hesitate to plunge the whole of Christendom into wars and chaos, in order that the earth should become their inheritance."*

Like many leading figures of that age, Von Bismarck understood the intrigues of the international bankers and was almost certainly correct in that assessment. Part of the bankers' "craftiness" involved financing the rise of a small group of oligarchs to control the key industries in the U.S. including petroleum, steel, transport, banking, and media. Oligarchs like J.P. Morgan, John Rockefeller, Henry Ford and Andrew Carnegie grew immensely rich and powerful. Just like the oligarchs in the 1990s Russia, these "robber barons" represented the interests of mostly European financiers who funded their ascent. However, securing control over America's key industries was only a part of their agenda. Beyond economic domination, they also sought to fashion the American society in ways that suited their long-term agenda. It is too far a digression for us to

---

[211] (Robinson 2009)
[212] Abraham Lincoln was assassinated on the 14th of April 1865, only five days after Confederation's army commander General Robert Lee surrendered to General Ulysses Grant.
[213] (S. Jones 2017)

discuss at length what that long-term agenda was, but I believe that the formulation presented by Carroll Quigley in his 1966 book "*Tragedy and Hope*," was spot on. Quigley wrote that the bankers' ultimate objective was, "*nothing less than to create a world system of financial control in private hands able to dominate the political system of each country and the economy of the world as a whole. This system was to be controlled in a feudalist fashion by the central banks of the world acting in concert, by secret agreements arrived at in frequent meetings and conferences.*" [214]

Scrubbing Russian-American friendship from history

To facilitate their long-term objectives, the money-changers sought to reform the American educational system, particularly the way U.S. history would be taught to future generations. This might seem like an outlandish conspiracy theory, but thanks to the investigations of the so-called Reece Committee, what we are about to explore is now a matter of record.[215]

In 1953, U.S. Congressman B. Carroll Reece set up the "Special Committee on Tax Exempt Foundations" which looked into the operations of various organizations like the Carnegie Endowment, Ford Foundation, Guggenheim Foundation and Rockefeller Foundation. The Committee's legal counsel René Wormser later wrote: "*It is difficult for the public to understand that some of the great foundations which have done so much for us in some fields have acted tragically against the public interest in others, but the facts are there for the unprejudiced to recognize.*" [216] In 1982, author and film maker G. Edward Griffin interviewed Norman Dodd who was Reece Committee's Director of Research. Dodd confirmed that his Committee's findings included "*the determination of these large endowed foundations, through their trustees, actually to get control over the content of American education.*" [217]

---

[214] (Quigley 1966)

[215] The U.S. Congress first investigated the large foundations in 1915 under the Commission on Industrial Relations. The Commission found that, "*The domination by the men in whose hands the final control of a large part of American industry rests ... is being rapidly extended to control the education and social survival of the nation. This control is being extended largely through the creation of enormous privately managed funds for indefinite purposes, hereafter designated "foundations", by the endowment of colleges and universities, by the creation of funds for the pensioning of teachers, by contributions to private charities, as well as through controlling or influencing the public press...*" (Taylor 2010)

[216] (Wormser 1958)

[217] (Griffin 1982)

During the course of his investigation, Dodd obtained access to the records of Carnegie Endowment from its inception in 1909. By examining the minute books of Endowment's deliberations, Dodd and his staff learned that the trustees of these foundations believed that the key to the success of their plans *"lay in the alteration of the teaching of American history."* In Norman Dodd's own words:

> *"They approach four of the then most prominent teachers of American History in the country -- people like Charles and Mary Byrd. Their suggestion to them is this, 'Will they alter the manner in which they present their subject' And they get turned down flatly. So they then decide that it is necessary for them to do as they say, i.e. 'build our own stable of historians.'*
>
> *Then, they approach the Guggenheim Foundation, which specializes in fellowships, and say, 'When we find young men in the process of studying for doctorates in the field of American History, and we feel that they are the right caliber, will you grant them fellowships on our say so?' And the answer is, 'Yes.' So, under that condition, eventually they assemble twenty (20), and they take these twenty potential teachers of American History to London.*
>
> *There, they are briefed in what is expected of them ... That group of twenty historians ultimately becomes the nucleus of the American Historical Association. And then, toward the end of the 1920's, the Endowment grants to the American Historical Association four hundred thousand dollars ($400,000) for a study of our history in a manner which points to what this country [should] look forward to, in the future."* [218]

It may seem odd that twenty young historians – designated future authorities on American history – should be sent to London to be instructed about *"what is expected of them."* We can better understand this in view of the fact that one of the main objectives of this oligarchic rewriting of history involved bringing about a rapprochement between Washington and London and scrubbing the 19-th century Russian-American friendship from memory and from scholastic curricula. The most influential of Carnegie Endowment's twenty hand-picked academics was J. Franklin Jameson, the domineering first President of the American Historical Association (AHA). Jameson made acquaintance with a Russian-speaking historian Frank A. Golder and commissioned him to go to St. Petersburg to conduct research in Russian archives and libraries. In

---

[218] Idem

1915, Golder published the article, *"The Russian Fleet and the Civil War"* in AHA's journal, *"American Historical Review."*

Golder put a dramatically different spin on the 1863 Russian intervention in the Civil War. Based on the premise that Alexander II sent his fleet to American ports in order to preserve them from a possible British attack, Golder went as far as suggesting that Russia deviously took advantage of her friendship with the U.S., and wrote that, *"Russia had not in mind to help us ... the United States was not conscious that it was contributing in any way to Russia's welfare and yet seems to have saved her from humiliation and perhaps war."* Contrary to Golder's intellectual innovation, historical record indicates that the friendship between the two nations was very real and deeply rooted in the public sentiment. Based on an extensive review of editorial articles written at the time, Thomas Bailey concluded that the most popular explanation for the Russian fleet's visit was, *"the one relating to friendship, alliance and succor..."* Bailey concludes that although other reasons for the visits were considered, it was the friendship-alliance hypothesis that took root. [219]

F. A. Golder's writing reveals just how vexed he and his sponsors were about this. He dismisses American friendship toward Russia as the consequence of Russia's clever cunning: *"The fact that this idea still has such strong hold on our country shows how skillfully the game was played."* Russia's game was in fact, so sly that Golder thought that *"there is probably nothing to compare with it in diplomatic history."*

The new-and-improved version of Civil War history had it that Russia never intended to help Lincoln preserve the Union against French and British conspiracy to break it apart. Rather, she craftily took advantage of the American friendship for her own welfare. The United States saved Russia from humiliation and even war, but since the Russians played their game with such masterful cunning, the Americans mistook their actions for genuine friendship. Thankfully, with the help of bought and paid for academics, America's oligarchs saved the nation from delusion.

Historian Howard Zinn cited George Orwell's words, *"Whoever controls the past controls the future,"* explaining that what Orwell meant was that, *"history is incredibly important in shaping the world view of the next generation of people."* Looking back over the century that lapsed since those events, we can start to discern why cultivating fear and loathing may have been expedient for the money changers. One of the most prominent ideologues of the American establishment Zbigniew Brzezinski formulated it as follows: *"As America becomes an increasingly multicultural society, it may find it more difficult to fashion a consensus*

---

[219] (Delahaye 1983-1984)

on foreign policy issues, except in the circumstances of a truly massive and widely perceived direct external threat." [220] As one of the world's most powerful nations, Russia was designated as that direct external threat that would make the American people consent to their economy becoming a permanent war economy and their military nearly permanently at war. This consensus on foreign policy has however been very unfortunate, both for the American and the Russian people.

Toward the new U.S. – Russian alliance

Since wars begin in the minds of men, it is in the minds of men that the defences of peace must be constructed

Archibald MacLeish

Enlighten the people generally, and tyranny and oppressions of body and mind will vanish like the evil spirits at the dawn of day.

Thomas Jefferson, letter to Pierre S. du Pont de Nemours

Perhaps more than at any point in history, the future of humanity lies in the hearts and minds of the people of the United States and the people of Russia. Do we dare imagine the world we could all build together if we rejected the needless fear and hostility? What might we achieve if we turned our talents and energies toward improving our world rather than producing arms of destruction? What if we chose beauty and harmony over power and dominance? Do we dare believe that it is our privilege to move humanity forward to a new, better, more gratifying ways of living?

Life is a magical gift and our present experience in the world of artificial scarcity and manufactured hostilities may not allow us even to fully envision what life could be like in its full splendor. Like people in a

---

[220] (Brzezinski 1997)

never-ending sandstorm, we cannot see the beauty that surrounds us, let alone enjoy it. Each and every one of us is vaguely aware that some important part of the human potential, perhaps something divine in us, remains unfulfilled yet eager for its own realization. The future is in our hands and we ought to strive to find and fulfill that potential. *That* is the struggle worth all of our earnest efforts, which must begin in mutual respect and friendship among nations and peoples so that we may begin to rediscover humanity for what it potentially is.

As utopian as these musings may sound, there can be little doubt that warfare wastes more than just economic resources. It also wastes human lives, it stunts and misdirects our creative energies and destroys the foundations on which we could build a far better future.

We have the choice and obligation not to leave our children the world in this state.

Vladimir Putin, I believe, understood these things perfectly well and I think this largely explains his unwavering disposition to engage with his American counterparts in a friendly and constructive dialogue. In order for us to avoid making a massive mess of things, it would be important for the American side to reject hysterical demonization shoved daily down their throats and to reciprocate Putin's disposition with friendship. As a human being and as a father, this is my fondest hope for the future. To begin with, this would be the first step to thaw the new cold war and prevent the hot one from erupting. Furthermore, in absence of hostility, the two powers could take steps to rid the world of nuclear weapons and end the senseless and costly global arms race. That would free up vast resources that could be allocated to building a future with far more prosperity and freedom than ever before.

I don't know whether we can attain utopia, but I do know that we don't have to destroy the world. Perhaps, just like in the 19th century, the future lies in the hands of the Russian and American people. In 1944, American mystic and reverend Edgar Cayce said that, *"In Russia there comes the hope of the world, not as that sometimes termed of the communistic, or Bolshevik, no; but freedom, freedom! That each man will live for his fellow man! The principle has been born. It will take years for it to be crystallised, but out of Russia comes again the hope of the world."* I believe that hope depends on what the world does with this hope.

But the most important struggle perhaps, is the struggle to engage the American people who I believe still hold the keys to the future of humanity. As Georg Friedrich Hegel prophesized, *"America is therefore the land of the future, where, in the ages that lie before us, the burden of the World's history shall reveal itself."*

Why I wrote this book

Bill Browder, a fellow hedge fund manager for whom I used to have hearty respect gave me a strong impression that he is a sinister conman. He wrote a book – a good book. But what of it? He would be neither the first nor the last conman to have done so, made outrageous false claims and lived happily ever after. For *garden variety* conmen I might have just tossed his book in the trash and contented myself to tell a few friends that I thought Browder was a lying liar and that his book is a self-aggrandizing con job. But something about this particular book prompted me to respond in a more thorough way precisely because I feel that Browder and his story hold a certain significance with regards to the question of war and peace that humanity might be facing in the near future. For one thing, Browder has devoted his life to demonizing Russia and Vladimir Putin and lobbying Western governments to toughen their hostile stances toward Russia to the detriment of both sides. He has been astonishingly prolific and successful in that campaign. In an interview in 2015, Browder has explicitly formulated his campaign's ultimate objectives: *"I think we are entering into a hot war right now, and that the best possible outcome is a*

Cold War."[221] I find it dismaying that a man who portrays himself as a human rights crusader could make such monstrously depraved statements.

In another display of that depravity, Browder used his book to announce to the world that if he should be killed in the future we must have no doubts that his killing was ordered by none other than Vladimir Putin: *"If I'm killed, you'll know who did it."*[222] I sincerely hope it doesn't come to that but if Mr. Browder truly does suddenly die in the near future I am virtually certain that his death will be exploited by all the usual suspects to blame Vladimir Putin or even to use Browder's death as *cause célèbre* for further escalation of hostilities with Russia. Browder reinforces the idea that Putin wants to have him killed when he writes, *"I am being pursued by the Russian secret police... The FSB doesn't just issue arrest warrants and extradition requests – it dispatches assassins."* But as I write these lines, it's been nearly 12 years since Browder had been expelled from Russia. During that time he's campaigned loudly and tirelessly against the country where he had made his killing and against President Putin whom he previously admired. If two process servers working for U.S. courts were able to approach Browder to serve him with subpoenas, a trained assassin could have done the same. If Vladimir Putin wanted Bill Browder assassinated, Mr. Browder could easily have been killed by now. The fact that the Russian state has filed three successive international arrest warrants for Bill Browder through the Interpol clearly shows their intent to pursue justice through legitimate legal channels.

At this time Browder is not yet a household name among the American or European people but I suspect that this might change if his plans to turn *"Red Notice"* into a Hollywood film come to fruition. In an interview with *"The Jewish Chronicle"* Browder said that, *"The most important next step in the campaign is to adapt the book into a Hollywood feature film... I have been approached by many film makers and spent part of the summer in LA meeting with screenwriters, producers and directors to figure out what the best constellation of players will be on this."*[223]

A Hollywood film about Bill Browder – if it turns out well produced and heavily promoted – could become a powerful propaganda tool in deceiving the unsuspecting Western public that Bill Browder is some sort of a hero human rights crusader and that Vladimir Putin is dr. Evil himself. Such a film could turn Browder into a household name and at that juncture his death *would* be very fortuitous for those elites in the West who long for a new war with Russia. Browder's death would suddenly give prominence

---

[221] (Ramani 2015)
[222] (Browder, Red Notice 2015)
[223] (Rashty 2015)

and credibility to his every utterance against Russia and against Vladimir Putin, particularly when he calls Putin "*a cold-blooded killer,*" and a "*criminal dictator who is not too different to Hitler, Mussolini or Gadaffi.*"[224]

All of this may sound far-fetched and incredible, but I have once lived through an outbreak of war. To the very last moments, most people in the former Yugoslavia thought that war was unthinkable and impossible. Its outbreak took nearly everyone by surprise, but once the war broke out it took a life of its own wreaking death and destruction on a large scale. People's psychology changed. It became fashionable to look at events in black and white and to wholly denounce the other side as enemies. Giving the enemy any benefit of the doubt and expressing empathy toward them suddenly became unpatriotic and suspicious. Mark Twain warned us long ago how the war psychology can creep into people's hearts and his words are worth pondering in full: "*The loud little handful--as usual--will shout for the war. The pulpit will--warily and cautiously--object--at first; the great, big, dull bulk of the nation will rub its sleepy eyes and try to make out why there should be a war, and will say, earnestly and indignantly, 'It is unjust and dishonorable, and there is no necessity for it.' Then the handful will shout louder. A few fair men on the other side will argue and reason against the war with speech and pen, and at first will have a hearing and be applauded; but it will not last long; those others will outshout them, and presently the anti-war audiences will thin out and lose popularity. Before long you will see this curious thing: the speakers stoned from the platform, and free speech strangled by hordes of furious men who in their secret hearts are still at one with those stoned speakers-- as earlier--but do not dare say so. And now the whole nation--pulpit and all--will take up the war-cry, and shout itself hoarse, and mob any honest man who ventures to open his mouth; and presently such mouths will cease to open. Next the statesmen will invent cheap lies, putting the blame upon the nation that is attacked, and every man will be glad of those conscience-soothing falsities, and will diligently study them, and refuse to examine any refutations of them; and thus he will by and by convince himself the war is just, and will thank God for the better sleep he enjoys after this process of grotesque self-deception.*"

The loud little handful in our midst is already shouting for war. But this time around our opposition must not be shy and deferential. It must be bold, determined and persistent. We would also do well to turn toward our Russian fellow men and women and tell them loud and clear that we want peace, not war. We must reach out to our soldiers and military

---

[224] Idem

commanders and ask them to refuse to fight, to refuse to launch bombs and missiles should such orders arrive. We must firmly put our thinking caps on and expect that the loud little handful might do devious things to get our consent for war. Such tricks are likely to include murdering prominent Putin critics and organizing false flag attacks to blame on Russia. We must start without delay to build the foundations for peace in our hearts and minds. There can be no justification for us to sleepwalk into another war. In addition to unprecedented scale of destruction and death, the economic, social and psychological damage from such a conflict would take many generations to repair. As I sit in my living room writing these words I can envision the two boys in the above photograph of World War II destruction being my own two sons. That photograph does not show the world I want them to inherit.

As a Croatian national, I have one more personal reason to publish this book: today, Croatia is regrettably a NATO member nation and I feel personally responsible for the fact that my grotesquely servile government has agreed to send a company of about 150 Croatian troops to the Russian border as part of a multinational battalion to serve under German command. Croatia has no quarrel with Russia – none that could come close to justifying a war. Our participation in the encirclement of Russia constitutes an irredeemable wrong and deserves a loud and unequivocal denunciation.

WAR AND PEACE

The best way to destroy an enemy is to make him a friend.

Abraham Lincoln

I envy you. You North Americans are very lucky. You are fighting the most important fight of all – you live in the belly of the beast

Ernesto "Che" Guevara

Thank you.
If you read my book through to the end, you have done me an honor and I thank you from the heart. I've put nearly three years of my life into writing it, working at night when I should have been sleeping because between a full time job and raising two small boys, that was the only time I could find peace to write.

At the end of this volume I will ask you for a small favor: if you enjoyed reading this book, please take a moment to give it an honest review on Amazon. For a self-published author, reader reviews are a valuable currency. Also, please recommend the book to your friends and acquaintances who might be open to seeing the US-Russia relationship from a different point of view. If you write, feel free to use any part of this book in your articles or blog posts. If we all apply ourselves to the cause of peace, we can make peace prevail.

Appendix I: Deflationary gap and the West's war addiction

To help answer the question of why one country has initiated more than 80% of wars over the past seventy years, I have reproduced here the article I posted on my blog, "*The Jubilee*" in 2011

Although I studied economics at the university, I don't recall coming across the subject of deflationary gap. The textbooks I still have don't mention it, and a search on the internet yielded close to nothing on the subject. Wikipedia doesn't even have an entry for deflationary gap. Answers.com provides a single vague sentence about it.

That's strange, for we're talking about a systemic flaw of the capitalist economic system that predictably corrodes the democratic framework of the society and leads to the rise of fascism and military conflagration. In his book "Tragedy and Hope," (by far the most fascinating history book I've ever read) Carrol Quigley devotes much space to deflationary gap as he meticulously traces the events leading to last century's two world wars. He considers the deflationary gap as "the key to twentieth century economic crisis and one of the three central cores of the whole tragedy of the twentieth century".

The subject of analysis is a closed economic system, in which the sum total of goods and services appearing in the market equals the income of the system and the aggregate cost of producing the goods and services. The sums expended by the businesses on wages, rents, salaries, raw materials, interest, lawyers' fees, and so on, represent income to those who receive them. The profits are entrepreneur's income and his incentive to produce the wealth in question. The goods are offered for sale at a price which is equal to the sum of all costs and profits. On the whole, aggregate costs, aggregate incomes and aggregate prices are the same, since they represent the opposite sides of the same expenditures.

However, the purchasing power available in the system is reduced by the amount of savings. If there are any savings, the available purchasing power will be less than the aggregate asking prices by the amount of the savings, and all the goods and services produced cannot be sold as long as savings are held back. In order for all the goods to be sold, savings must reappear in the market as purchasing power.

Normally, this is done through investment. But whenever investment is less than savings, purchasing power will fall short of the amount needed to buy the goods being offered. This shortfall of purchasing power in the system, the excess of savings over investment, is the deflationary gap.

Methods of bridging the deflationary gap

The deflationary gap can be closed either by lowering the supply of goods or by raising the supply of purchasing power, or by a combination of both methods. The first solution will stabilize the economic system on a low level of economic activity. The second will stabilize it on a high level of economic activity. Left to itself, a modern economic system would adopt the former alternative, resulting in a deflationary spiral: the deflationary gap would lead to falling prices, declining economic activity, rising unemployment, and a fall of national income. In turn, this would cause a decline in the volume of savings, until savings reached the level of investment, at which point the economy becomes stabilized at a low level of activity.

This process was not allowed to unfold in any industrialized country during the great depression of 1929-1934 because the disparity in the distribution of income between the rich and the poor was so great that it would cause a considerable portion of the population to be driven to absolute poverty before the savings of the richer segment of the population could decline to the level of investment. Moreover, as the depression deepened, the level of investment declined even more rapidly than the level of savings. To avert social uprisings, governments of all industrial nations attempted to generate a recovery through two kinds of measures: (a) those which destroy goods and (b) those which produce goods which do not enter the market.

Averting depression through destruction of goods

The destruction of goods will close the deflationary gap by reducing the supply of unsold goods. While this is not generally recognized, this method is one of the chief ways in which the gap is closed in a normal business cycle. In such a cycle, goods are destroyed by the simple expedient of underutilizing the system's production capacities. The failure to use the economic system at the 1929 level of output during the years 1930-1934 represented a loss of goods worth $100,000,000,000 in the United States, Britain, and Germany alone. This loss was equivalent to the destruction of such goods.

Destruction of goods by failure to gather the harvest because the selling price is too low is a common phenomenon under modern conditions, especially in respect to fruit and vegetable crops. While the outright destruction of goods already produced is not common, it has occurred in the depression years 1930-1934: stores of coffee, sugar, and bananas were destroyed, corn was ploughed under, and young livestock was slaughtered to reduce the supply on the market. The destruction of goods in warfare is another example of this method of overcoming deflationary conditions in the economic system.

Producing goods that don't enter the market

The second method of bridging the deflationary gap, by producing goods which do not enter the market, supplies purchasing power in the market (the costs of production of such goods enter the market as purchasing power), while the goods themselves do not drain funds from the system, as they are not offered for sale. New investment would be the natural means to accomplish this, but modern economic systems in depression do not function this way. Rather, private investment tends to decline considerably. Alternatively, purchasing power must be supplied to the system through government spending. Unfortunately, any program of public spending quickly leads to the problem of public debt and inflation, which tends to compound the problems rather than solving them.

War: the irresistible solution

Approaches to public spending as a method of financing an economic recovery can vary depending on its objectives. Spending for destruction of goods or for restriction of output, as under the early New Deal agricultural program is hard to implement in a democratic country, because it obviously results in a decline in national income and living standards. Spending for nonproductive monuments or prestige projects like space programs is somewhat easier to justify but is not a long-term solution. The best approach, obviously is investing in productive capital goods, since it leads to an increase in national wealth and standards of living and constitutes a long-run solution.

Unfortunately, this approach runs into ideological head-winds in modern economies as it constitutes a permanent departure from the system of private capitalism. As such, it is easily attacked in a country with a capitalistic ideology and a private banking system. Instead, developed nations tend to favor the most dangerous method of bridging the deflationary gap: spending on armaments and national defense.

The appeal of this method is always rooted in political and ideological grounds. Military spending tends to help heavy industry directly and immediately. Heavy industry, which absorbs manpower most readily (thus reducing unemployment), suffers earliest and most drastically in a depression. This tends to make it very influential in most countries.

DEFLATIONARY GAP AND WEST'S WAR ADDICTION

Defense-related spending is also easily justified to the public on grounds of national security.

But increasing defense spending enhances the political clout of the military-industrial complex and tends to increase a nation's reliance on the military in the conduct of its foreign policy and an escalation of conflict which leads to further increases in military spending. The vicious cycle ultimately results in the emergence of fascism: the adoption by the vested interests in a society of an authoritarian form of government in order to maintain their vested interests and prevent the reform of the society.

In the last century in Europe, the vested interests usually sought to prevent the reform of the economic system (a reform whose need was made evident by the long-drawn depression) by adopting an economic program whose chief element was the effort to fill the deflationary gap by rearmament. Quigley's analysis, based on the historical developments in the aftermath of the economic depression of the early 1930's closely parallels today's events.

The economic crises which germinated from the same systemic feature present in the modern economic system, followed a similar pattern in economic and political developments that we are witnessing today.

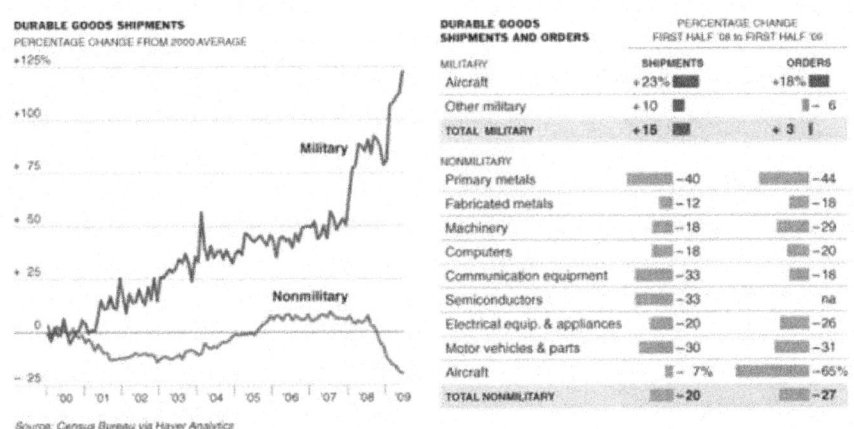

Figure 0-1: To avert a depression, US Government ramps up military spending

In the last century, we have seen these developments lead to two world wars, the second of which included the use of nuclear weapons. Today, as we seem to be heading in the same direction, the question is: do we even know how to arrest this escalation of armed conflicts? If the most trigger-happy actor in this drama is a nobel peace-prize laureate (sorry, I can't bring myself to capitalize "nobel peace prize"), I fear we have little grounds for optimism.

Nevertheless, if there should be any hope for humanity to avert further conflagration, a better informed, truthful debate just might lead the way to the needed economic and political reforms.

Appendix II: The top of the pyramid

One of the more interesting articles about Russia, that had been memory-holed is the following one, published in the Sunday Times in 2003, barely a week after the arrest of Mikhail Khodorkovsky. It represents a rare piece of evidence that Russia's young oligarch class of the 1990s were agents representing the interests of Western financiers. The article has been scrubbed from the internet.

Rothschild is the new power behind Yukos

Simon Bell in Moscow, Lucinda Kemeny and Andrew Porter
From The Sunday Times
November 2, 2003

A SENIOR MEMBER of the Rothschild banking family has emerged as the key figure in the battle for control of Yukos, the Russian oil giant.

The Sunday Times can identify **Lord (Jacob) Rothschild** as the secret holder of the large stake in Yukos that was previously controlled by **Mikhail Khodorkovsky**, the oil company's chairman.

Khodorkovsky, reputed to be Russia's richest man, was last week arrested by Russian prosecutors on charges of fraud and tax evasion. His imprisonment has triggered a trustee agreement he put in place with Rothschild a few months ago.

Rothschild, 67, now controls the voting rights on a stake in Yukos worth almost £8 billion. This places him at the centre of a dispute with the Russian state. It is widely believed that the charges being brought against Khodorkovsky are a response to his political ambitions to succeed **Vladimir Putin** as Russia's president.

Russian prosecutors tried to freeze a 44% stake in Yukos on Thursday. Their move highlighted the previously unknown arrangement that allowed voting rights to be transferred to an unnamed foreigner — Rothschild — should Khodorkovsky be unable to "act as a beneficiary" of the shares. It is thought that Khodorkovksy, 40, took this precaution when he realised he was facing arrest. The shares are held via the Gibraltar-based Menatep Group.

Khodorkovksy has known Rothschild for years through their mutual love of the arts and their support for Russian development via the Open Russia Foundation. Rothschild is a multi-millionaire in his own right, with a fortune estimated at £400m. He has not been involved with NM Rothschild, the City investment bank, since walking out during a furious row 22 years ago. Rothschild went on to build his own investment empire through firms such as RIT Capital Partners, St James's Place Capital and J Rothshild Assurance.

It is thought that Khodorkovsky could remain in prison until at least the end of the year. He is accused of illegally obtaining $1 billion through fraud and tax evasion. If convicted, he could face 10 years in jail.

The Yukos affair has provoked a crisis in Russia's fledgling capitalist system. Russian shares fell heavily last week and the value of Yukos slumped by a third as foreign investors fled the market. Khodorkovsy broke an agreement that Putin's government would not investigate the controversial circumstances in which the oligarchs made their money as long as they stayed out of politics. Instead, Khodorkovsky funded opposition parties.

Russia's economic revival has been soured in recent months by disputes over the ownership of leading companies. One of these involves a disputed 25% stake in Megafon, Russia's third-largest mobile-phone network operator, which was planning a flotation in London early next year. **Mikhail Fridman**, a Russian billionaire oil tycoon who has just com-pleted a $7 billion joint venture with BP, will this week step up his efforts to prevent IPOC, an obscure Bermudan investment company, blocking the flotation.

Fridman's Alfa Group bought a 25.1% stake in Megafon in August from LV Finance, a company registered in the British Virgin Islands. The transaction was made through a number of offshore companies set up by LV Finance and by Alfa.

IPOC, the investment company, says this deal should not have been allowed to take place since it had already paid the money needed to exercise an option over the same block of shares. IPOC already held a 6.5% stake in Megafon.

In the latest of a series of court hearings, IPOC will next week present its case in the British Virgin Islands. Fridman, through Alfa's telecoms subsidiary, will contest IPOC's claims. He will argue that IPOC has presented itself as an independent company with some western interests that invests in publicly quoted vehicles. But Fridman will say its only major stake is in Megafon and, rather than being backed by western investors, it is a vehicle for unnamed Russian interests.

Other shareholders in Megafon include TeliaSonera, the Scandinavian telecoms group with a 44% stake, and Telecominvest, one of the founders of Megafon set up with the help of **Leonid Reiman**, Russia's minister for telecommunications.

Separately, this week there are plans for the listing of Irkut, one of Russia's largest manufacturers of military aircraft, on the London Stock Exchange.

Source: http://business.timesonline.co.uk/tol/business/article1101531.ece

Bibliography

Alburt, Lev. "Vladimir Putin, America's Reluctant Foe." *Chess-News*. 22 June 2015. http://chess-news.ru/en/node/19343 (accessed June 26, 2017).
Boris Yeltsin - the Formation of a Leader. Directed by Alante Alfandari and Daniel Leconte. 2001.
Armstrong, Martin. "So who really tried to blackmail Yeltsin & takeover Russia - NSA-CIA-or investment bankers?" *Armstrong Economics*. 12 July 2013. https://www.armstrongeconomics.com/uncategorized/so-who-really-tried-to-blackmail-yeltsin-takeover-russia-nsa-cia-or-investment-bankers/ (accessed April 12, 2017).
Ash, Timothy Garton. "Putin must be stopped. And sometimes only guns can stop guns." *The Guardian*. 1 February 2015. https://www.theguardian.com/commentisfree/2015/feb/01/putin-stopped-ukraine-military-support-russian-propaganda (accessed April 11, 2017).
Aslund et al., Anders. "An Open Letter to the Heads of State and Government." 28 September 2004. http://www.journalofdemocracy.org/articles-files/gratis/Documents-Open-Letter-16-1.pdf (accessed June 20, 2017).
Atkisson, Rodney. "Putin and Russia: Decent Man, Reformed Country." *Free Nations*. 31 May 2016. http://freenations.net/putin-russia-decent-man-reformed-country/ (accessed March 18, 2017).
Austin Fitts, Catherine. "Letter to Editor of Boston Globe Re: Harvard." *The Solari Report*. 22 April 2002. https://solari.com/blog/letter-to-editor-of-the-boston-globe-re-harvard/ (accessed December 30, 2016).
Bauman, Rachel. "What Really Killed Sergei Magnitsky?" *The National Interest*. 16 June 2016. http://nationalinterest.org/feature/what-really-killed-sergei-magnitsky-16612?page=show (accessed May 29, 2017).
BloombergBusinessWeek. *Table: Boris Jordan: The Buying and Selling of Russia*. 30 April 2001. https://www.bloomberg.com/news/articles/2001-04-29/table-boris-jordan-the-buying-and-selling-of-russia (accessed May 20, 2017).
Black October '93: Tanks in Moscow, Blood on Streets. Directed by Pavel Bodykov. 2013.
Broder, David S. "How Obama Might Recover." *Washington Post*. 31 October 2010. http://www.washingtonpost.com/wp-dyn/content/article/2010/10/29/AR2010102905810.html (accessed June 2017, 2017).
Browder, Bill. *Red Notice*. London: Transworld Publishers, 2015.
Browder, Bill. *The Hermitage Case: Organized Crime and Legal Nihilism Inside the Russian Government*. Private document briefing, London: Hermitage Capital Management, 2009.
Brown, Catherine. *Deconstructing Russophobia*. 16 June 2016. https://off-guardian.org/2016/06/16/deconstructing-russophobia/ (accessed January 13, 22017).

BIBLIOGRAPHY

—. "Deconstructing Russophobia." *Off Guardian.* 16 June 2016. https://off-guardian.org/2016/06/16/deconstructing-russophobia/ (accessed April 21, 2017).

Brzezinski, Zbigniew. *The Grand Chessboard: American Primacy and its Geostrategic Imperatives.* New York: Basic Books, 1997.

Campbell, Mary. "Q&A: Hermitage Capital Management Founder Takes On Russia's Putin." *FinAlternatives.* 29 May 2013. http://www.finalternatives.com/node/23784 (accessed May 31, 2017).

Carden, James. "By Screening 'The Magnitsk Act,' the Newseum Stood Up for the First Amendment." *The Nation.* 20 June 2016. https://www.thenation.com/article/by-screening-the-magnitsky-act-the-newseum-stood-up-for-the-first-amendment/ (accessed May 29, 2017).

Chossudovsky, Michel. "KNOW THE FACTS: North Korea lost close to 30% of its population as a result of US bombings in the 1950s." *Global Research.ca.* 27 November 2010. http://www.globalresearch.ca/know-the-facts-north-korea-lost-close-to-30-of-its-population-as-a-result-of-us-bombings-in-the-1950s/22131 (accessed March 17, 2017).

Claffey, Mary, and Sara Sikes. "The First Ambassador: John Quincy Adams in St. Petersburg, 1809-1815." *Russian Life.* September/October 2008. http://www.russianlife.com/pdf/adamsinrussia.pdf (accessed July 12, 2017).

Cloughley, Brian. "Make No Mistake: Russia Remains the Only Target Country of NATO's Nuclear Weapons." *Strategic Culture Foundation.* 5 December 2016. https://www.strategic-culture.org/news/2016/12/05/make-no-mistake-russia-remains-only-target-country-nato-nuclear-weapons.html (accessed June 18, 2017).

—. "The Beneficiaries of Conflict With Russia." *CounterPunch.org.* 31 March 2017. http://www.counterpunch.org/2017/03/31/the-beneficiaries-of-conflict-with-russia/ (accessed June 17, 2017).

Cottrell, Robert. "Russia: Was There a Better Way?" *The New York Review of Books*, 4 October 2001: Volume 4, Number 15.

Cowen, Tyler. "The Lack of Major Wars May Be Hurting Economic Growth." *New York Times.* 14 June 2014. https://www.nytimes.com/2014/06/14/upshot/the-lack-of-major-wars-may-be-hurting-economic-growth.html?_r=1 (accessed June 23, 2017).

Delahaye, Tom. "The Bilateral Effect of the Visit of the Russian Fleet in 1863." *Loyola University Student Historical Journal.* 1983-1984. http://www.loyno.edu/~history/journal/1983-4/delehaye.htm (accessed July 12, 2017).

Djurdjevic, Bob Altzar. "Russia's privatization: a financial crime of the century?" *Truth in Media.* 14 March 1998. http://www.truthinmedia.org/Bulletins/tim98-3-8.html (accessed February 8, 2017).

Doctorow, Gilbert. "Agent William F. Browder: the Smoking Gun." *Russia Insider.* 13 April 2016. http://russia-insider.com/en/politics/agent-william-f-browder-smoking-gun/ri13858 (accessed April 20, 2016).

Dunkerley, William. "Operation Beluga: A US-UK Plot to Discredit Putin and Destabilize the Russian Federation." *OpEd News.* 27 March 2016. https://www.opednews.com/populum/page.php?f=Operation-Beluga-A-US-UK-

BIBLIOGRAPHY

by-William-Dunkerley-Antiterrorism-Database_France_Litvinenko_Putin-160327-385.html (accessed May 26, 2017).

Durden, Tyler. "Europe Has A Modest Proposal For Greece: "Don't Pay Wages For One Or Two Months"." *ZeroHedge.* 13 March 2015. http://www.zerohedge.com/news/2015-03-13/europe-has-modest-proposal-greece-dont-pay-wages-one-or-two-months (accessed March 22, 2017).

Eisenstein, Charles. *Sacred Economics: Money, Gift, and Society in the Age of Transition.* Berkeley: North Atlantic Books, 2011.

Engdahl, William F. "How 'shock therapy' has ruined Russia." *Executive Intelligence Review.* 14 May 1993. http://www.larouchepub.com/eiw/public/1993/eirv20n19-19930514/eirv20n19-19930514_006-how_shock_therapy_has_ruined_rus.pdf (accessed November 8, 2016).

—. "Reply to a Reader's Complaint about Anti-American Pro-Russian Bias." *New Eastern Outlook.* 30 April 2015. http://journal-neo.org/2015/04/30/reply-to-a-reader-s-complaint-about-anti-american-pro-russian-bias/ (accessed 12 30, 2016).

—. "Russia's Remarkable Renaissance." *New Eastern Outlook.* 9 March 2015. http://journal-neo.org/2015/03/09/russia-s-remarkable-renaissance-2/ (accessed August 16, 2016).

—. "What if Putin is Telling the Truth?" *New Eastern Outlook.* 15 May 2015. http://journal-neo.org/2015/05/15/what-if-putin-is-telling-the-truth/ (accessed March 4, 2017).

Expat, SF. "Russia Has Shot From 124th to 40th in 'Ease of Doing Business'." *Russia Insider.* 27 October 2016. http://russia-insider.com/en/business/central-bank-sees-russias-moving-doing-business-rating-good-sign/ri17246 (accessed March 18, 2017).

Fedorov, Boris. "Reform of the Soviet Banking System." *Communist Economies journal*, 1989, vol. 1, no. 4: 455-461.

Friedman, Robert. "The Money Plane." *New York Magazine*, 22 January 1996: 24-33.

Gerber, Theodore P., and Michael Hout. "More Shock Than Therapy: Market Transition, Employment and Income in Russia." *American Journal of Sociology*, 1998: Vol. 104.

Glinski, Dmitri, and Peter Reddaway. *The Tragedy of Russia's Reforms: Market Bolshevism Against Democracy.* United States Institute of Peace Press, 2001.

Goldman, Marshall I. "Putin and the Oligarchs." *Council on Foreign Relations.* November/December 2014. http://www.cfr.org/world/putin-oligarchs/p8018 (accessed 12 10, 2016).

Goodman, Melvin. "David Ignatius, the CIA's Apologist-in-Chief." *CounterPunch.* 27 January 2017. http://www.counterpunch.org/2017/01/27/david-ignatius-the-cias-apologist-in-chief/ (accessed January 27, 2017).

"Gorbachev: Putin saved Russia from disintegration." *RT.com.* 27 December 2014. http://rt.com/news/217931-gorbachev-putin-saved-russia/ (accessed March 6, 2017).

Grenier, Paul R. "Distorting Putin's Favorite Philosophers." *Consortium News.* 27 March 2015. https://consortiumnews.com/2015/03/27/distorting-putins-favorite-philosophers/ (accessed April 2, 2017).

BIBLIOGRAPHY

Griffin, G. Edward. "Transcript of Norman Dodd Interview." *SupremeLaw.org.* 1982. http://www.supremelaw.org/authors/dodd/interview.htm (accessed July 18, 2017).

Harding, Luke. "Bill Browder: the Kremlin threatened to kill me." *The Guardian.* 25 January 2015. https://www.theguardian.com/world/2015/jan/25/-sp-bill-browder-kremlin-threatened-to-kill-me-vladimir-putin (accessed April 25, 2017).

Harding, Luke, Sean Smith, and Phil Maynard. "Sergei Pugachev Putin's former banker in exile - video interview." *The Guardian.* 28 July 2015. (accessed September 10, 2015).

Helmer, John. "THE THINK-TANK THAT BLASTS FROM THE PAST – THE CASE OF CASE, CRONIES AGAINST SELF-SACRIFICE IN EUROPE." *Dances With Bears.* 2 February 2015. http://johnhelmer.net/the-think-tank-that-blasts-from-the-past-the-case-of-case-cronies-against-self-sacrifice-in-europe/ (accessed June 14, 2017).

Hiatt, Fred. "After the fall of the Soviet Union, the U.S. tried to help Russians." *The Washington Post*, 4 May 2015: Editorial Board.

Hlavaty, Craig. "When Boris Yeltsin went grocery shopping in Clear Lake." *Chron.com.* 7 April 2014. http://blog.chron.com/thetexican/2014/04/when-boris-yeltsin-went-grocery-shopping-in-clear-lake/ (accessed December 19, 2016).

Hofheinz, Paul. "Let's do Business." *Fortune*, 23 September 1991.

Hollingsworth, Mark, and Michael Bow. "Accused turns accuser against Bill Browder's claims of corruption." *The Independent.* 9 December 2015. http://www.independent.co.uk/news/business/analysis-and-features/accused-turns-accuser-against-bill-browder-s-claims-of-corruption-a6767376.html (accessed May 31, 2017).

Holodny, Elena. "Putin Describes the Meaning of Life." *Business Insider.* 7 November 2014. http://www.businessinsider.com/putin-meaning-life-love-2014-11 (accessed April 2, 2017).

Hudson, Michael. *Dr. Michael Hudson's Testimony Before the Russian Parliament.* 15 March 1999. http://michael-hudson.com/1999/03/dr-michael-hudson-testimony-before-the-russian-parliament/ (accessed December 12, 2016).

Ignatius, David. "Innocence Abroad: the New World of Spyless Coups." *Washington Post.* 22 September 1991. https://www.washingtonpost.com/archive/opinions/1991/09/22/innocence-abroad-the-new-world-of-spyless-coups/92bb989a-de6e-4bb8-99b9-462c76b59a16/?utm_term=.0e91fe06d01a (accessed November 30, 2016).

Jeffreys-Jones, Rhodri. "Decades of failures: Why the CIA keeps blowing it." *Salon.com.* 24 August 2013. <http://www.salon.com/2013/08/24/decades_of_failures_why_the_cia_keeps_blowing_it/ (accessed 11 24, 2016).

Jones, Jeffrey M. "Americans Increasingly See Russia as Threat, Top U.S. Enemy." *Gallup.com.* 16 February 2015. http://www.gallup.com/poll/181568/americans-increasingly-russia-threat-top-enemy.aspx (accessed June 22, 2017).

Jones, Stack. "An Essay On The History Of Banking." *The Banking Swindle.* 1 April 2017. https://criminalbankingmonopoly.wordpress.com/2017/04/01/essay-on-banking/ (accessed July 12, 2017).

Klein, Naomi. *The Shock Doctrine - the Rise of Disaster Capitalism.* Picador, 2007.

BIBLIOGRAPHY

Komisar, Lucy. "Institute for Advanced Study in Princeton bans Lucy Komisar from Wm Browder speech." *The Komisar Scoop.* 2 December 2016. http://www.thekomisarscoop.com/2016/12/institute-for-advanced-studies-in-princeton-bans-lucy-komisar-from-wm-browder-speech/ (accessed May 28, 2017).

—. "NY Review of Books reports this comment, but won't print it." *The Komisar Scoop.* 15 January 2015. http://www.thekomisarscoop.com/2015/01/ny-review-of-books-reports-this-comment-but-wont-print-it/ (accessed May 24, 2017).

—. "Russian Sanctions Highlight Role of Western Enablers." *100 Reporters.* 21 May 2014. https://100r.org/2014/05/russian-sanctions-highlight-role-of-western-enablers/ (accessed May 23, 2017).

Kouprianova, Nina. *Glamorizing Catastrophe.* 24 November 2015. https://souloftheeast.org/2015/11/24/glamorizing-catastrophe/ (accessed January 13, 2017).

Kramer, Michael. "Rescuing Boris." *Time.com.* 15 July 1996. http://content.time.com/time/magazine/article/0,9171,984833,00.html (accessed January 5, 2017).

Krieger, Michael. "Meet the 77th Battalion – The British Army is Mobilizing 1,500 "Facebook Warriors" to Spread Disinformation." *LibertyBlitzKrieg.* 2 February 2015. https://libertyblitzkrieg.com/2015/02/02/meet-the-77th-battalion-the-british-army-is-mobilizing-1500-facebook-warriors-to-spread-disinformation/ (accessed April 11, 2017).

Kroenig, Michael. "Time to Attack Iran: Why a Strike Is the Least Bad Option." *Foreign Affairs.* 1 January 2012. https://www.foreignaffairs.com/articles/middle-east/2012-01-01/time-attack-iran (accessed June 23, 2017).

Landler, Mark. "Film About Russian Lawyer's Death Creates an Uproar." *New York Times.* 9 June 2016. http://www.nytimes.com/2016/06/10/world/europe/sergei-magnitsky-russia-vladimir-putin.html?_r=1 (accessed June 1, 2017).

Likoudis, Paul. "The Plunder of Russia in the 1990s." *The Happy Wanderer.* 24 March 2011. https://paullikoudis.wordpress.com/2011/03/24/the-plunder-of-russia-in-the-1990s/ (accessed January 18, 2017).

Lindgren, Dan Joseffson and Stefan. "Shock Therapy: The Art of Ruining a Country." *Josefsson.net.* 1 April 1999. http://josefsson.net/artikelarkiv/51-shock-therapy-the-art-of-ruining-a-country.html (accessed November 13, 2016).

Louis, Federal Reserve Bank of St. "M3 for the United States." *FRED - Federal Reserve Economic Data.* n.d. https://fred.stlouisfed.org/series/MABMM301USM189S .

Lundberg, Kirsten. "CIA.gov." *CIA and the Fall of the Soviet Empire: the Politics of "Getting it Right".* 1 June 1995. https://www.cia.gov/library/readingroom/docs/19950601.pdf (accessed 11 20, 2016).

MacDonald, Bryan. *RT.com.* 30 July 2015. https://www.rt.com/op-edge/311174-media-russia-putin-pugachev/ (accessed January 13, 2017).

McClintick, David. "How Harvard lost Russia." *Institutional Investor*, 27 February 2006.

BIBLIOGRAPHY

Mercouris, Alexander. "The Magnitsky Case - A Trial At Last?" *Russia Insider.* 20 January 2016. http://russia-insider.com/en/society/magnitsky-case-trial-last/ri12298 (accessed April 25, 2017).

Miller, Merlin. "A New Russian Revolution; Merlin Miller Visits Mother Russia." *American Free Press.* 12 July 2015. http://americanfreepress.net/a-new-russian-revolution-merlin-miller-visits-mother-russia/ (accessed March 15, 2017).

Morris, Ian. "In the long run, wars make us safer and richer." *Washington Post.* 25 April 2014. https://www.washingtonpost.com/opinions/in-the-long-run-wars-make-us-safer-and-richer/2014/04/25/a4207660-c965-11e3-a75e-463587891b57_story.html?utm_term=.85e779cc1216 (accessed June 23, 2017).

Motlagh, Jason. "Fighting Putin Doesn't Make You a Saint." *New Republic.* 31 December 2015. https://newrepublic.com/article/126760/fighting-putin-doesnt-make-saint (accessed April 2017, 2017).

Secret Government: the Constitution in Crisis. Directed by Bill Moyers. 1987.

Murray, Craig. "The Surveillance State Should Be Targeted on Cows." *Craig Murray.* 18 April 2016. https://www.craigmurray.org.uk/archives/2016/04/the-surveillance-state-should-be-targeted-on-cows/ (accessed May 30, 2017).

New York Times. "OUR NAVAL VISITORS.; THE RUSSIAN FLEET IN THE HARBOR. SKETCHES OF THE VESSELS, OFFICERS, ETC." *New York Times.* 26 September 1863. http://www.nytimes.com/1863/09/26/news/our-naval-visitors-russian-fleet-harbor-sketches-vessels-officers-etc.html?pagewanted=all (accessed July 14, 2017).

Osipovich, Alexander. "William Browder's war." *Institutional Investor's Alpha.* 9 December 2011. http://www.institutionalinvestorsalpha.com/Article/2945489/Operations-Administration/William-Browders-war.html (accessed May 31, 2017).

Pace, Eric. "William Casey, ex-C.I.A. head, is dead at 74." *New York Times*, 7 May 1987: Obituaries.

Pace, Julie. "8 years after hope and change, voters are angry, anxious." *AP News.* 18 July 2016. https://apnews.com/f832c94c7c2c431380839d1f21a7d9c3 (accessed April 21, 2017).

"Perverted history: Europeans think US army liberated continent during WW2." *RT.* 28 April 2015. http://rt.com/news/253753-europeans-wwii-victory-poll/ (accessed June 29, 2017).

Petras, James. "The Soaring Profits of the Military-Industrial Complex, The Soaring Costs of Military Casualties." *Global Research.* 24 June 2014. http://www.globalresearch.ca/the-soaring-profits-of-the-military-industrial-complex-the-soaring-costs-of-military-casualties/5388393 (accessed June 27, 2017).

Popov, Yevgeniy. "Операция "Дрожь": тайная переписка агента Навального." *Последние Новости (YouTube channel).* 10 April 2016. https://www.youtube.com/watch?v=Pjv48NPdst4 (accessed December 18, 2016).

Quigley, Carroll. *Tragedy and Hope: A History of The World in Our Time.* New York: MacMillan, 1966.

Ramani, Samuel. "Interview With Prominent Putin Critic Bill Browder, CEO of Hermitage Capital Management." *HuffPost.* 5 March 2015.

BIBLIOGRAPHY

http://www.huffingtonpost.com/samuel-ramani/interview-with-bill-browder_b_6849828.html (accessed May 31, 2017).

Rashty, Sandy. "Be careful of Putin, he is a true enemy of Jews." *The Jewish Chronicle.* 5 November 2015. https://www.thejc.com/culture/books/be-careful-of-putin-he-is-a-true-enemy-of-jews-1.61745 (accessed April 12, 2017).

Richter, Greg. "Bill Clinton: Putin 'Kept His Word' in Deals." *NewsMax.* 25 September 2013. http://www.newsmax.com/Newsfront/clinton-putin-kept-word/2013/09/25/id/527736/ (accessed March 30, 2017).

Robinson, Jerry. *Bankruptcy of Our Nation.* Green Forrest: New Leaf Press, 2009.

Romer, Paul R. et al. "Doing Business." *Doing Business 2017.* 25 October 2016. http://www.doingbusiness.org/reports/global-reports/doing-business-2017 (accessed March 18, 2017).

Russian Mafia. *Boris Jordan.* n.d. http://www.rumafia.net/en/dosje/401-boris-yordan.html (accessed 05 20, 2017).

Sachs, Jeffrey. "What I did in Russia." *JeffSachs.org.* 14 March 2012. http://jeffsachs.org/2012/03/what-i-did-in-russia/ (accessed November 13, 2016).

Sailer, Steve. "The Rape of Russia explained by Anne Williamson." *Steve Sailer: iSteve.* 2014 February 2014. http://isteve.blogspot.com/2014/02/the-rape-of-russia-explained-by-anne.html (accessed December 4, 2016).

Satter, David. *Boris Yeltsin.* 24 April 2007. http://www.wsj.com/articles/SB117737318737979751 (accessed January 13, 2017).

Schumer, Charles E. "The Money Plane." *Congressional Record Volume 142, Number 19 - Tuesday, 13 February 1996.* Washington D.C.: Government Publishing Office, 1996. E196-E197.

Shuster, Simon, and Carlos H. Martinelli. "What it's like to grow up under Putin in Chechnya." *Time.* 22 Jun 2015. (accessed March 21, 2017).

Simes, Dimitri K. "Losing Russia: the Cost of Renewed Confrontation." *Foreign Affairs.* November/December 2007. https://www.foreignaffairs.com/articles/russia-fsu/2007-11-01/losing-russia (accessed January 5, 2017).

Sputnik. "US Federal Appeals Court Suspends First Lawsuit Filed Under Magnitsky Act." *SputnikNews.com.* 26 January 2016. https://sputniknews.com/us/201601261033706366-magnitsky-act-us-lawsuit/ (accessed April 25, 2017).

Sterling, Rich. "Gorbachev Warns of Growing Danger." *Consortiumnews.com.* 17 May 2017. https://consortiumnews.com/2017/05/15/gorbachev-warns-of-growing-danger/ (accessed May 29, 2017).

Stooge, Kremlin. *Sergei Magnitsky, Bill Browder, Hermitage Capital Management and Wondrous Metamorphoses.* 19 January 2011. https://marknesop.wordpress.com/2011/01/19/sergei-magnitsky-bill-browder-hermitage-capital-management-and-wondrous-metamorphoses/ (accessed May 15, 2017).

Streeto, Mike. "From Russia With Money." *The Independent.* 23 08 1997. (accessed 12 10, 2016).

BIBLIOGRAPHY

Stulb, David L. et al. "Corporate Misconduct - Individual Consequences." *EY.* 2016. http://www.ey.com/Publication/vwLUAssets/EY-corporate-misconduct-individual-consequences/%24FILE/EY-corporate-misconduct-individual-consequences.pdf (accessed March 18, 2017).

Taibbi, Matt. "USAID: Jerks, Perks and Propaganda." *JanineWedel.info.* 4 June 1997. http://janinewedel.info/harvardinvestigative_exile.html (accessed 12 10, 2016).

Talbott, Strobe, and Steven Pifer. "Ukraine needs America's help." *Washington Post.* 29 January 2015. https://www.washingtonpost.com/opinions/ukraine-needs-more-help-from-the-west/2015/01/29/462b1ea4-a71b-11e4-a7c2-03d37af98440_story.html?utm_term=.353813432942 (accessed April 11, 2017).

Tarpley, Webster G. "American Banker Wharton Barker's First-Person Account Confirms: Russian Tsar Alexander II Was Ready for War with Britain and France in 1862-1863 to Defendn Lincoln and the Union - Americans "Will Understand"." *Tarpley.net.* 23 September 2013. http://tarpley.net/2013/09/23/american-banker-wharton-barkers-first-person-account-confirms-russian-tsar-alexander-ii-was-ready-for-war-with-britain-and-france-in-1862-1863-to-defend-lincoln-and-the-union-americans-will-und/ (accessed July 12, 2017).

—. "U.S. Civil War: The US-Russian Alliance that Saved the Union." *VoltaireNet.org.* 25 April 2011. http://www.voltairenet.org/article169488.html (accessed July 12, 2017).

Taylor, Daniel. "Tax Exempt Foundations and Think Tanks: The Process of Invisible Power." *Old-Thinker News.* 11 December 2010. http://www.oldthinkernews.com/2010/12/11/tax-exempt-foundations-and-think-tanks-the-process-of-invisible-power/ (accessed July 19, 2017).

Tennison, Sharon. "Putin, by Sharon Tennison." *The Vineyard Saker in Oceania.* 14 September 2014. http://www.vineyardsaker.co.nz/2014/09/17/putin-by-sharon-tennison/ (accessed March 25, 2017).

—. "Sharon Tennison: "Russia Report on Putin"." *Johnson's Russia List.* 14 April 2014. http://russialist.org/sharon-tennison-russia-report-on-putin/ (accessed March 15, 2017).

Treisman, Daniel. "Blaming Russia First." *Foreign Affairs.* November/December 2000. https://www.foreignaffairs.com/reviews/review-essay/2000-11-01/blaming-russia-first?page=4 (accessed December 09, 2016).

Walsh, Robert. "The Plague of Money Laundering The Greatest Danger to America." *European Financial Review.* 11 June 2017. http://www.europeanfinancialreview.com/?p=16572 (accessed July 27, 2017).

Watson, Paul Joseph, and Yihan Dai. "RAND Lobbies Pentagon: Start War To Save U.S. Economy." *Prison Planet.* 30 October 2008. https://www.prisonplanet.com/rand-lobbies-pentagon-start-war-to-save-us-economy.html (accessed June 23, 2017).

Wedel, Janine R. "The Harvard Boys Do Russia." *The Nation.* 14 May 1998. (accessed December 3, 2016).

Weed, Thurlow. "Tsar Alexander II of Russia pledges support for the Union." *Reformation.org.* n.d. https://www.reformation.org/czar-alexander.html (accessed May 2, 2017).

BIBLIOGRAPHY

Wight, John. *The Demonization of Vladimir Putin.* 29 January 2016. http://www.counterpunch.org/2016/01/29/the-demonization-of-vladimir-putin/ (accessed January 13, 2017).

Wiist, William H., et al. "The Role of Public Health in the Prevention of War: Rationale and Competencies ." *American Journal of Public Health.* 13 May 2014. http://ajph.aphapublications.org/doi/abs/10.2105/AJPH.2013.301778 (accessed June 23, 2017).

Wikipedia. "1993 Russian constitutional crisis." *Wikipedia.* n.d. https://en.wikipedia.org/wiki/1993_Russian_constitutional_crisis (accessed January 3, 2017).

—. *David Ignatius.* 29 December 2016. https://en.wikipedia.org/wiki/David_Ignatius (accessed January 12, 2017).

Williamson, Anne. *Don't Cry for Boris Yeltsin.* 4 May 2007. https://www.lewrockwell.com/2007/05/anne-williamson/dont-cry-for-boris-yeltsin/ (accessed December 12, 2016).

—. *Russia's Fiscal Whistleblower.* 16 June 1998. http://www.motherjones.com/politics/1998/06/russias-fiscal-whistleblower/ (accessed December 12, 2016).

Willige, Andrea. "Which countries are on the right track, according to their citizens?" *World Economic Forum.* 12 January 2017. https://www.weforum.org/agenda/2017/01/which-countries-are-on-the-right-track-according-to-their-citizens (accessed March 14, 2017).

Wood, Todd L. "Look In The Mirror America!" *ZeroHedge.* 22 February 2014. http://www.zerohedge.com/news/2014-02-22/look-mirror-america (accessed March 15, 2017).

Wormser, Rene. *Foundations: Their Power and Influence.* New York: David-Aidar Co., 1958.

CPSIA information can be obtained
at www.ICGtesting.com
Printed in the USA
LVOW13s0954081017
551661LV00011B/699/P